WORDS ARE PEOPLE TOO!

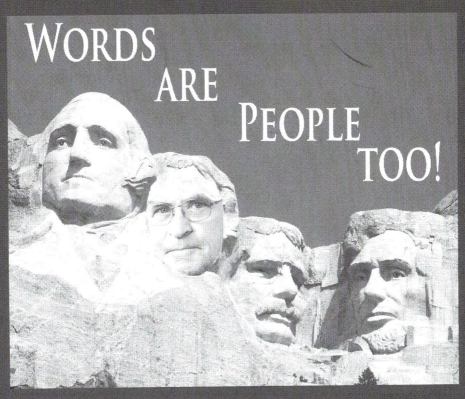

**Bob's rarely used...
and rarely useful**

"Encyclobodomy"

of words and phrases.

*"...A complete
and definitive
fabrication..."*

by Bob Pitta

Words Are People Too… is fiction. All of the references to acts or activities of persons cited in this pseudo-reference book are fictitious. Any reference to any actual person, living or dead, is a fictional reference with the exception of all nonfiction persons mentioned on this and the following page.

Jacket Design: Rich Draper and Jan Dove
Jacket Image: Rich Draper

Library of Congress Control Number: 2013910079
Waptoo, Rio Vista, CA

DEDICATION

"All Dead-Occasions can be observed at the end of what we like to refer to as Life-o-Suctions."

To Jan & Tom

Bob Pitta

CREDITS

Thanks to my loving wife and best friend Charlene, who puts up with my "jocularity"(read: "wit")—especially when she is knitting.

(TRANSLATION: *I am her KNIT-WIT*).

Thanks to my sister Jan and my good friend Rich for performing solo acts of cover art.

Thanks to Cheryl Lucas, who inadvertently asked me to write a brief history of the Broadway musical and who got what she asked for—at which time my muse was born, afterbirth and all.

FOREWORD

Words are man's only form of both spoken and written communication—notwithstanding pictographs, cuneiforms, hieroglyphs, and #2 pencils. In the early days of written communication, words had to gestate in the minds of men before they could gesticulate (as it were). That means that, at some point, before any word was spoken out of the mouth of man, it had to float around in the mind of man, along with innumerable other words and mental images, in a fight for survival, recognition, and then as acceptance as a shared sound in the float space used by all. That is a lot of "float" space. Only after we discovered the storage space (now referred to as the Cloud) did we realize that not only could that space in your brain cloud your memory, it was also apparent that the words used to communicate to your neighbors or family were always available to be arranged into a specific combination so that any idea that you wanted to communicate was cogent—no matter how verbose (much like this sentence). *(Please note that no cogent verbalizations of ideas were harmed in the production of this compendium.)*

For instance, if in a previous eon, you felt threatened and wanted to respond to a challenge such as "This spearhead is momentarily going to be integrated fully into your cell structure if you don't share some of that mastodon," you might not want respond with "Over my dead body!" when you had the vocal option to respond with the less aggressive "Come **over** to **my dead** (mastodon) **body**, and let's eat while we talk this out." Specific words, therefore, had to be specifically grouped and evocated if one was to communicate effectively (and as a result possibly stay alive to hunt another day).

As you may have imagined by now, we use words to interact with other humans. They tend to have little effect on animals, minerals, or plants, though not necessarily in that order. Early man made the occasional exception when he found himself backed into a cave by a saber-toothed tiger (which is where the phrase "Nice Kitty!" came from). Consequently, the effective use of words may typically involve at least one mouth, or the substitution of a stylus if the interaction is being recorded. Additionally, ink, paint, or grease, along with a surface such as papyrus, rock wall, or chalkboard would be helpful.

Nevertheless, for some, questions arise regarding the need for written communication. After all, with such a rich and loquacious oral tradition, why should we go through the huge and seemingly insurmountable process of inventing written symbols to represent every oral expression used throughout history? One of the answers is that humans are vain creatures and need beauty products (see: **ETYMOLOGY of SHAMPOO**). The memorializing of words into writing feeds into that vanity. It allows for the creation of a history—not only of the words and ideas, but also, in some cases, of the person or people who helped create specific words **(see: ETYMOLOGY of ANOREXIA)**. Another very basic but important reason to write stuff down is to create and document laws that we agree upon—in an effort to prevent chaos (or at least marginally improve the chaos we are now living in). Once we agree upon rules, they become a part of our written communication and can be referred to as many times as needed to decide if a social contract has been broken. Imagine that whole process without the written word. It would be bureaucratic chaos (which is considered by some - a redundancy).

When we read *WORDS ARE PEOPLE TOO!* we will come to understand that individuals and small groups throughout human history lived the words and phrases that they created. Those same people have left us with complex tomes laden with a complete and intricate documentation of all words, justly created, so that all of mankind can surround itself with essential beauty products and the laws we use to govern the sale of those products.

So, as stated before: words are mankind's only form of written communication—be they sprayed on walls, written down on paper, hung up in cyberspace, or even scratched into the sand with the twig from the branch of a tree. It is, therefore, incumbent on me to provide you, loyal reader, with a lexicon of words and phrases detailing their origins. Please note that the term "origins" is used loosely in this context and as such is not meant to actually represent any officially sanctioned origin or etymology of any given word. "Origins," for our purpose, is anything that I was able to make up that might or might not have been how the word originated (if we all lived in straitjackets).

Most etymologists (word-history geeks) will parse each word or phrase and try to find root derivations documented in scholarly tomes—and usually end up quoting the most deadly of all languages: Latin (sorry, Italy!). Therefore, I hereby solemnly promise to you that I will not waste your time with scholarly research, but will, with little or no respect for examination, take you to the place where real words were born, suckled, and grew up to young adulthood—and then sent into the world to make letters longer, complicated phrases harder to understand, and in general, confuse how we communicate with one another. (In the interest of full disclosure, I must hereby mention that for those people who never learned to read or write, the opposite is not necessarily true. New words will simply add to their confusion, move us all one step closer to chaos, and in general create sores on the wall of the Cloud that will fester until the end of time.)

In closing and for your benefit—since the term **Encylobotomy (En-Psych-Lobot-Toe-Me)**, as referenced on the cover, is such an uncommon word, we will henceforth refer to the explanation of the origin of individual words and phrases as simply their **ETYMOLOGY (Et-Toe-Maul! Ah-Gee!)**. This guide will take you, with stunning simplicity, through the startling history of the creation of words and phrases by making highly questionable assumptions.

This guide is in geological order. Each word has its definition, followed by a semi-rational explanation of where it came from (as best as I can guess). If for some reason you become shocked or offended by definitions that seem too bizarre, please keep in mind that you need to get out more.

With that codicil, I wish you much joy in the clearly astonishing and exclusive discoveries you are about to uncover in this book.

Bobdotcalm

DISCLAIMER...

Etymology, as well as Encyclobodomy, as every preschooler knows, is a reference to the study of the origin of words. Any etymologies or encyclobodomies herein found to be factual or consistent with the actual etymology or encyclobodomy of the word under discussion is a complete and utter coincidence and, as such, was not intended by the author. Warning: This is not the play space of the "factually driven." (For your convenience, and in the event that you are using some of this material on your thesis, you will find a complete, historically referenced Table of Chronological Contents at the other end of this book.)

AMBITIOUS!

Engaging in some idle thought, the times are

Often more than not, that subtle light of

Clear insight—my mind enfolds—no less

Delights. And in a fashion quite profound,

The thoughts are told in lyric sound.

Through my head they weave and climb,

Enlighten me in simple rhyme.

Now, comfort is the element one needs for

Thought's development.

So after pen and pad are there, I bring along

The softest chair. Into a quiet room I glide

Then realize my hungry side.

And all the while my mind, it pounds

With proverbs new to be renowned.

In haste, soft music I prepare,

To prod my mind—make rhythm fair.

Prepared, complete with pad and pen

And food to solve my eating yen—

Ambitious! I sit on my flank

When all at once my mind goes blank!

CHRONOLOGY ONE:

THE INQUISITARIUS PERIOD

(FROM 250,000 BC THROUGH 101,000 BC)

‹ *THE EARLY YEARS* ›

"...WITH GRUNTS AND GROANS, NEW WORDS HE HONES..."

HUMAN
(FIRST USED: 250,000 BC)

Definition: Of the species: Sapiens, and the genus: Homo—Latin meaning wise (or knowing)—man.

Etymology: Over the years, archeologists have made some discoveries about the origins and development of the so called: Human Being. In an effort to not belabor all of the baby steps that were required to evolve into the camp of "Man," let us begin with a brief expostulation on the origins of the "Human" being.

It is generally posited by Archeologists that **Homo Habilis** was the first of the upright biped creatures to use what we now call tools. This was over two hundred million years ago. These tools were made of stone, and were used to dig, chop, and, we can guess, not infrequently were used to mash the heads of predators and/or competitors.

And it was a beginning. While it took many millions of years for these "ape-men" to modify into the fully cogent and self-aware (HA!) "Man" that we know today, it was many millennia before he perfected the use of tools. Even the Neanderthal had a hand in the process.

Somewhere in the beginning of biblical time, around 6,000 BC, the Bronze Age jumped into the headlines, and the use of tools began to broaden. Concomitantly, the improving skills of the crafters and users began to change the world. It was also the time when we could say without a doubt that the Human Animal had come to stay.

Our focus, and the original purpose of this verbose pre-amble, is to direct you to the etymological underpinnings of the term HUMAN—which we can now do.

The development of the stone axe and its usefulness as a defensive weapon, as well as its use as a tool for foraging and chopping wood, is legendary. We have determined that the primary use of the axe was as a tool for chopping and digging. Those activities were commonly referred to as **HEWING**. That is to say that to chop trees or to chop wood was to **HEW**—as it still is today. Because these Bronze Age Men were now bearers of tools with which they could **HEW**, it seemed only natural to call them **THE HEW MEN**. Thus the contraction to **HUMAN.** The name **HUGH**, as in **HUGH** SWARTZ, is also a related phrase (May the Swartz be with Hugh). Additionally, to this day, Hugh is associated with the common yet less subtle term **HACK** (as in "to Hack into Hugh").

HIDE
(FIRST USED: 249,702 BC)

Definition: Seeking cover so as not to be seen.

Etymology: On hot days, early men were so horrified at seeing their bodily juices *(sweat)* leaking from every crevice and cranny that some actually fainted. Others were nauseated, which not infrequently, induced vomiting. That only added to the general chaos. Most decided that the only way to avoid the trauma of sweat was to stay in the darkened caves and simply wait to die. Some simply averted their eyes—to avoid looking at themselves or their companions dripping away their precious bodily fluids. Some scanned the treetops in an attempt to send a signal that they were not in the least concerned. But the first great heat wave that they experienced produced the first great hysterical reaction in the history of man. It also produced an innovative way to avoid having to face their fear of "leaking" to death.

Of course, we understand now that the panicked reaction was caused by something that we all now know helps us avoid heatstroke. It is, of course, the physiological function that we refer to as sweat (or perspiration). And sweat scared the new humans. Amazingly, their solution to the anguish and fear that they experienced would ever change how we see one another—even into the twenty-first century.

The men and women of 249,702 BC began hunting those big furry animals that prowled at night in search of prey. Once they had surrounded and killed a lion or a buffalo, they would strip it of its skin and its fur and barbecue what was left over. They fashioned the skins and furs into something that the tribes people could drape over their naked bodies. The wraps served two very important purposes:

a) They were used as a body cover so that they (and their neighbors) wouldn't be traumatized by the sight of "sweat," and

b) The coverings would absorb the vital bodily juices so that they wouldn't have to walk around on warm days dripping the stuff all over the ground.

The wraps were referred to as HIDES, which was a description of their purpose that is: to HIDE the sweat. As it turns out, that term has stayed with us even until the present. It now refers to the animal coats we still collect and still use to cover ourselves. We still shave the Hides of wooly animals and fashion them into garments to HIDE our own sweat glands.

As a final note before we close this discussion on HIDES: It is important to point out that when the HIDES were fashioned into suitable coverings, the term CLOTHES was first coined as CLOSE, in a reference to what early man wanted to do about any discussion of their initial fear of sweat—that is, CLOSE the discussion. It was only after the needle and thread were invented that CLOSE became CLOTHES (which were mostly knitted from threads made of cotton). And while we have all suffered under the delusion that the term HIDE was about hiding our nakedness, it was again, in fact, more about "hiding" the abomination called sweat.

DISPROPORTIONATE
(FIRST USED: 240,012 BC)

Definition: Unequal and excessive share when compared to another.

Etymology: When the Ogg family first sat around the dinner campfire in their cave in the south of France, Lester Ogg was the first to take a portion of the severely roasted three-toed sloth that Emma Ogg had slaved over all afternoon, basting it, as she did, in its own blood. Lester was not much of a "group" thinker, and he took both forelegs of the sloth for himself—which, by the way, included all six toes. That left less tempting portions for Emma and their five children, Icky, Offal, Whiff, Tag, and Dennis. Gourmands usually discarded the hindquarters because even in the early cave-dwelling days, everyone knew what came forth from the posterior. Consequently they had no desire to consume that section of the animal. That left the hind legs (tough and sinewy), the head (tossed before cooking), and the midsection (usually overcooked). Lester tended to brag to his fellow hunter-gatherers about how much of the meal he had consumed. Over grog or two, he would belch out, hand gestures and all, in primitive Neanderthalese: **"Dis proportion ate!"** Ultimately, his boast came to mean: "more than your fair share" or **DISPROPORTIONATE.***

> * It should also be noted that the term **deliberate** also came from Lester Ogg during this period of gastric discovery. However, none of Lester's five

children were ever heard to utter the phrase, and in fact, whenever **LIVER** *was served, they all came down with a mysterious pre-dinner flu, and much to their gratification were ultimately sent to bed without supper.*

INTERNAL COMBUSTION
(FIRST USED: 236,725 BC)

Definition: Self-generating process in which a substance reacts vigorously with oxygen to produce heat and light.

Etymology: Internal Combustion is so named because:

a.) All combinations of consumables become combustibles upon consumption, and are, without exception located internally, and

b.) The combustions are frequently manifested in the form of an audible explosion followed by a bright flame emanating from the posterior vent hole, often referred to as the tail pipe.

DESPICABLE
(FIRST USED: 235,312 BC)

Definition: Contemptible, meriting scorn

Etymology: The term DESPICABLE found its origin during the early development of language. In an interesting union of linguistics and nasal hygiene, early man's first utterance upon finger-mining his left nostril was in the form of the primitive exclamation "Dis pickable!"

After he showed off his discovery, general revulsion ensued, followed by a mighty heaping of scorn. Thus did the phrase: **DIS PICKABLE**! morph into the term **DESPICABLE** and come to be synonymous with **CONTEMPTIBLE**.

FOOTSTOOL
(FIRST USED: 230,612 BC)

Definition: A device that allows you to step up, a "chair" for your foot.

Etymology: One of the most commonly shared experiences of man (dating back into the stone age) has been the one in which we inadvertently step in pet poop while engaging in some innocent endeavor—such as walking across the floor or the lawn. Most people, as recorded history shows, had the need and discipline to take the time to train the pets to yowl at the cave door if they need to go out. Others have gone to decidedly borderline extremes to avoid the possibility of tracking poop all over the floors of our homes.

These people are descendants of eons of mankind who squeamishly avoided even the slightest possibility of the inadvertent step in the mud. Avoiders of shoe poop limited themselves to stepping on strategically placed boxes so that they never have to be concerned about accidental "smutch" on the business side of their shoes. While it does make navigating around the house less than optimal, it also guarantees that any pets wandering about will not poop where their human companions might accidentally step.

And so the term **FOOTSTOOL** came into our language in the year 230,612 BC. It was then that an enterprising hominid relative of ours decided to step up on what appeared to be a twelve-inch-high rock. His intention was to get a better view of the mastodon that had just passed through. He wanted to determine whether or not it was a male or a female. Females were good hunting and good eating when barbequed and basted in their own juices. The males, on the other hand, tended to be tough and overly chewy. However as he stepped up onto the "rock," he found that it was quite soft. He stumbled and fell and almost opened himself up on his own spear. This stumble was a common experience for mastodon hunters in 230,612 BC.

A survey taken of all North American Mastodon hunters on June 14 of that year produced the following results:

Question:

A. Have you ever stepped on a rock that was soft and mushy? Response: Yes: **82%** of all responders.

B. Which rocks are more conducive to a successful hunt? Response: Hard Rocks: **67.2**%. Soft and Mushy Rocks: **21%.** Do Not Care: **11.8%**.

C. Have you ever considered that some of those "Soft Rocks" might be Mastodon Stool? Response: 55%: No Comment. 45%s: Huh?

D. Would you be willing, in the future, to refer to piles of Mastodon poop as "Foot Stool"? Response: 83%: Eeeeewwwwwuuh. 17%: What-now?

By May 14* the results of the survey were compiled and considered. It was determined that there would be no progress without a com-promise. Just when negotiations were deadlocking, a group of con-cerned women suggested someone invent a fake foot stool. It was suggested that it could be constructed out of branches, and as such would cost pennies.

The suggestion was adopted, and the device to "step up and peer farther" was invented. Now, instead of stepping "into" a foot (1') (of) stool, you could, if so equipped, now step "onto" a (1') stool. Other benefits included:

a.) The reeking stench of the "hunter's feet" slowly dissipated.

b.) The delicate sensibilities of the women were assuaged because shoes had yet to be invented, and even the most focused of the ladies, somehow, still mistook the mastodon stool for a step-up stool every once in a while.

The progress of this historical data began in June in the year 236,725 and ended in May of that same year. (To avoid confusion please note that BC time records moved backwards, as it were, toward 1 AD and as such December 31 was the first day of every year, and January 1 was the last.)

LAPSE
(FIRST USED: 205,986 BC)

Definition: Something overlooked or not remembered; a requirement before having a relapse.

Etymology: As we all know from our study of prehistory, the life of the caveman was less desirable than most of our own. A standard part of every prehistory teacher's lesson plans is the study of caveman domiciles and their furniture (or lack thereof). It is accepted by most scholars that furniture, as we know it, was nonexistent. However, depending on the topography of a given cave, one could find ledges that may have been used as beds and boulders that may have been used as seats (around a fire pit, for example). It is also commonly accepted that the cave ladies were much more fragile than their male counterparts; and whereas the cavemen sat on the hard and unforgiving rocks, it was the privilege of the ladies to sit on the cavemen laps to avoid the bumps and bruises common to rock seats.

And it came to pass that when furniture was invented, one of the first things that the cavemen purchased were comfortable chairs to replace the boulders.

Chairs were made available to everyone living in the cave.

Occasionally, an errant and forgetful cavewoman would catch herself hovering over the male, about to revert to her earlier training regarding sitting on the laps of the guys. She was usually gently reminded that she had a chair of her own. After that, the tale of her forgetfulness occupied many conversations around the fire pit. Reverting to any old abandon behavior was forevermore referred to as a **Laps**. (When language was invented later in the same eon, the spelling was mistakenly recorded as **LAPSE.)**

HERD
(FIRST USED: 191,323 BC)

Definition: Typically refers to a large group of domesticated animals.

Etymology: As man transitioned from the safety of the cave dwelling to a more agrarian society, he was left to devise ways to protect himself and his family from the predators that roamed the prairie during the night. After a number of failed experiments, it became clear that the options were narrowed down to either sleepless nights or some sort of warning system that would rouse him from his sleep prior to being eaten.

It was much too dangerous to post a member of the family to watch during the night because by the time you heard her screams, it was often too late to do anything about it. The resolution to the problem was to collect, and keep intact, a group of grazing animals—such as the nice bovine creatures from which marauders occasionally "borrowed" milk. With the crowd of animals resting at night alongside the humans, every time a predator came along the animals would become unsettled and call out warnings to one another in the night. Those cries would be heard by the sleeping herders, who would awaken and help drive off the hungry predators.

Because they **heard** the animals' night terrors, they rather clumsily referred to their domesticated pals as their **HEARD**. It wasn't until 1937 that a little-known government commission that was created to **Fix the Language** changed the reference from H**EAR**DS of animals to **HERDS** of animals—oddly taking the "**EAR**" out of the equation.

IMPUNITY
(FIRST USED: 153,003 BC)

Definition: Exemption from consequence or punishment

Etymology: A visit to any monkey cage in a zoo mixed with some quiet observation will lead to the accurate assumptions that some monkeys, like some young human kids, revel in disruption and delight in chaos. The thing about the little imps is that the more of them there are, the less likely that any guiding authority (like parents or zookeepers) will or can have an impact on their behavior. Think back to the last time you watched monkeys in a cage. There was always the handful of them that were jumping and screaming and generally disrupting the peace and tranquility that one might ordinarily expect in a re-creation of the forests and savannahs. Their group chaos makes it difficult to determine which monkey (or kid) perpetrated the disruption. So it is this unity of the monkeys, or the little imps (our own kids), acting in concert with one another, that came to mean freedom from consequence—as associated with the two words **Imp Unity**—which, as we all know, when combined is **IMPUNITY.**

PITY
(FIRST USED: 127,992 BC)

Definition: Usually defined as a sympathetic emotional response to the misfortune of another person or people.

Etymology: It is commonly held that the game of golf had its origins in Scotland toward the end of the fifteenth century. While that may be true in the strictest sense of the term, it of course is not the whole story. Golf did have its origins in Scotland. However, the version portrayed in our history books is blatant fabrication.

It was in the spring of 127,992 BC (roughly) that we have evidence of a game played by the Neanderthal, with a roundish rock and a tree branch (later referred to as the "golf club"). Most scientists held that the Neanderthal was unable to stand up right—that he was "stooped of shoulder." It is interesting that while they defined him as "stooped," they named him Homo erectus (Hello!). In any event, it is obvious that the "stooped" shoulder issue was not one of physical differences between Homo erectus and Homo sapiens. In fact, the so-called "stooped" shoulder was a result of the Darwinian theories concerning the origins of the species.

It is clear that the "stooped" shoulder was a genetically adjusted change in the physique of early man to allow for the best position in which to hit a golf ball. It has since been scientifically proven that the "stooped shoulder" position does not really optimize hitting the long ball, but the game of golf had not yet progressed in its evolution to long fairways. In addition, the courses in those early days were "rougher" than the more evolved "fair"way courses that we are accustomed to today.

The main issue with golf courses in those days in ancient Scotland was that the terrain was not accommodating to any sport. The ground was rough like the lunar surface for as far as the eye could see. The rocky terrain was covered with little pits—as though the area had been trapped in a shower of tiny meteorites. The game was played using a tree branch that was as straight and thick as could be found. It was termed the Club. Only one club was required. The object was to hit a round stone along the ground in the hope that the stone would fall into one of the designated little pits on the landscape. The stones (balls) were launched from any small twig (tee) that the player could find that would hold the stone off of the ground. Eighteen holes (or pits) later, the player who managed to get his rolling stone into all of the designated holes with the least number of "strokes" of the club was declared the winner.

The most difficult part of the game (much like today) was to balance the stone (ball) on a twig (tee) before hitting it. Frequently, if not always, the twig would break or be wedged at just the right angle for the stone to fall to the ground with each attempt to balance it. These attempts to set the game in motion caused much frustration and, dare I say it, anger among the players (*It is fair to say that lives were taken when twigs were breakin'*…). The spectators would whoop and holler each time a twig broke and referred to the player's reaction as: "getting teed off." The phrase stuck, and the twig was named the tee. The name of the game was originally referred to as **Pit-Tease** and was later shortened to **Pit-Tee.** The name **Pit-Tee** wasn't changed to "Golf" until the fifteenth century, nearly a half a million years later. The term **Pit-Tease** was shortened to **PITY** to refer to the heartfelt condolence of fellow players when your stone would miss the pit you were aiming for. Somewhere in the neighborhood of 125,000 BC, the term **PITY** referenced any heartfelt emotion for the misfortune of others.

HEIRLOOM
(FIRST USED: 115,084 BC)

Definition: an object so treasured that it is passed from one generation to the next.

Etymology: Archeologists, anthropologists, and etymologists have determined that one of the first words to be uttered in the year 115,084 BC was the word **HEIRLOOM**. The early cave man, known to scientists as The Pilt-Down Man, was, as we have seen in historical museum dioramas, covered with hair. This was nature's way of providing him with a coat. The biggest complaints, in and out of caves, in those days were: "What no pockets?", and "Lots of mattes!"

One rainy day, a bored Pilt-Down man, who was trying to comb out some of his mattes, began to closely study the nature of the matte and discovered that if you cut it off with some sharp rocks, it retained its ability to cover a "Human" and to keep him warm. It was also good for cleaning up messy kitchen spills.

In any event, long story short, our Pelt-Down matte scholar developed a crude machine that, if fed with long strands of hairs, could make artificial mattes of any size. That development led to the invention of hair shirts, which, of course, were the precursor to clothes.

Where there were clothes, there could be pockets—and soon, long lines of Pelt-Down men formed at the barbershops to be sharp-rock shaven and have their hair turned into the first article of clothes ever—a Hair Shirt, which was referred to as a **Smocket** (a contraction of the words *smock* and *pocket*). The machine that wove the hair was called a hair loom. The hair looms were so amazing back then that they were the single most important treasure a family could own, and they were passed from one generation to another. As everyone now knows, the word **HAIR** was misspelled on the patent application for the original Hair Loom, and thus came to be the term **HEIRLOOM**, which to this day refers to a thing of importance passed on through the generations.

Some scientists have decided that the Piltdown Man was a hoax and a ruse. We know that it was not a ruse because it is an established and heavily subscribed-to fact that the invention of clothes actually happened—thus the certification of our etymology.

CLUB
(FIRST USED: 101,862 BC)

Definition: A group of people formed for a specific purpose with specific meeting times.

Etymology: This term dates back to the Stone Age and the first use of a tool often described as the portion of the thickest part of the limb of a tree. Certain men of the day felt that they had, with a thick tree branch in hand, a better bargaining tool to smooth out the little wrinkles in life. Those men who used the "threat of force" tool tended to hang out together. (Some speculate that this group was the beginning of what we now know as Major League Baseball.

In any event, somewhere it was decided that the tree limb would be called a **CLUB**—partially because language at the time was fairly monosyllabic. The men who used the "club" began hanging out with each other as a natural function of mutual interests, and as a group were nicknamed **the Club**. Not much has changed since those times.

Clubs are still identified as groups with common interests.*

> * The **club** as a weapon has changed in form, but not in intent (except for Major League Baseball). However, when planning a party, some **Clubs** indelicately refer to parties thrown by the club as a **Bash.**

CHRONOLOGY TWO:

THE PALEOSPECIFIC ERA

(FROM 100,000 BC THROUGH 17,999 BC)

‹ THE POST-EARLY YEARS ›

DURING THE "PRE-LANGUAGE" EPOCHS OF MAN...EVERYONE COULD BE SAID TO BE "SPEECHLESS."

MANIFESTOES
(FIRST USED: 89,520 BC)

Definition: A statement of objectives or principles upon which one stands.

Etymology: During the Paleospecific Era, ancient Man was transitioning from the hominid stage to the human stage. With this transformation came the loss of some of the anthropoid hair that was characteristic of the apes (*The term* Paleospecific *was, in fact, coined as the human hair receded, revealing skin tones—and therefore, Paler creatures*). These people were saddled with the problems of whittling their own tools out of stone, fighting off the savage attacks from beasts of prey, foraging for food, and creating enough one-syllable words to name their all of their children. They nonetheless found time for friendly interaction with others.

One of the highlights of their time together was what they referred to as the **Man Fest**. The **Man Fest** was basically a group picnic. It was held each August in front of one of the homes of the group. (Homes, in those times, were usually referred to as Man Caves—but Homes could also refer to anyone from the "Neighborhood"—as in, "My Homeys.")

The event was simple. Food and games made for good times. The food usually comprised a fresh kill and barbecue. The games were simple and fun. Who could roll a boulder down the hill the fastest? Who could find their way, blindfolded, back to their cave without drawing blood...and who could name and physically identify all of their own children from among every child in the group!

The closing ceremony of the **Man Fest** ritual was the **Proclamation**. Each Cave Man would stand in the entrance of his home and proclaim (in one syllable words) the sanctity of his cave, his property, and his community. He would symbolize his commitment to home, family, and fellows by **"digging his heels"** into the dirt, just leaving his toes exposed. He would then pound his chest and wiggle his **TOES**, declaring his home sacred.

This rite was called the **Man Fest Toes**, and it helped foster a sense of tribalism and unity. To this date, the term **Manifestos** refers to a public declaration of principle or intention.

POROUS
(FIRST USED: 73,697 BC)

Definition: A property that allows for seepage

Etymology: In the olden days, prior to the establishment of science, and before real doctors, most people had a personal problem with seepage. Seepage, even in the days of oldie, was defined as fluid passing through small openings in the human body. In the days when man was new to the world—his birthplace is what we now refer to as Africa—man (*this generic term includes women*) followed the herds of animals that guaranteed him a protein diet. The closer man, in his pursuit of meat, wandered to the equator—the warmer the air became (because of proximity to the sun). The closer man came to the sun, the hotter man's external temperature became. Man's body, in a defensive reaction to the heat, began pumping fluid through what is now known as his Pores (*which make up the natural body coat we refer to as skin*). As we all now know (thanks again to science), the body, by exuding water, is just protecting itself from the ravages of heat. It reacts much the way an air conditioner coil does, or much like the effects of a cool breeze on a warm day at the beach.

The problem was that this group we refer to as the "First Men" didn't know what was happening, so they freaked out. Their first thought was that they were leaking! They had no indication of whether or not the leakage would cease and desist (See etymology for HIDE). Quite frankly and understandably, they panicked. There was much weeping and gnashing of teeth. Happily this was prior to the invention of clothes, so as to eliminate the obvious problems associated with the renting of garments (obviously if you cannot buy clothes, you certainly cannot rent them!).

In any event, the water springing forth from these human bodies caused stress and self-pity. The most commonly heard lamentation was "Poor Me!" and "**Poor Us**!" That exclamation, though short lived, became the term we now refer to as **POROUS**—which is a property that allows for liquid to seep through.

HYDRANT
(FIRST USED: 62,006 BC)

Definition: Usually a surface valve available to firemen to access water under pressure.

Etymology: In 62,006 BC, the term *hydrant* had a different meaning then it does now. Typically, when a cave person grew too fat for his or her clothing (*which were usually made out of the hide of some animal* *that they had consumed)*, they would grow restive and ill at ease. This discomfort frequently resulted in a moment of rage. The bulky clothes wearer would "rent" (tear) his (her) garments in disgust at the weight gain. The person would throw the now-too-small animal hide at the nearest animal (which was nearly always a domestic dog). Dogs, of course, will do what dogs do, which would be to "mark" (pee on) the cast-off wardrobe with their scent. At that point, the angry cave person would go into another furious rant, thus burning calories and ultimately losing some of the unwelcome weight. This activity was referred to as peeing on the **Hide Rent (or "Rant**"). The word, if not the concept, is still in use today as **HYDRANTS**, which are structures that are installed in towns and cities across the world to give a dog a place to pee.

CITRIC ACID
(FIRST USED: 44,000 BC)

Definition: A mild acid that occurs naturally in many fruits and other foods.

Etymology: It has been established that as early as 44,000 BC (give or take), the cave men and their cronies would urinate pretty much anywhere that it was convenient. The discovery was a stunner—especially the evidence that many of them would pee against the nearest tree, just as their dogs did on hydrants.* Because the men used trees as potty posts, most of the other cave people (women) stayed away from the trees, if for no other reason than to avoid the smell.

However, at some point, one or more of the locals realized that the orange-and-yellow balls that seemed to grow on, and then fall from, the trees might be eatable. They determined this from the fact that birds, insects, and larger animals all fed from the hanging and fallen orbs. The tribal leader, Sid, urged one brave soul to test the tree's fruit to see if it could be a source of food. The tribesman picked one of the fruits from the tree with yellow fruit. Using a sharpened stick, he broke open the small yellow orb. Yellow juices ran across his fingers and hand. He tested the juice with the tip of his tongue. And then he screamed. He flung the broken fruit into orbit and ran for the nearest stream, where he rinsed out his mouth for the next several hours.

Once he had settled down, he began to accuse the tribal leader, Sid, of playing an evil trick on him. "What was wrong?" his friends asked. "It had a horrible taste…" the tribesman said. "It tasted like the pee that we water our tree with… those orbs are little yellow balls filled with our urine." "It was a sick trick! Ask Sid!" The fact is that it was an unripened lemon that the tribesman/taster sampled and declared urine-ated. (*The question that still haunts the historians who studied this "event" was: How did the tribesman know what urine tasted like?*)

It was not until the dawn of 10,000 BC (*May 13*) that the lemon, or the orange, pear, peach, or cumquat would ever again be tested as a source for food. And the reason, when anyone asked, was always quoted as: **"IT WAS A SICK TRICK! ASK SID!"** Even today, that tangy taste in some of the fruits we eat is still referred to as **A Citric Acid**.

*See Etymology for: **Hydrants***

ISLAND
(*FIRST USED: 38,019 BC*)

Definition: land surrounded by water.

Etymology: In the days just before the language was formalized and hand-scratched onto stone tablets for all to study, we were much less ready—let alone able—to have words that were spelled differently but kept the same sounds as other words. That is because if it was not written down, how was one to determine which word the speaker was referencing? (Some examples: gate or gait; to or too or two, pair or pare or pear.)

In any event, aside from context, it could be next to impossible to determine what someone was saying when words collided. It is appropriate here to note that the very term "context" is derived from the Latin to mean "con" or "with" text. That meant that you had to be able to read the individual words to understand which word was actually being used.

The term **ISLAND** has history, etymologically speaking, in that the use of the term generated confusion about language, context, and spelling. Its use generated such frustration that people paired spoken language with scratches and characters on stone tablets in order to understand the meaning. As such, those scratches and characters constituted the *first use* of written language.

But back to the etymology: When early man transversed the great seas and oceans of our planet, they could and did spend many months at sea without a glimpse of land. Since the word *sea* was already taken, the term *see* was therefore not available to indicate something visual, so the word *eye* was used to refer to something you see, or saw. As a consequence, when land was spotted after months at sea, the deckhands would shout "**I EYE LAND**!" Confusion reigned (not rained) as shipmates tried to determine whether the deckhand had been infested with a serious case of the stutters or he was repeating himself intentionally. In any event, the result was that the crew eventually got the boat to shore and then argued about how they were to understand each other if there was stuttering on the most important issue of the journey. Because of this confusion, spelling, and then writing and documentation were invented. However, before written language took hold universally, several other important etymological issues made landfall.

a.) "**I EYE**…" was changed to **"AYE AYE"** as an acknowledge-ment by the sailor that he understood such sounds as "**I EYE LAND.**"

b.) "**EYE LAND**" was changed to "**ISLAND**" but was still pro-nounced "**EYE LAND**," even though for all intents and purposes, it could have been spelled **I LAND,** as in I land on the Eye Land.

c.) Saying: "**SEA**" twice (**SEA-SEA**) was changed to "**SI, SI!**" and in Spanish meant the same as "**EYE EYE**" (now changed to "**AYE, AYE!**")

d.) It became apparent (not "*a parent*") that **SEA-ING** was **BELIEVING** (not *bee leaving*) regarding the choice between spoken and written language.

*(It is important here to note that the aforementioned term **ISLAND** was totally appropriate because even though it was surrounded by water, it still **IS LAND**.)*

FOUL
(FIRST USED: 36,227 BC)

Definition: something that is not nice, totally uncalled for, disgusting, a smelly mess.

Etymology: Since the beginning of language, man has had a sense of the unfair, the unpleasant, the vulgar, and over-the-top rudeness. In point of fact, he copywrited the word **FOUL** because he felt that the very sound of it exemplified the feeling of the soul when encounter-ing unpleasantness. One even had to scrunch up one's face to prop-erly mutter the word.

Historically speaking, all was well until the invention of the chicken. After living with a couple of chickens for a couple of years, the native terrians (hominid earth dweller of the Cro Magnum persuasion) became disgusted with the personal habits of the egg layer. Most birds came around occasionally, left their poop in tiny concentrations, and then flew or wandered off unless they were sitting on a nest. As opposed to other birds, the chicken spent all of its time clucking around the cave and leaving "chicken debris" wherever it dropped. Over time the sediment built up and reeked, both when the air was still and when the wind kicked the dust up.

In an effort to not overburden the meaning of the term **FOUL**, early man created a special word for some specific unkempt winged creatures. It is the term that you and I know as FOWL, which includes chickens, ducks, and geese. Proof of the existence of FOWL DROPPINGS even into prehistory is evidenced by archeological digs. The strata from the era that we now call the Crustaceous Period is made up entirely of what, in geology, is referred to as CRAP (Chicken Remains and Poop). Most importantly, however, the foresight of early man helped to free up space around the term **FOUL**. By unburdening the term **FOUL** from all of the weight of the bird-poop effluvia, an entire area has been freed up to apply a whole subset of sports applications, including the three most time-tested iterations: **Foul** Ball, **Foul** Line, and **"What's that Smell?"**).

PRAY
(FIRST USED: 25,126 BC)

Definition: Supplication, requesting assistance from God

Etymology: To **PRAY** is a term (or phrase) used since the beginning of mankind, and it still used today. It is used as a direct result of not wanting to fall **prey** to the wild beasts or the searing heat of a thermonuclear war.

The theory behind the new term was that in order to remain competitive in the world of things that "live to eat," one must be one "preyer" ahead of the things that "eat to live." And, then, essentially, if all else failed, **PRAY** to God that you are not, nor do you want to become, **PREY**.

CATASTROPHIC
(FIRST USED: 22,717 BC)

Definition: A calamity, a disastrous result.

Etymology: This is one of those words that was handed down from primitive man. It is clear from archeological digs that big cats such as the saber-toothed tiger were indigenous to the tropics. And since man was armed with that knowledge, the big cat was not a threat. If you lived near the big cats, it was considered wise to move to another climate. In making that simple move, you would eliminate having to deal with the unpleasantness associated with being neighbors to a hungry and unfriendly predator.

The message uncovered on cave walls in the tropics was "Cat is Tropic"; a terse, blunt, and quite clear warning that living in the tropics was a serious risk with the obvious Cat-**is-Tropic** results—i.e., you may be on the menu for lunch; hence, the origin of the term **CATASTROPHIC**.

BURDEN
(FIRST USED: 22,051 BC)

Definition: a heavy load to bear, a difficult task

Etymology: Prior to the completion of the evolution of birds, their predecessors, who lived among the dinosaurs, were also egg layers. Birds hollowed out nesting dens in the hard scrabble of earth to incubate and nurture their young, just like the dinosaurs. Birds were den nesters also, which put into question their ability to survive as a species. That is to say that despite learning how to fly to escape predators, they remained mostly helpless when trying to protect their eggs or nestlings. Digging dens in the cold hard scrabble did nothing to achieve that goal. The best they could do was screech and poke the predator's head with their pointy beaks in the hopes of running the poachers off. The birds struggled with this aspect of their lives but knew that in order for their species to survive, they must dig or perish (*it should here be noted that some species of owl and penguin still do dig dens*).

Many eggs were pillaged by many hungry predators. At a certain point, in one of the heretofore unnamed epochs, an enterprising bird determined that this den-nest thing was foolish and unlikely to add to the quality of life, as such things go. And in that moment, a pivotal change came about that altered the future of birds and predators everywhere. This particular bird built its nest out of twigs and branches as usual, but it was off of the ground and up in a crook of branches in a tree. As a result, **the bird den was lifted**—and life was forever altered for birddom. It was then that the phrase **BIRD DEN** became the word **BURDEN** meaning "a task too difficult."

SHAMPOO
(FIRST USED: 21,797 BC)

Definition: a product used to clean hair.

Etymology: It is frequently overlooked that long before pharmaceutical and cosmetic companies got into the game of selling special soap for the washing and rinsing of hair, the cave men, despite their caricature in movies and cartoons, also needed to clean and groom their hair. It has been determined, through DNA testing and other scientific studies, that the cave men and women actually washed their hair in the sticky poo of the mastodon.

The mastodon poo

a) served to coat the hairs with its sticky content

b) served the secondary purpose of giving the hair some added thickness, and

c) gave the hairdresser a medium with which to form and style the hair into those magical shapes that belonged to the "New, Clean Hair" image of the cave men and women.

Archeologists' conjecture that at some point, while leaning over a pond to drink, a heretofore unknown cave person saw his or her reflection in the pond and was jolted to the realization that mastodon poo was totally and completely gross. We find evidence that the first real hair product created to actually clean hair was apparently made of citrus juices and mashed bananas. When rinsed off of the hair, it miraculously did not stick, stink, or leave a poo stain on everyone's pillows, as well as everything else that it touched. But best of all, it smelled sweet.

As the new product gained in popularity, there was a demand for a name for this new substitute for the old Mastodon Hair Poo. It was at that point that the term **Sham** (*or fake*) **Poo** was established, and it has stayed in our lexicon to the present day.

LICENSE
(FIRST USED: 19,222 BC)

Definition: A legal document granting a right, as earned through a regimen of study and testing (example: a lawyer has earned the right to pass the bar on the way home).

Etymology: The natural order of things, as pertaining to man's progression from Epithphilanthrupus to the Homo sapiens as known about the twenty-first century BC is:

a) A single man evolved who was both bi-dexterous and bi-sexual—which meant that he could procreate both male and female offspring with one hand tied behind his back.

b) As extended and distended families developed from him, they typically stayed together as a homogeneous group, largely out of embarrassment about Dad's "situation." As those groups got larger they found more interesting things to do, and they developed into tribes, which can be defined as groups of individuals and families with common interests.

c) The final step in the evolution of man as a social being was man attempting to stay organized—typically through surrogates, who were authorized to "govern" societal activities.

The first thing that the "governors" attempted to do was make sure that the activities of all of the individuals in the society conformed to a general plan that insured everyone's safety. There were a lot of failed attempts to get control of dangerous activities—especially the actions of those who wished to sell fish.

The problem with fish sellers was that they did not always sell the "catch of the day." It became increasingly evident that many of them sold fish that might have been caught as many as five or six days before the sale (refrigerators were not invented for several very, very long centuries). The obvious problem was that people were getting sick from the aging fish, and some people were dying even before the process of die-gestion was complete.

It seemed, to those charged with keeping the eating public safe, that there should be a way to keep all fish sellers honest. They decided to hire "inspectors," whose job was to check each fish seller to determine whether the fish were fresh enough to eat. Fish sellers who were found to be lying about the freshness of their product would be slapped with one of their own fish and assessed a fine.

There was a fairly easy way to determine whether the fish seller was guilty of selling old fish. First, upon asking about the freshness issue, one would often notice the eyes of the fish seller darting to the left and the right and looking at the sky while responding to the query. But more typically, the inspector could smell the old fish as soon as he entered the establishment. The smell could be fairly nauseating. Nonetheless, their sense of smell usually helped inspectors determine a violation. The nasal tool used to detect this crime was known as a **LIE SCENTS,** or in some situations as a simple **LIE SENSE**. Those fish vendors who were **SENSIBLE** were deemed to be in good standing and were awarded with a **LIE-SENSE** (later transposed as **LICENSE**), which allowed them to operate without fear of being slapped with a week-old fish.

The term **LICENSE** is a direct result of the early days of fish marketeering and was expanded to include all aspects of "**sellers**

versus consumers"—from practitioners of alchemy to space rocket engineers.

THISTLE
(FIRST USED: 17,985 BC)

Definition: A thorny stemmed desert plant of the Aster family.

Etymology: The Aster family dates back to prehistory, and it is only through a strongly developed habit of oral tradition that we are able to present the etymology of the term **THISTLE**. The Aster family originated in the high desert plains of south eastern California (then known as **Fornia**, which translated into modern English means **For Nia**, the name of the wife of Adam Aster, and to whom he had promised to bequeath the entire Mojave Plateau.

Adam Aster, the first of his line, was generally considered an "OK" provider for his extended family. The very name Aster came about when Adam asked his wife a question. (Thus the etymology of the phrase "**asked her**…"[Aster] becomes intertwined in the etymology of the term **THISTLE**.) In any event, on any typical morning, Adam sought out his wife and asked her (Aster) what she wanted for dinner. And typically, Nia would reply that they would be grateful for anything that Adam could bring home.

Adam would go out to hunt for food each day, and as likely as not, he would come home with a bundle of prickly plants to make into a soup (game was not especially plentiful in the high desert). Nia would often end up boiling the thorny flowering plant and feeding the entire clan with it. The plant came by its now-familiar name of **THISTLE** because when Adam came home with vegetable matter for dinner instead of the coveted game meat, all he would say was "**THISTLE** have to do…."

CHRONOLOGY THREE:

<THE PREDACIOUS EPOCH>

(FROM 17,999 BC THROUGH 2,799 B.C)

< *THE PYRO-ARSONEOUS ERA* >

"...A CINDER CONE IS OFTEN REFERRED TO AS A VOLCANIC ASH HOLE..."

DEFICIT
(FIRST USED: 16,680 BC)

Definition: The lack of something essential

Etymology: Over the course of the ages and as man evolved, he developed the five senses in a specific order. First there was the sense of smell, a direct result of which was that soap was invented. Following the sense of smell was the sense of sight, which directly led to the development of shampoo (see Etymology of Shampoo) and conditioner. Next came the sense of touch, which went a long way toward the propagation of the species. It was followed by the sense of taste, which was the engine that instigated the invention of salsa. Oddly enough, salsa played, and still plays, a significant role in the destruction of the very sense that fostered its existence.

Finally, we come to the evolution of the fifth sense, the sense of hearing, or lack thereof. As we know, there are some people who are born and go throughout life without the ability to hear. One of the sad aspects of the loss of that sense is explained by the etymology of the term **DEFICIT**.

In the days of the caveman, British developmental psychologists who happened upon an alleged deaf person would ask (rather loudly): "**DEAF, IS IT?**" If the person responded in the affirmative, that person was said to have a liability—or "the ability to lie" (see Etymology of

Liability) because the response is in itself empirical evidence that the person's sense of hearing exists. However, the subject who responded to the question with a blank stare was said to be "**DEAF, IS IT?**" The spelling of the term was shortened to **DEFICIT**—that is, to be lacking something (in this case—the ability to hear).

LAWN MOWER
(FIRST USED: 16,308 BC)

Definition: a device (requiring manual labor or other power source) that trims or cuts grassy areas.

Etymology: Prior to the invention of the wheel, when primitive man ventured out of his caves and broke from the hunter-gatherers, he learned to plant his own crops and employ the aid of domestic animals with a number of his outside chores. His solution to what would become the age-old problem of trimming the lawns that he planted in front of and behind his primitive caves, shacks, and lean-tos was both simple and ingenious. He employed one of his domesticated animals, typically a cow, to nibble the lawns down to an appropriate length. At that time, only the best ruminating bovine was given the sole and specific chore of trimming the lawns of the newly "landed" cavemen.

These beasts were referred to as **Lawn-Mooers** and as indicated, held that exalted position for several hundred years. It was only when the wheel had been developed and the Iron Age was in full swing that a device built specifically to replace the **Lawn Mooers**—i.e., the newly named **LAWN MOWER**—came along and replaced the **Mooers**. The **Mooers** were sent back to the milking barn, and the **MOWER** became the most prized possession in primitive man's garage. The term **LAWN MOWER** was, of course, in homage to the aforementioned **Mooer**.

SWEAT
(FIRST USED 13,480 BC)

Definition: To perspire, to exude moisture

Etymology: The word **SWEAT** evolved as a contraction of the two words "It's wet!," or "sss-wet!" **SWEAT**, as we have documented, was a common complaint uttered by the early cavepersons who chose to live in the tropics and feared the loss of their own bodily fluids.

❖   ❖   ❖

TALENTED
(FIRST USED: 10,000 BC)

Definition: Possessing an aptitude or the ability to do something that others can't; to do something better than most.

Etymology: It was not long after the first caveman discovered his own ability to think and plan that his skills at hunting improved remarkably. However, he did not discover the real limits to his skills until he spent some time observing the beauty and muscled strength of the hawks and eagles who hunted from the air. It was during one of those periods of observation that a nearby squirrel, working on opening a walnut, became the target of a circling bird of prey. As the caveman watched, the hawk tucked in its wings and dove like an arrow in flight. It silently dropped through the air until it was nearly upon the unsuspecting squirrel. In a simple move of extraordinary grace and strength, with full-wing engagement the bird reversed itself and in the same instant opened its deadly talons and dispatched the squirrel in the blink of an eye. The sight of those astonishing razor-sharp talons grabbing and then hauling the squirrel carcass off into the top of a nearby tree both stunned and excited the caveman. He spent many evenings around the fire extolling the exquisite skills of the special hawk. He even gave the bird the name: **TALON-TED**. The name ulti-mately came to mean having extraordinary abilities. Sadly, due to a shortage of classroom spelling bees, the term **TALON-TED** was mis-spelled when it was recorded in *The Caveman Annals* as: "**TALENTED**."

WHEEL
(FIRST USED: 9,989 BC)

Definition: Any disk-shaped object used to convey other objects

Etymology: The spherical disks that were used as far back as recorded time, surprisingly, were not called **WHEELS**. Despite the disparity of languages around the world, in known and unknown habitudes, the thing that we have come to now know as the **WHEEL** was always referred to as the Spherical Round Thing, or the SRT. The first histori-cal references to the term **WHEEL** comes from an unexpected place.

Think of the Andes Mountains, which are the dominant geographi-cal feature of present and ancient Peru. Because of the geography and other generally lackadaisical issues, the Spherical Round Things were not employed as labor-saving devices. Peru, as in most of South America, had no beasts of burden—no donkeys, no camels, no horses, no elephants, and no slaves. Consequently the Spherical Round Things had no place in their society—except for the children. The Spherical Round Things were used as toys for the tots of Peru.

The children loved to get up in the morning and play. Even before breakfast, they could be found outside having races to see who could roll the Spherical Round Things the farthest using small tree branches to keep them upright. Parents would wake in the mornings to the delighted shrieks of their offspring. They would shout and yell: "**WHEE**!" as they ran alongside their SRTs (*Spherical Round Things*).

It became such a common yell that parents began to refer to their children's call to play as the **WHEE YELL**.

The term stuck. It spread around the world primarily because it was easier to say than Spherical Round Things. The **WHEE YELL**, of course, has become more common than dirt and is now spelled **WHEEL**. It has also been reduced to one syllable in an effort to simplify the language.

CATALYST
(FIRST USED: 9,500 BC)

Definition: A **CATALYST** is usually considered to be the thing that causes another (important) thing to happen when that change does not impact the thing that caused it. It is the causal agent.

Etymology: Over ten thousand years ago, man discovered cattle. The discovery changed the development of man in a profound way. Prior to herding and husbanding, early man was a hunter. Two key events caused man to hunt. One was the need for protein, and the second was the need to protect himself from the primary urges of predators. When man realized that cattle couldn't care less about eating him yet it cooked up on the "Barbie" with mouthwatering satisfaction, man stopped chasing predators and took up collecting large groups of grass munching cattle.

So cattle, in effect, caused the switch from man as hunter to man as herder. The one problem that remained was how each tribe was going to tell whose cows were whose. Because of the similarity of any one cow to all others, it was determined that each tribe should have its scribe draw up a parchment that listed each animal and the tribe that owned it. This list was called the **CATTLE-LIST**, or **CATALYST*** for short. The term eventually came to mean, as it does today, something that causes a change.

> **The Cattle-Lists eventually became so unwieldy that man was urged into the Bronze Age for no other reason than to hasten the discovery of the branding iron, which in turn solved the problem of cattle identification. The scribes tore up all of their cattle lists as the herders branded their herds with rudimentary combinations of Xs and Os.*

MELANCHOLY
(1ST OF 2) 9,372 BC; (2ND OF 2) 1937 AD

(Think about it. We live in a very stressful world. Wars, pests, and petulance, gas prices at an all-time high, the occasional hole in our socks— and all with no end in sight! It is under this raggedy umbrella that many of us develop what can be best described as MELANCHOLY).

Since **MELANCHOLY** *has become somewhat of a national pastime, it is appropriate to examine what we are dealing with so as to better understand how to face these moments of depression. And so, as a public service, I have done very little research into the historical underpinnings of this term because, as they say knowledge is power—and with proper understanding comes the ability to objectively recognize the onset of* **MELANCHOLY*** *and have the etymological tools to resist any temptation to fall into that depressed state.*

Definition: a state of mind resulting in mild to severe depression; a sad, sometimes empty feeling.

Etymology: *There are two schools of thought on the development of the term* **MELANCHOLY**. *We will herein explain both etymological* *camps' positions in their chronological context and let the reader be the judge of which explanation best invokes the actual historical under- pinnings.* The first etymological school of thought on this term is as follows:

This term was first used in the early agrarian era during the develop- ment of man as a gatherer rather than a hunter, and it is thought that the process of the gathering of melons led in part to the paradigm shift from hunter to gatherer. It was the custom for early gatherers to call out—or in effect, pray—that food would be found with the help of a "melon deity."

In any event, the male provider would wander the plain in search of food to carry home to his family for consumption. In the temperate zones, it was not uncommon for wild melons to be the staple food (as corn was to the Cornish, or as grapes were to the people of Grape Briton). As the season progressed and the melon "crop" decreased, the gatherers could often be heard to call out to the "great melon spirit" for help in discovering as-of-yet unfound melons. The fewer melons found, the more the melons were "called out" for. As the melon "crop" disappeared, the more desperate and depressed the melon gatherers became, and the louder became their cries, the louder the empty echoes delivered the sad replies. It was in these desperate days at the end of harvest season that melon calls echoed across the valleys. Observers referred to these wails as the sound of the men becoming "all melon-calley," a term later truncated and associated with a depressed state—i.e., **MELANCHOLY**.

*See 1937

FLEECE
(FIRST USED: 8,965 B.C.)

Definition: The coat of a sheep. Wool that is harvested through shearing

Etymology: The word **FLEECE** is much more complicated than it appears at first glance. As we know from our dictionary, **FLEECE** is the word used to describe what is basically the fur that covers the animal that we call a sheep.

> (*One has to wonder why it is that when the fur is attached to the animal and it rains, the fur does not shrink. Why then, one would ask, does the fur* [which we call wool after removing it from its original owner] *shrink when it is converted to a sweater and then placed in the washing machine?*)

In any event, returning focus to the complicated term **FLEECE**, it is interesting to note that we have named the insect most commonly found in the coat of a sheep: **FLEAS**. (While it has a completely different spelling from **FLEECE**, it is yet pronounced almost identically.) Then there is the reaction of most humans who come in contact with a large group of gregarious fleas camping out in the coat called **FLEECE**. He or she **FLEES**. (Again, a different word, and yet an almost identical pronunciation.) Finally, should you buy a nice sweater from the street vendor downtown, and it has a label proclaiming Wool, and you determine two weeks later that it is horse hair, you can be said to have been **FLEECED**.

(*And just for the record, the process to refine sheep's wool by removing all of the short brittle hairs should not be called worsted! It should be called bested unless you are looking at it from the sheep's point of view!*)

HYDRATE
(FIRST USED: 8,960 BC)

Definition: The capacity of living things to consume, maintain, or lose water.

Etymology: Early man, as agrarian, typically determined whether flocks and herds were getting enough water by carefully monitoring the coats of the animals. If, for instance, the animal was dead, it was clearly under **HIDE RATED**—that is, the hide of the bovine was so dry that it could exist only as a dead thing. However, for the living animals, a simple dust-to-mud test was in order.

With a mouthful of water, they would "spit-spray" a portion of the **HIDE** of the animal. They would then rub the wet section of **HIDE**. If their hands came back muddy, it was an indication of an extremely dry animal. That was because the coat would be filled with dust and dirt (a sign of dryness). If their hands came back dry and relatively clean, typically it meant that the animal's fur was healthy. A healthy animal was an animal that was getting adequate fluids.

Early man referred to these manual tests (muddy or dry hands) as **HIDE RATING** (or rating the moisture content of the animal's hide). We now have more efficient and effective tests to determine if an animal has appropriate fluid levels, but we refer to all things "water" as **HYDRATE**— and all things "slaughter" as **HIDE RATE**—i.e., rate per hide.

LEFT
(FIRST USED: 7,564 BC)

Definition: On the side of, or in the direction of west, when the subject or object is facing due north

Etymology: In the early days of history, after man had crossed over from the monkey phase to the early human phase, some men began the rudimentary study of the human eye. Back then ophthalmology could only dream of being a science, and optometry was not yet a twinkle in ophthalmology's eye.

The first eye doctor was a somewhat smug pretender who was ultimately credited with the "invention" of the term **LEFT**, (as in the opposite of **Right**). That was because in those days, as is true today, right-handed persons considered themselves "normal" and everyone else abnormal, specifically, those unfortunates who favored "the other" hand. At that time there was no official designation for "everything not **RIGHT**," such as "the other foot," or "leg," or "arm," etc. It was the first eye specialist, Doctor Sean Cite, who caused the term **LEFT** to come into widespread use as a description of those things "not **Right.**" His historic words were: "If you lose your right eye—you will only have what's **LEFT.**" And, of course, everything not **Right** from that day forward became "what's **LEFT.**" Ultimately, the "what's" dropped out of the phrase, and thereafter the designation became the **LEFT** eye, or arm, or leg.

SNAKE
(FIRST USED: 6,000 BC)

Definition: A reptile without limbs

Etymology: When the biblical chapter on Adam and Eve was edited for publication, the story of Adam's brother, *Trevor,* was edited out. It is from that unpublished information that we can trace the etymology of the term **SNAKE**. As we are all aware, the snake played a pivotal role in the story of Adam and Eve, but it also played a role in the short life of Trevor as well. Trevor was said to actually have discovered these limbless creatures when he inadvertently fell into one of their pits while roaming on the outskirts of the Garden of Eden. He fell onto the largest of the group of these limbless reptiles, which at the time were preparing to head out to the garden to hunt down dinner. The monster unhinged its jaws and clamped down on Trevor's ankle, releasing a toxic portion of its stored-up venom.

Trevor screamed so loud that both Adam and Eve came running. The reptiles slithered away just as Adam found Trev, who by now, as a result of the venom, was beginning to suffer blurred vision and slurred speech—both precursors to imminent death. Adam hugged his brother, and seeing the swollen puncture wounds on Trev's ankle, asked him what kind of pain he was feeling. Trevor tearfully looked at his brother and said in barely audible slurred speech: "…sssss—an—ache!" And then he died.

Neither Adam nor Eve understood Trevor's last words (which were "It's an ache") and decided he was describing the creature that bit him. And so it came to pass (as we say in Bible Speak), that the limbless reptile, which would later play such a pivotal role in the remaining years of human history, was from that day forward called a **SNAKE**—which, of course, was a contraction of Trevor's last words.

DO NOT ENTER
(FIRST USED: 5,996 BC)

Definition: A phrase meaning Do Not Enter (this place).

Etymology: Interestingly, this phrase has roots that place it back just a month and three days after the recording of history was begun. The first Greek historian, Horrid, tells us that back when man was just beginning to run out of caves and just beginning to create the first tent neighborhoods, some friction developed between the landed cave dwellers and the new tent cities. Not surprisingly, the cause of the friction was that the tent dwellers were not much more respected than squatters, and disputes were alarmingly escalated because the cave people were afraid that their hunting grounds would be diminished with each new tent erected. The Cave Council paved the way for the posting of signs (in areas of dispute) that read: Do Not Tent Here! *(The Southern Cave Council—SCC—allowed for the postings to read: Do Not Tent! Y'All HEAR?—but that has no real bearing on the basic history).* Over time and with a lot of wind, some of the signs (which were made out of sticks stuck to the trunks of trees with a bit of tar) lost a few letters, and the message came to read: Do Not en ter—with the missing *T* and *H* and *e* left blowing in the wind. And so, as history tells us, the phrase **DO NOT ENTER** was contracted from Do Not Tent Here! It ultimately kept its original meaning, which was Stay Out!

The Cave Council was so enamored with their authority that they gave somewhat guarded permission for the Cave Peoples to engage in fisticuffs and other violent sorties to press their point—which was to preserve hunting grounds. They even implied that an imposition of death was allowed if no other recourse was available. That led to a number of actual deaths and the disenchantment of the Cave People with the Cave Council. The problem was not with the actual deaths, but rather with the disregard for property rights. Specifically, dead individuals were being buried where they dropped, mostly without the permission of the landholder. The Cave Council responded by making signs (free upon request) that read: Do Not Inter. The net result was that an entire bureaucracy was formed around the signs—specifically DO NOT TENT HERE, DO NOT ENTER, and DO NOT INTER.

TREATS
(FIRST USED: 5,987 BC)

Definition: An unexpected tasty snack

Etymology: This term dates back to the days of Adam, Eve, Trevor, Cain, and the ever Abel—who, as you are aware, lived in Eden, which was entirely too far from civilization (epoch-wise) to be able to run out to the grocery store to buy candy bars or chips. It was indeed trees that provided the sweetest fruits, including the pear, the juiciest of oranges, and the ever "tempting" apple. The very term **TREATS**, in fact, came from the contraction of two terms: Tree and Eats….or **"TREE EATS"** which was, later on, sensibly contracted to **TREATS**.

AGREED
(FIRST USED: 5,897 BC)

Definition: Generally speaking, the term references two or more parties with separate interests conceding lesser issues in an effort to achieve common goals.

Etymology: Covenants, goals, contracts, and stipulations are all tactics used by individuals who are intent on providing themselves with the best options and results on a given issue. The only thing that separates humanity from chaos and anarchy is man's willingness to accept the lesser evil to establish the greater good.

Having said all of that, it should be noted that the only reason to enter into partnerships with others is to make sure that the individual needs of each partner is met. Therein lays the basis of the term **AGREED**. For each person signing in to the compact there is a need or desire being filled. That need or desire can be defined as an individual "greed." If each "greedy" need is being fulfilled, then the consent is commonly characterized as "**A GREED**"—from whence we derive the term **AGREED**.

❖   ❖   ❖

MUCILAGE
(FIRST USED: 5,812 BC)

Definition: Sticky paste

Etymology: Oral history indicates that before written history, some people witnessed a moose fall from a high ledge onto a rocky surface below. They raced to the scene but all that was left was a sticky paste and some fur. They used the sticky paste to hold things together and the fur to paint the sticky stuff onto surfaces that needed to be held together. In their primitive language they referred to the paste as **MOOSE-LEDGE**, or what we now fondly refer to as **MUCILAGE**.

❖   ❖   ❖

CHOPSTICKS
(FIRST USED: 4,726 BC)

Definition: Tools (wooden or plastic sticks) with which to pass food from a plate or bowl into the mouth.

Etymology: Chopsticks have been around (Asia) for the past six (plus) thousand years in wooden form and were used originally to disprove the theory that man evolved from the apes. Chopsticks were introduced to the populace exactly 6,737 years ago as a tool for eating without getting food all over your fingers. This was important because once you settled down to sleep at night, there were many a carnivore on the prowl, sniffing around for tasty morsels. And what could be more enticing than still-attached finger-food that smelled and tasted just like the evenings culinary delights?

It is therefore clear that the idea of using wooden sticks to eat with may have saved countless* lives. As noted, it also served to establish that the rumors started by the apes, suggesting that we were "cousins," were lies. And if that weren't enough, the suggestions were so patently false and demeaning that even the thought of such an abomination, did, in many cases, lead to dyspepsia and shortness of breath.

The argument was: if "man" could, using his prehensile-spatchilosum muscles, demonstrate the manual dexterity required to transfer food from plate to mouth using two simple sticks called food-sticks (which could double later in the evening as conducting batons at the orchestra, or sticks for the drummer in the back row)—then the ape should be able to perform the same with the same dexterity. Because there was no evidence that any ape had ever, or could ever, successfully manipulate "the sticks" without getting food wedged in his nose, let alone bring an entire orchestra to crescendo— man could be said to be superior and unrelated to the "other" hairy creatures.

The use of the food sticks suffered a near-fatal collapse when people began complaining that they were having some difficulty in restaurants. When they ordered such things as rib-eye steaks** or prime rib, the diners would typically attempt to savage the meat with jabs from the "food sticks" to break it into smaller eatable pieces. And when that failed, they would simply pick up the slab of meat and eat it out of their hands like a piece of watermelon. This disturbing trend was clearly a setback. The regression required decisive action. At the Annual Asian Emperor's Counsel (AAEC) in the year 4726, it was established that henceforth, all cooks would be required to serve food that had been chopped into small nuggets to facilitate the mechanics of eating with the "sticks" utensils. It was also decreed that because of the compatibility of the newly decreed chopped-up food, there was no good reason not to return to the daily use of the Food Sticks to attempt the impossible (cutting meat). From that day forward the utensils became " **CHOPSTICKS** (clearly referencing the "chopped-up food).***

Math hadn't been invented yet.

Ordering rib-eye steaks was frequently misunderstood due to the fact that the first **CHOPSTICKS were actually named rib-eye Stakes.*

**** It should also be noted that rice balls are a direct result of the **CHOPSTICK** controversy. It was difficult to pick up individual grains of rice with the sticks, so it was decreed that rice be cooked so that it was sticky. The stickiness helped bind two or more rice grains, which in turn made the target larger when probing with **CHOPSTICKS**. One unsung cook-hero made the concoction too sticky—with the now-popular rice ball as a result.*

CHRONOLOGY: FOUR

THE HELLACIOUS PERIOD

(FROM 2700 BC THROUGH 300 BC)

‹ *THE AGE OF PHIL OSSO* ›

"PLEASE LEAVE MY TEA OOLONG."

TEA
(FIRST USED: 2,700 BC)

Definition: Ancient liquid refreshment derived from the boiling of leaves and, more recently, certain types of herbs

Etymology: One of the well-kept secrets of human history is about to be revealed to you—and it is about the relationship between tea, Arabic numerals, and keeping track of our daily lives.

It is widely agreed upon that **TEA** was discovered by the Chinese Emperor Shen Nung in 2700 BC. Immediately following that discovery, **TEA** was introduced to Japan at about 4:00 o'clock in the afternoon of the year 805 AD. It seems like only yesterday that **TEA** was introduced to Europe by the Dutch in 1610. In any event, between 2700 BC and 1610 AD, the Chinese and the post-805 AD Japanese had years to experiment, play with, refine, and invent new types, tastes, and textures of **TEA**.

In the meantime, back in Rome, the use of Roman numerals was becoming something of a problem due to the huge amounts of parchment required to write a check for sums much bigger than $DCCCCXXXXVIII.00 (which was $948.00), not to mention the problems with mistakenly adding in one too many Xs or Cs.

Back in China and subsequently Japan, they were so busy inventing new kinds of **TEA** that it was determined that they were running out of names for the thousands of different **TEAS** coming out of the leaf-shredding machines. To resolve this problem, they adopted a simple numeric system to name their **TEAS**.

This involved assigning groups of numbers (most of which were just lying around waiting to be put to some use) to identify various **TEAS** and **TEA** groups. As an example: they adopted twelve general categories into which they could group **TEAS**. The number-one category might be black **TEAS**, the number two category green **TEAS**, the number three category diet **TEAS**, and so forth. From that point forward, any tea with the number one in its name belonged to the category of black **TEAS** So, for instance, twen-**TEA**-one might be a mild black **TEA**, while number thir-**TEA** three might be a bellicose diet **TEA**. The "teens" numbers (thir-**TEA** "N" through nine-**TEA** "N") were all new experimental **TEAS** and would either advance to the permanence of having a place in one of the other categories (otherwise referred to as "certain **TEAS**") or would be flushed down the drain like so much **TEA**-pee.

Very soon after the first ninety-nine **TEAS** were developed, categorized, and slotted by number—the Far East communities got word from their foreign scouts that the Huns were pillaging and lying to ruin the great capitals of the West. As a reminder to be ever vigilant, the **TEA** Commission decided that the next 999 types of tea to be developed would be assigned numbers in sequence, but that the **TEA** identifying number would be preceded by the descriptive words "Hun" and "Dread," as in One Hun Dread and Twent-**TEA**! This brilliant, forward-looking step kept the Asian communities alert and ready for an invasion from the dreaded Huns at any time.

It was not long before those **TEAS** were developed. It was time for the **TEA** Commission to plan the naming of future **TEAS**. In a move to honor the consumers of **TEAS**, the commission decided that each new **TEA** would refer to the consumer as "Thou" for the individual, and

"Sand" to represent the vast Asian populations ("*as like unto the sands of the earth*"). So **TEA** names such as "Two Thou-Sand and Twent-**TEA**-Two" came to be. It was during this period of **TEA'S** development that the West discovered **TEA** in a big way through the Far Eastern Trading Companies of the Dutch. However, there was no practical way to import tens of thousands of **TEA** types, so the Dutch trading companies decided not to go forward with an import program. The pooh-bahs, caliphs, and emperors of the Far East convened in an attempt to develop a strategy to entice the West to get into the **TEA** trade.

At the same time, the Dutch were looking at an entirely different issue, in light of the discovery of the Asian use of Arabic numerals. It occurred to them that they (the Chinese and Japanese governments) should co-opt Arabic numerals to replace the hugely complex and space-consuming so-called Roman numerals. To that end, the Dutch proposed that they select a limited variety of **TEAS**—to be purchased in massive ongoing quantities—for the right to use the Arabic numeral system.

An agreement was reached by all sides on of February 30, 1202 BC—and history was made. It took about four hundred years to develop **TEA** names that didn't have a number attached to them and that people would buy to drink. Additionally, a number of new **TEA** names were added to the lexicon, though not always necessarily in keeping with norms of good taste.

Some examples are listed below:

Hast **TEA** / Heft **TEA** / Haught **TEA** / Heart **TEA** / Lust **TEA** / Plent **TEA** / Par **TEA** / Special **TEA** / Impetuosit **TEA** / Subtle **TEA** / Tranquila **TEA** / Abilita **TEA** / Faul **TEA** / Royal **TEA** / Devot **TEA** / Bestialit **TEA** / Timidit **TEA** / Duplicit **TEA** / Guilt **TEA** /and, of course, in honor of the British—the name: Proper **TEA**.

ASSAULT
(FIRST USED: 1,712 BC)

Definition: This term refers to the infliction of bodily harm onto a person, or to an attack upon a group of people, a city, or nation by a person or persons intent on harming the person(s) or property involved.

Etymology: The first use of this term is documented in Genesis 19:23. The specific reference is to a man named Lot, who with his wife and children were warned by two angels to flee the environs of the ungodly cities of Sodom and Gomorrah. Lot was somewhat stupefied by the message and just stood there. It took some of his friends to manhandle him into fleeing into the hills with his family. Lot and troop had been warned by the angels not to look back. And so it came to pass that as soon as they were clear of the area and climbing into the hills, the Lord rained brimstone and fire upon the cities.

For whatever reason, Lot's wife, who was always forgetting something, turned to look at the destruction and was immediately turned into a "pillar of salt," as we are told in Genesis 19:23. It becomes apparent, though not stated, that someone else must have turned to look as well. How else would we have verification that Lot's wife was actually turned into a salt mound? What we do know for sure is that this was the inception of the term **ASSAULT**. When whichever person turned and saw Lot's wife, he or she must have shouted: "Oh Lot! Your beloved wife has been turned into a salt mound!" (We still don't know if others were being "**A SALTED**" on that day.)

Yet from that day forward, any reference to someone having bodily harm inflicted unto them was said to have been **"A SALTED,"** or as we now say it, **ASSAULTED.**

YACHT
(FIRST USED: 601 BC)

Definition: Lightweight vessel used for sailing or navigating waterways.

Etymology: The term yacht is, not surprisingly, one of our oldest known biblical terms; and not surprisingly, it has its genesis in the great flood of biblical lore, which, in turn, had its genesis in THE BOOK OF GENESIS. Prior to the actual sailing of the ark, Noah (who was quite old—look it up) was said to have been somewhat of a cantankerous character. It was widely reported that he was a man who found it necessary to have the last word on every subject. Because of his "special conversation," he was constantly insisting that every man should now be constructing an ark like the one he was building. He said that arks were necessary to save all of the animals from the coming deluge. Of course, every man with whom he had that conversation walked away with a knowing sneer, having decided that Noah had "rounded the bend" and soon would be escorted to the "home." Another thing that they all agreed on, and the history books relate, is that his annoying accent made things even less bearable (socially speaking). Noah would harp about the flood—and over and over he was heard to say in his annoying twang: "**YA OUGHT** ta build yerselves a beeg boat" and "**YA OUGHT** ta git ready for the beeg flood." Every sentence started with the declarative "**YA OUGHT**..." and ultimately, people began referring to his boat not as the ark, but as the "**YA OUGHT,**" which, as we know, was later contracted into the present day term **YACHT**.

WEIGHT
(FIRST USED: 561 BC)

Definition: A measurement of mass

Etymology: Early moms would show concern for their fat children by frequently telling that they "**eat way too much**" and that they should stop making pigs of themselves because it reflected poorly on the mom. Over the years, and as the "children of mass" grew-up to be "trim-challenged" adults, their doctor would repeat the advice that the patient might consider dieting. He reminded them that they were eating "**way too much.**" However, as medicine and the practitioners thereof matured over the years, they streamlined the phrase "**You eat way too much!**" to the simpler phrase "**You way to much!**" The spelling of **WAY** was changed to **W-E-I-G-H** so as to not confuse it with any other "way."

BASTARD
(FIRST USED: 500 BC)

Definition: A pejorative appellation; one born out of wedlock; not particularly considered a term of endearment.

Etymology: In the tradition of mainstream big-game hunters who track their prey by following the spore of the tapir or wildebeest, the lesser esteemed fish-chasers of the Papua Islands would work their way upstream, in pursuit of the largemouth bass. They would do this by attempting to track the bass spore (or turds, as they were referred to by the uncouth ancestors of today's sports-fishermen). It was usually the outcasts of the Papua culture who would turn to fish chasing, in an attempt to regain some status in the primitive culture. However, the very concept of fish chasing as a substitute for the big game hunt added to the scorn heaped upon them by their more daring "hunter" cousins. They became the butt of Papua jokes, and ultimately their watery activity became synonymous with the term **bass-turds**—which later was truncated to **BASTARDS**. Today the term has common usage as a pejorative, listing among its references not only "fish chasers" but also any unliked person, or any person of dubious parentage.

ACCORD
(FIRST USED: 469 BC)

Definition: Bringing people together to agree

Etymology: It is difficult to pinpoint the first use of the term **ACCORD**. However, we do know that as early as 469 BC, amid the battling Greek city-states, that the term was used to describe the movement of military prisoners. Typically, after a battle, the victors would move large groups of prisoners. They bound five or six men together with a **CORD**, which they tied to a mounted soldier's horse. Then they dragged the prisoners by the **CORD** to the holding camp, where they executed the prisoners as a group by requiring them to drink hemlock. It should be noted that the ancients had a different philosophy then we do now, and voluntarily drinking hemlock was the honorable thing for soldiers to do upon capture. It was clear that all of the prisoners were of a mutual understanding with regard to their city-state's interests and their philosophies

But above all they shared their beliefs and helped each other muster the courage to die honorably.

It was said that they were in **A CORD** as they were dragged to their final moment and then to their final resting places. It was understood that the **CORD** was what brought them together to agree to, and share, the same fate.

The words appear to have morphed into today's version: *****ACCORD**.

*(It has also been suggested that the term **ACCORD** was derived from the musical term **A CHORD**—which describes a series of notes that essentially "agree" with one another and play nice with other **CHORDS**. Whichever argument you choose to use during your etymological discussions, these histories share the same tone, and that is to say that things in **ACCORD** work together toward a common end.)*

PLATO
(FIRST USED: 427 BC)

Definition: Ancient Greek philosopher, a molder of minds. He is often confused with Play-Doh.

Etymology: It's his name!

PREAMBLE
(FIRST USED: 369 BC)

Definition: a reference or explanation of what is to come; a term specifically used to define an introduction for what is to follow.

Etymology: Preamble was the precursor to the term **forward**.

Let's break this word down:

a) **AMBLE** references more of a saunter and slightly less of a walk.

b) **PRE-** indicates "before."

So putting the two together we get "Before the saunter (or walk)."

It is said that this term dates back to the days that Aristotle, Plato, and, of course, Socrates roamed the known world (which was typically referred to at the time as Greece.)

As we all know from our grammar-school philosophy studies, all Greece was divided into three parts: The Platonic Gates, The Socratic States, and the Aristolic Metropolic. Each of these learned gentlemen (from whom came those city-state names) were, early on, associated with the founding of the Great Roaming Empire (better known at the time as Greece but later co-opted by Roam for one of their ad campaigns). It is, however, no coincidence that growing up, their two best friends were the half men/half gods Romulus and Remus (both born in Alba on the Italian Peninsula), and neither of whom were particularly happy children, having been suckled by a she-wolf and fed by a woodpecker. (The veracity of this story is clearly in the answer to the question: "Who could make this stuff up?")

Both of the brothers wanted to serve as king(s), if for no other reason than to acquire a more interesting diet (woodpeckers and demigods have entirely different ideas regarding what makes an interesting meal). However, the leaders of the Sheep Herders International Local .005 were not as enthusiastic about the idea of these two scrawny "wolf-men" discovering the delights of a fine lamb chop, so they "politely" prodded Romulus and Remus to continue to roam until they could discover a land of their own, name it anything they wished (except Greece), and then take it unto themselves. It should be no surprise to anyone where the name of the capital city of Italy—i.e., Roam—got its name, however poorly spelled. And of course, the rest, as we say, is history…except for this next part, which is hugely speculative.

Some have said that Aristotle, who was not much of a geographer, assumed that Alba (the birthplace of Romulus and Remus) was a part of Greece—and being in need of a good **AMBLE** at the time, decided to walk over there to see if it might indeed be a good place to raise wolves.

During this **AMBLE**, a group of Aristotle's devoted students followed and listened to his prattling about philosophy and its oranges (sometimes spelled *Origins*). It was widely held that Aristotle was primarily responsible for the Oranges of Philosophy. That theory has since been genuinely disproved, and it has been subsequently verified that the Oranges of Philosophy actually began in Indochina and then shipped, via the Chinese navy, to Greece—from whence came the now popular navel oranges. It was, however, once documented that Aristotle, who rarely washed his navel, did, one morning, find a sprout of *Citrus Reticulata* growing within the aforementioned belly button, apparently nurtured from a fine matte of body hair and linen fibers. Such documentation was later disproved when it was determined that oranges, navel or otherwise, did not come into common usage until the disease referred to as scurvy was invented as a WMD during World War One.

In any event, the term **AMBLE** actually came from these long walks, as did the abhorrent, unending, relentless, mind-numbing studies later to be named philosophic dissertations—which, in fact, sprang from Aristotle's mindless ramblings on these twelve-hour forays into the Greek countryside looking for Alba (which, as you may have guessed, was, and remarkably still is, on an entirely different peninsula in the Mediterranean Sea).

However, to get back on point, Socrates, and later Plato, were both given to these walking lectures in imitation of their young and more studly student Aristotle. They too, were followed by their students. The students called these walking-talking excursions **RAMBLINGS**—later shortened to **AMBLINGS**, and finally, shortened again to **PRE-AMBLES** because they knew that the walking-talking excursions would extend into longer, more detailed lectures once they arrived at the Universe Cities (the so-called scholastic environments of early Greece).

Another etymological offspring of these great thinkers was, of course, the term **Universe Cities**—later changed to the phrase **Universe Sit-Ease** because once there, you could actually **SIT** and learn rather than walk to learn. From that beginning, of course, came the modern-day term **UNIVERSITIES** and **UNIVERSITY**.

So to recap: Romulus, Remus, Plato, Socrates, Aristotle all played a part in the development of several modern-day words, among which are:

1.) The development of the term **AMBLE**—followed by its metamorphosis into the term **PREAMBLE**.

2.) **Rome**—more informally referred to as **Roam.**

3.) And finally, the development of the term **Universe Cities** and its subsequent adjustment to the term **Universities**.

TENTACLES
(FIRST USED: 365 BC)

Definition: generally refers to a series of appendages common to certain species of marine life.

Etymology: Surprisingly, Aristotle (384–322 BC) was said to be secondarily responsible for bringing this term into the lexicon. Aristotle felt that observation was the key to understanding, and to that end he spent each summer from 364 BC through 360 BC with his young son exploring the coastlines and shallows of the Aegean Sea. They were looking for, collecting, recording, and speculating on the nature of each sea creature they found.

Aristotle had a small boat, and he and his six-year-old son, Eapeus, loaded it with supplies (drawing and measuring implements, food, and a raggedy old tent in the event that they should need shelter from a storm). During their wanderings they discovered, captured, and measured several types of coral, octopuses, squid, and anemones. It was during these voyages that Aristotle was also able to categorize many species of worms, mollusks, crustaceans, and fish.

In an attempt to keep his six-year-old son involved in the process, he told Eapeus that he could name the strange appendages that emanated from many of the marine animals, including the octopus and squid. Eapeus was stumped but nevertheless stalled his dad from naming and closing the book on those multi-armed creatures. Then one night, when a storm was blowing in from the west, Aristotle set up the ragged little tent they were carrying to protect them from just such weather. And while it protected them during the storm, Eapeus couldn't sleep because the wind blew some severely frayed strands of canvas material from the disintegrating tent back and forth across the side of his face as he tried to sleep. After a while, and in frustration, he cried out to his dad: "Papa! The tent tickles." His father turned and looked—and the thought broke through at the same time for both of them.

In the morning Aristotle bundled the frays so that they would no longer bother the boy, and he entered into his records that the multi appendages of certain sea-creatures would forever be called **TENTACLES** in memory of the night that the tent tickled.

PHILOSOPHY
(FIRST USED: 312 BC)

Definition: a search for a general understanding of values and reality by chiefly speculative rather than observational means; an analysis of the grounds of, and concepts expressing, fundamental beliefs; the most general beliefs, concepts, and attitudes of an individual

Etymology: The great unsung hero of those who are fascinated by the intricate and complex concepts of the somewhat ethereal and intoxicating analytical study now called philosophy was a man by the name of **Philip of Osso. Philip of Osso** lived in ancient Greece from 419 BC until his death in 322 BC. He was the teacher of such men as Plato, and Aristotle. He taught them the life value concepts that made them such great thinkers. His very successful business was based on a series of manuscripts (or books) that he wrote, lectured on, and sold for a fee. The discipline that he wrote about was eventually named locally as the "**Phil Osso Fee**" but came to be known worldwide, and for the rest of time, as **PHILOSOPHY.**

RECTANGLE
(FIRST USED: 312 BC)

Definition: the science of two-dimensional shapes, based on postulates and axioms (if A is equal to B and B is equal to C, then A is equal to C—unless, of course, this is sophistry). See?

Etymology: It was early on in the study of geometry, as introduced by Pythagoras with his theorems and elucidated in the 300s BC by Elucid (whose name was later misspelled as Euclid) and propagated in academies organized by Plato, that geometric words began to severely clutter the language. Geometric elders, with undying devotion, seemed intent on establishing as much confusion as possible when introducing the plethora of new words into the lexicon. The skin crawls when one hears the terms parabola, octagon, quadrant, hectare, trapezoid, cylindrical, bisector, and on, ad nauseam.

However, the real trouble developed when the Geometric Word Police discovered what they thought was an inappropriate breach of patent and a misuse of geometric terminology. It began innocently enough when a young married couple found themselves involved with the third person, who was secretly the old lover of the female and the best friend of the other male of this threesome (names are withheld to protect the innocence of families involved). In any event, a bitter break-up came at the most inopportune of times, as there were no news stories of any titillation value greater than the awful disruption of these three young lovers. The press gave full cover-page disclosure of the mess and probed deeply into the psychological aspects of these forbidden practices. They headlined each hit-piece with the title **"FORBIDDEN-PRACTICE POLICE WRECKED TANGLE OF AMOROUS TRIANGLE."**

The Geometric Committee for Patent Controls was instantly up in arms. Fortunately, this episode happened before modern court systems were in place, and the only solution available came as a compromise wherein all future references to threesomes were required to use the lesser term triangle—and the term **WRECKED TANGLE** was to be returned to its former glory as a good old geometric **RECTANGLE.**

CHRONOLOGY: FIVE

THE VEXATIOUS ERA

(FROM 310 BC THROUGH 02 BC)

< WORDS TO LIVE

OR DIE!

BYE >

THEY THOUGHT IT WAS EGG-WHITES, BUT WE KNEW IT WAS SNOT...!

WOE
(FIRST USED: 203 BC)

Definition: term used to express calamity or great sorrow.

Etymology: Somewhere between the discovery by Hannibal that the elephants weren't "cutting it" and the installation of four tires on the Mustang in 1964, many a person died or was severely injured as a result of the riding, or the attempted riding, of horses. Up until the Mustang, the reference to HC (horse carnage) was common. It is clear that horses had a positive effect on the lives of some men, but for others, the interaction could result in anything from a mild tail whipping to impotence.

All of the negative interactions were a direct result of

a) an "independently minded" horse

b) failure on the part of the horse to hear or understand the command **WHOA**

c) failure on the part of the horse to assent to the command **WHOA**

d) failure on the part of the rider to stay off of the horse

e) failure on the part of an innocent bystander to understand that you cannot, without consequence, step out in front of a large quadruped that is galloping toward you.

Nonetheless, one or all of these events has happened frequently over the last seven thousand years. Happily, these calamities have provided us with the etymological underpinnings of the term **WHOA.** It is a word that commands a horse to stop. For any number of reasons, it has apparently been translated by the horse to mean DUMP THE RIDER or GO FASTER or STOP ON A DIME. In any event, the result of the command, more often than not, means that disaster is forthcoming. Thus was introduced into the lexicon the oft-used term **WOE** (and sometimes **WOW**) as a description of the end result of the juxtaposition of man and horse.

ALARM
(FIRST USED: 189 BC)

Definition: Apprehension; fear of danger; a sound machine that warns or alerts.

Etymology: Many people throughout the ages have passed on to their own children the tales and stories of their ancestors. When brought together, folklore, fables, forecasts, and narratives seem to come from a simmering pot of wonderment stew, each ingredient of which may or may not be based in reality. The truth is that through science and the inquisitive mind, some of the "meat" of each story appears to have at least a soupcon of basis in fact. For example, Noah's Ark—science now can point to a great flood in a region that supported the life of a large population of man and animals during the century under discussion. Another example is the story of the lost continent of Atlantis. It is only recently that science has laid claim to the ability to posit that such a specific place could have existed—even though the tale is multicultural.

During exhaustive studies and research on the etymology of the term **ALARM,** I have uncovered some fairly breathtaking, if not unreliable evidence, to cement the concept of the lost continent onto the Highway of Darwinian Evolution.

Everyone has, no doubt, seen and discussed the Darwinian chart that shows, from Darwin's perspective, the Ascent of Life, including man. It begins on the left lower corner with the amoeba as the first form of life, which leads to a tadpole, a fish with fins, and then a fish with legs walking out of the water…and on up the evolutionary ladder to Homo Sapiens—and then finally, modern-day man. The lost continent of Atlantis confirms my supposition that a step in the evolution of life is missing a key component, and that component was a form of man that could breathe underwater. Surely if a fish can walk out of water, then man can walk into it—and stay until he's done with whatever he set out to do!

For years there have been debates about the missing continent of Atlantis. Most people believe that it lies somewhere at the bottom of the sea between the American and the Euro-African continents. Treasure hunters have scoured all accessible diving spots. They have produced some notable evidence of man's existence on this submerged continent. Oddly, however, they have never produced the continent.

In the search for the origins of the word **ALARM**, I have uncovered irrefutable logic, subject to all of the rigors of questionable judgment that puts to bed forever the tiresome guessing game regarding Atlantis. If there were physical evidence of men living on Atlantis, it is evidence that will never be discovered because I posit that Atlantis existed during that missing link in the evolutionary charts. That missing link is the one where man is a creature that was able to breathe underwater. No one can claim that Atlantis is a fairy tale without proof. If Atlantis existed underwater where no one could see it, the burden of proof lies with the naysayers.

So it becomes obvious that man lived underwater on the "lost continent," which was also underwater. As an underwater breather, man would still need pots to carry his food in and would still produce art to hang on his walls. These pots and artworks that are found by divers and declared to be from Atlantis most certainly are from there. The saddest part of this story is that between the years 200 and 100 BC, a great disaster befell the "Lost" Continent and its underwater inhabitants. Everyone occupying this Shangri-"L-agua" was, alas, lost because of a threat posed by less friendly and far hungrier creatures.

This is where etymology comes in.

As you may know, the great squid and the octopus are considered to be the macaws of the oceans. If you have ever taken a close look at a squid or octopus, you might get the impression that they had just eaten a macaw and that the only thing left to chew on was the beak. But do not be fooled. That beak, apparently waiting to be swallowed, is actually the "mouth" of these great oily undersea creatures. They can snap or shatter bones in a heartbeat—and swallow them whole as well!

We know, from the papyrus records of the time, that in the year 189 BC there was a great migration of giant squid and octopus from the Mediterranean region to the mid and west Atlantic ocean. It is believed that this migration settled near, and in, the area of Atlantis that was then, and still is, an undersea "continent." These tentacle creatures (comrades in arms) began to prey on the inhabitants. The people (referred to as the Atlantisnickians) had never encountered creatures such as these and were very concerned.

It was less than two weeks after the migration was complete that the assault began. An Atlantisnickian gentleman would round the corner of the garage to empty the trash—only to be grabbed by three of six or eight arms and pulled into the oblivion of the great macaw-like beak. Before long, way too many people were disappearing. The only advantage the Atlantisnickians had was that the creatures fed only at two in the morning and four in the afternoon. A general meeting of the Atlantisian National Security Force (ANSF) rallied all of the remaining citizens to establish some protocols and, in general, protect themselves from the marauders.

A professor of unapplied science algorithms (USA) offered a potential stopgap. He claimed to have a theoretical solution. It was a mechanical device that might, at the least, warn the citizens when to be wary. With the needed approval from the ANSF, he got the go-ahead to finance and develop a prototype. He called it the **ALL ARM** CLOCK because it was able to alert the citizens when an attack of the "**ALL ARMED CREATURES**" was imminent. The device was prepared and set with a loud internal bell at both 1:45 a.m. and at 3:45 p.m. At the same instant that he plugged the device into the wall socket, it occurred to him that water and electricity do not mix.

But alas, the electric circuit was opened, and everyone on Atlantis was fried. The **ALL ARMS** creatures (squid and octopus) that were not in the vicinity had their eyebrows singed so badly that they up and left the area altogether.

You can still find some of the ancestors of the **ALL ARMS** creatures (that almost got fried) in the Gulf of Cortez and Baja. If you dive at night, you will see them still shuddering with a lingering electrical pulse as they swim away from you—to this day fleeing from potential electrocution.

The device that led to the destruction of the Atlantisnickians has had a name change from the **ALL ARM** clock to the more simple and direct **ALARM** clock. It should only be used in water-free environments.

IRRELEVANT
(FIRST USED: 186 BC)

Definition: Disconnected; not pertaining to, not needed; serving no useful purpose

Etymology: Hannibal's hatred for the Romans was legend, and he spent most of his adult life (from 229 BC to 182 BC) in the pursuit of the destruction of the Roman Empire and the protection of the Carthaginian way of life. The most recognizable achievement of his life was the oft-repeated stories of his crossing of the Alps on elephants in the conquest of Rome and her allies.

The sight of five hundred elephants moving inexorably southeastward over the Alps must have been an incredible sight, and it is said that with all of the men and provisions on the backs of those elephants, nothing could withstand the onslaught. The term **IRRELEVANT** came into being during just one such onslaught when one of Hannibal's generals, upon looking back at the long line of men and animals winding down a mountain trail, was heard to say that the rear elephant was of no use to them in battle because by the time it reached the battle site, the battle would be over. It was a windy day, and it was difficult for the soldiers to hear the general, so when he shouted to them of the uselessness of the **rear elephant,** it sounded like he said **"IRRELEVANT."** Thus a word was borne (on the wind), and came into use meaning not needed, or serving no useful purpose.

CAESAR
(FIRST USED: 71 BC)

Definition: An historical Ancient Roman patrician family name; later to become the title of Roman emperors

Etymology: It is said that Aurelia, the mother of Julius **CAESAR**, often told the story of how the **CAESAR** family name came to be. It was said that Caius Julius **CAESAR's** grandfather on his father's side was named Disgustus Julius Paturnicus. Disgustus apparently was somewhat of a pirate king and commanded a band of five thousand, including family and friends. Disgustus was not without his charms. However, it was frequently mentioned that he was completely unattractive to the opposite sex. The only means available to have his way with the fairer sex was to select the one he most pined for and then have his pirates heed his command to "**Seize Her**!" He used this command frequently during pirate "road trips" (also referred to as "plunder runs"). The term "**Seize Her**!" became Disgusts' nom de plume and, through the power of the transcribed word, was an instant hit with the general rabble. Disgustus Julius became Disgustus Julius "**Seize Her**!" "**Seize her**" was, of course, spelled "**C-A-E-S-A-R**" in the original Latin.

DAM(N)
(*FIRST USED: 67 BC*)

Definition: A structure placed across a waterway to block the flow, usually resulting in the formation of a lake—where before there was only a stream or river; a curse word.

Etymology: It was not uncommon, anywhere in the world, to hear the term **DAMN** used as a sign of frustration or amazement—for anything from staring into a results-laden toilet to seeing your favorite quarterback sacked in the Big Game. The fact is that there are two terms—both pronounced identically—that fill those vocal frustration voids. The appropriate approbation to vent frustration is the term damn (**D A M N**), which technically is considered a "curse" word. Its engineering cousin is the term **DAM** (D A M)—which, as everyone knows, refers to an erstwhile construction and technical marvel that backs up free-flowing water, provides a source of potable water as well as fulfilling the recreational needs of summertime play.

The first earthen dam constructed by man was an unintended result of an attempt to see farther across a river valley where a competing tribe was poaching game that the indigenous tribe claimed as its own. The tribe, which for identifying purposes we will refer to as the Shovelers, clearly understood that information about one's enemy was the key to success in any battle, and for years had employed a strategy they called Dig and Mound. This military technique consisted of digging a trench and mounding the dirt alongside the trench so that the soldiers stand or move around behind the mound without being seen. Additionally, it was a mound from which they could visually access their enemy or prey where no such access had been available before. They also liked to speak in code lest the enemy infiltrate and have advance warning of their war game. Consequently, the Dig and Mound operations were truncated to the anagram: **DAM**.

The perfect conditions were met for a military application to augment a civil endeavor when a rogue storm swept the valley and dumped copious quantities of water not only in the valley but also on the surrounding hillsides. The result of this unseasonable assault from Mother Nature was to create a bog where a serene meadow had once been—which, as happenstance would have it, was a definite disadvantage to THE SHOVELERS, who now were literally "bogged down" in the mud. However, the waters also wreaked havoc with the new and suspect tribe, who were now hiding below the **D.A.M.** structure and were themselves standing in water that was seeping out from under the earthen mound and deepening.

The good news was that the **D.A.M.** MOUND burst, releasing tons of impatient water downstream and carrying along with it the ill-fated newbie's and their military strategies. The bad news was that virtually everyone's shoes were ruined.

And so, from 67 BC onward, the term **DAM** came into general use and abuse as men had to hand dig and mound each and every **DAM** they constructed. This type of work was hugely burdensome but necessary to provide defense and a clean water source to the diggers. But alas, it was tiring work, and along with every shovelful of dirt and rubble that they had to dig and mound could be heard the muttered word "Nasty!" Over time the two words **DAM** and nasty were heard being spit out of the tired diggers each time they muscled their spades into the dirt. All day long it was "**DAM**!", then "Nasty!" and they would shake the sweat off of their heads and faces and plunge the shovel in again.

"**DAM** Nasty! **DAM** Nasty!" Over and over it was repeated until the "hand-made" excavations were complete. At a point nearing exhaustion, the word "Nasty!" was dropped, and only the capitol letter *N* was muttered, resulting in the new expletive: **DAM...N**! And so it was that the new term "**DAMN**!" sprang forth from the old term **DAM**.

DAMAGE
(FIRST USED: 71 BC)

Definition: Destruction from any cause.

Etymology: Destruction from any cause is no consolation if you lose your house or your Rolls Royce to a flood, or to a rainstorm of brimstone and fire. The term **DAMAGE** has come to signify all such events.

However, in the beginning, when the word was just being formed, it had a quite simple foundation. In those days, before concrete and beavers, most dams (*as detailed in the etymology of the term **Dam***) were hand constructed with pick, shovel, and crew boss, and was a work of sweat and labor. It could be said in those days that not a lot of detail went into the science of engineering. Consequently, as the man-made dams became older, they became less stable and would typically fail. As the entire backed-up water supply simply washed away all evidence of an earthen berm, the wall of water would find its way down the steepest path—sweeping away hamlets and villages—until it found its natural course again and peacefully flow on toward the nearest ocean.

To the remaining citizens, who typically stood, albeit woefully, on higher ground, and who surveyed the losses of their relatives, homes, shops, horses, barns, churches, bars, bus stops, et al, the only way to explain the catastrophic calamity was to blame the dam's age. Then with heavy hearts and heavier shovels, they would begin again to rebuild the dam. It was a task that had to be completed before they could reconstruct their homes and businesses. Thus was the first use of the term **DAM AGE** established, and the word came to mean, as time moved on, anything that might be marred or broken by an outside cause.

(Author's Note: It never occurred to these early people that as a means of avoiding a repetition of the destruction, they should rebuild their homes and lives on higher ground. Perhaps someday, in the distant future, a practical-minded generation will discover the "higher ground" as a means of assuring that Mother Nature has to work a little harder to confound homeowners.)

ANNIHILATED
(FIRST USED: 38 BC)

Definition: The process by which a person or thing becomes nonexistent, obliterated, or generally extinguished.

Etymology: It was during the reign of Cleopatra of Egypt and before her fateful trip to Rome to be with Marcus Antony that the term **ANNIHILATED** came into common usage.

In Ancient Egypt the term Nile meant river. The Nile itself was thought to be the longest river in all of civilization at that time (no one, to date, has challenged that assumption).

The experience most commonly felt by the inhabitants of the Nile shorelines was the loss of a loved one at the watery hands of the river. Also and not infrequently there was the slight and slippery sound of the shuffle of sand beneath the webbed feet of the creeping crocodiles crawling within tasting distance of a third cousin or a beloved pet cat. At times it was the rapid rise of the river that claimed human victims, or an unsuspected leak of one or more of the reeds from which the water taxies were constructed.

Whatever the case, people were disappearing as fast as the evaporation of water in the humid sunshine of the Nile valley. When the Ancient Egyptian police came by to inquire about this or that missing person (or dromedary, or cat, etc.), citizens began explaining the loss with the same trepidation as third graders who, when asked about their missing homework, would respond "My dog ate it!" The grief-stricken relatives would tell rescue authorities that their cousin or their pet goat was gone because "**a Nile ate it**." Ultimately the term morphed in to our current use, and something that is destroyed is **ANNIHILATED**.

CHRONOLOGY: SIX

`THE TOXIN-FECTOUS EPOCH

(FROM 01 AD THROUGH 900 AD)

< "ONE MAN'S PETULANCE IS ANOTHER MAN'S PESTILENCE" >

THE REASON THAT PEOPLE HAVE TROUBLE LOSING WEIGHT IS THAT THE SMELL OF BURNING FAT MAKES THEM HUNGRY.

BARBARIAN
(FIRST USED: 3 AD)

Definition: Tribes of warriors intent on the destruction of the Roman Empire in the fourth century AD

Etymology: The Huns attacked the Roman Empire from the east. The tribe of Belghis Inna was only one of many tribes united in a common purpose. However, fomenting the Dark Ages was not something that they planned. Nonetheless, their inclination was to turn back the militant and aggressive Roman invaders, drive them back to Rome, and then destroy their Roman social and political systems.

One Hun in particular stands out because of his progeny. Belghis Inna was a leader of his tribe and was a man's man. He "got down" and partied with his "guys" at the end of each grueling day of battle. All local pubs were protected from pillage by the invaders so that they (the invaders) could spend the evenings with a sense of camaraderie and conviviality in the drinking establishments along their arduous trek to Rome. Belghis had a son by the name of Barry. Barry was a fine lad—pushing twenty-two years, as the story goes. Barry, despite all of his battle-fierce countenance, turned into a happy drunk each night when pub hopping was available.

Oddly, after several pints, Barry would spend the remainder of the evening roaming about the town or village turning out lights that had been left on. He loved to turn out every light he could find. Everywhere that Barry went, the expectation was that the place would go dark after a few ales. No one but Barry knew what was the causing the darkness, and (we speculate) it was Barry who was ultimately credited with turning the whole of Europe from its place in the sun—to what, from then on, would be known as the Dark Ages. But shutting down the lights was not Barry's biggest impact with respect to the plight of the Roman Empire. He was eliminating the ability of the rest of the Huns and their Honeys to participate in their evening rest and recreation rituals (what with the constant putting out of the lights). Once it was discovered that Barry was responsible for the "Dark Ages," Belghis Khan, who was leading this expedition halfway across the known world—to squash the Romans—decreed that henceforth all drinking establishments should bar Barry Inna from drinking anything other than water. Word spread far and wide, and every pub and drinking establishment was posted with a huge sign that read:

BAR BARRY INNA.

It was not long before that wording became a catchphrase for the Romans. When they saw the invading hordes, they knew that the dark ages were just a short horse gallop away. They would shout in alarm: "Here comes the Bar Barry Innas!"—which, of course, was later truncated to **BARBARIANS.**

❖   ❖   ❖

SEXTANT
(FIRST USED: 345 AD)

Definition: An instrument used to view and track celestial bodies.

Etymology: It wasn't until 345 AD that the distasteful issue arose regarding the highly suspicious, high-traffic activity around the Bedouin **TENTS** that had inauspiciously been set up on the edges of the great city of Alexandria. Ostensibly, the permits had been issued so that scientists and other interested parties could study the night sky away from the bright lights that the city fires and pyres provided.

As it turned out, the instruments used to measure the celestial spheres were, in fact, measuring celestial bodies right here on earth. The quiet movements and the barely audible moans suggested that the term Bedouin meant more than most people expected. The discovery of the tawdry enclave inspired the wrath of the Pharaoh—and the **SEX TENTS** were dismantled. Nonetheless, the instrument used to "scan" the **celestial bodies** thereafter became known, after a minor spelling adjustment, as the **SEXTANT**.

PARANOID
(FIRST USED: 358 AD)

Definition: A psychiatric condition in which the subject is unduly suspicious.

Etymology: The science of psychiatry can be traced back to the ancients. Plato, in the fourth Century BC, talked about the separation of the physical sphere from the mental in referencing the soul. The term **PARANOID**, in fact, originated in 358 BC when two of Plato's students offered one of the first dissertations on what caused some people to distrust, or fear, their neighbors and friends when they talked to each other.

The Dissertation, entitled *Distrust, or Fear of Neighbors and Friends When They Talked to Each Other"* held that such a mental state was not caused by physical presence so much as by an unhealthy state of mind. It was a state of mind that feared, and was angered, by **two or more** people talking to each other. During these "Distrust" events, the subject's misguided perception was that **the two people** were conspiring against him (or her). The deranged mental state was called **PAIR-ANNOYED**, and has been with us for better than two millennia in the form **PARANOID**.

IGNORANCE
(FIRST USED: 377 AD)

Etymology: the opposite of intelligence; without benefit of fact

Definition: People who have a point of view that they insist is valid and should be held so by all rational beings are sometimes stymied by opposing views. Typically, and nonetheless, many of these zealots feel it is their mission—their destiny, if you will—to promulgate their opinion at whatever cost. There is no evidence, however, to suggest that they are correct in all of their statements, nor is there any evidence that everything that they say is wrong. The only evidence, as such, is formulated in the oft-heard shouted attempts to drown out anyone with opposing views.

The sometimes vehement postulations have, at their core, some value—and it is, by careful weighing and consideration of all that has been said, that balanced and well-rounded views come to moderate our thinking and our acts. That, in turn, influences legislation that compels how we behave as a societal unit. It is when ideologues ignore these so-called rants that stupidity prevails and less-than-sound-and-principled legislative precepts are promulgated.

Only by paying close attention to all public discourse, whether reasoned or irrational, can we rest in confidence knowing everyone's view is fairly considered. It is therefore essential to social well-being that all good citizens listen to the rants of zealots rather than ignore them. The very term **IGNORANCE** long ago was assigned to individuals who chose to **IGNORE RANTS** and thus not understand the root causes of discord. (As Socrates said in the year 377, "I know nothing except the fact of my ignorance.")

PERIL
(FIRST USED: 541 AD)

Definition: A dangerous state; a specific time or place where one is at risk

Etymology: The "Dark Ages" was a horrible time to live. Aside from the fact that there was no light (a problem that was only corrected during the coming Age of Enlightenment), people were no sooner convinced that the Dark Ages were over and the Age of Enlightenment at hand when they were struck with the bubonic plague—which was referred to as the black death.

As the black death swept across Europe from the east, people became aware of the contagious nature of the disease. They were extremely suspicious of any neighbors who had two or more sick people living together. Curiously, such an event was thought to be a harbinger of the horrors of the bubonic plague. Word spread that the best defense against catching the fatal disease was first to identify any two ill persons, and second, to avoid them at all costs. Obviously, the term **PAIR ILL**, used in common parlance today and spelled **PERIL**, is a direct result of those events and a measure of how desperate folks were for medical assurances (which later became the basis for the oft-used phrase medical insurances).

FAIRYTALE
(FIRST USED: 620 AD)

Definition: Stories told about the whimsical fairy creatures that inhabited the enchanted forest of ye oldie.

Etymology: The term Dark Ages generally refers to the period between the fall of the Roman Empire (about 500 AD, give or take) and the dawn of the Middle Ages (about 1000 AD). Some say we call it the Dark Ages because no one who was credible wrote stuff down (creating a recording of what happened during that time). The fact is that it was called the Dark Ages because people couldn't see well due to the lack of light. Again: Because few were left who were "enlightened" after the Fall* of Rome, and because all of the partying was done at night, it never occurred to most people that it made more sense to spend their waking hours during the daytime. Consequently, most folks fell into the habit of staying up all night and sleeping during the day. Thus: the Dark AGES.

That is precisely why people began seeing things. Like **FAIRIES**. The problem with nighttime sightings of gossamer-winged **FAIRIES** was that you could not clearly identify the wings, and such, and ended up describing the "beasts" as creatures with bright eyes and **TAILS** that could lunge at you out of the darkness, sit on your shoulder and munch on your neck.

In fact, there were no **FAIRIES**. During the Middle Ages, scientists stayed up all night to try to capture one of these creatures. What they found were wingless, **TAILED** creatures, moving from person to person, chewing on chin waddles. On the first night, two of these creatures landed on the scientists' shoulders. Even though their noshing made for a pretty creepy sound, they were, nonetheless, captured, bagged, and tagged until morning. It was then that they were determined to be nocturnal "Flying…"(Leaping actually) Lizards," which is where the old refrain of surprise "LEAPING LIZARDS!" came from. The **TAIL of the FAIRY** was also put to rest and from then on recounted as a **FAIRYTALE**.

(It was called the FALL OF THE ROMAN EMPIRE because it took place on October 23, 476 AD which is, pretty much, the middle of fall around the Mediterranean.)

THAT
(FIRST USED: 620 AD)

Definition: A non-specific reference to the subject under consideration

Etymology: Talk about conspicuous consumption—especially in times of fiscal insecurity! It has come to my attention **that** if you type in the word **"That"** and do a Google search, you get 5,740,000,000 hits. I am appalled (as you should be) at such flagrant consumption of what, clearly, is our ever-dwindling ether (Ether is where we store everything that we produce and consume aboard the Internet, also referred to as the Cloud). Consequently, I am sworn to heretofore mitigate the overproduction and use of the word **"That"** until further notice. And **that's *(sorry)*** not going to be all **that** easy.

This whole imbroglio gave me pause (*if I'd have meant paws, I'd have typed paws*)**,** as it were, and triggered my curiosity. I began researching the whole unfolding, insidious, potentially ether-cramping, mass consumption, wasteful disregard and abuse of the term **That**.

It is clear to anyone with an understanding of language that the word "That" that we are speaking of came from the Southeast Asian surname: Pfthat (***pronounced That***). In particular, it is my understanding **that** Pfhelchur (***pronounced Feltyour***) Pfthat was the first to use the term Pfthat (transcribed as *That*) in a complete sentence in the year 620 AD Pfhelchur had been held back in grammar school for four consecutive years because of a lack of ability to add, subtract, or even count numbers. Pfhelchur asked his father Pfathom (pronounced *Fathom)* Pfthat to help him understand the difficult abstract concepts of math. Pfathom, in an attempt to simplify the basis for the math formulas—i.e., that one is one, and one more is therefore no longer one—sat Pfelchur down and asked him to pfocus. He then began by pointing to his sister Pfholly (*pronounced Holly*) and saying, "Pfthat is one, right?" It was then that Pfhelchur locked in on Pfholly Pfthat with a look of wonderment.

Pfathom pfelt encouraged, so he stepped in next to Pfholly and, pointing at himself with one hand and at Pfholly with the other, said to Pfhelchur: "Now, how 'bout Pfthat and Pfthat?" Pfhelchur said: "Yes, Pfthat and Pfthat," pointing and clapping his hands with glee. Pfathom raised his hands in exasperation and proclaimed Pfhelchur a pfailure. Pfelchur, for his part, referred to everything and every person, from thence forward, as "Pfthat" (or as we now pronounce it, **That**).

Despite its dubious origins, the word "**That**" has become almost impossible to avoid—and each time it is spoken, written, or thought, a little piece of our limited storage becomes ever more finite, notwithstanding the Pffact **that** each additional use creeps us more closely to a possible **BLACK WHOLE** of inphffinity. **That** has not always been the case. There was a time when **that** never would have happened—**that** we would ever even conceive of the danger of the cataclysmic collapse of our lexicon, clouding the consciousness, and at the same time clarifying the clarion clamoring for a calamity **that** is to close for comfort.

What is **that**...Who is **that**...Why is **that**...When is **that**...They say **that**... Been there...done **That**... WE NEED TO STOP **THAT**! **THAT** WILL ABOUT COVER IT! **THAT'S THAT** AND ENOUGH OF **THAT**!

ARE YOU TIRED OF **THAT**?

DO YOU NEED PROTECTION FROM **THAT**?

WHAT ABOUT YOUR GRANDCHILDREN...DO THEY NEED ANY MORE OF **THAT**?

SEND COPIOUS QUANTITIES OF CASH, CHEQUES, CHEQUE-BOOKS, SAFETY DEPOSIT BOX KEYS, AND UNUSED COUPONS TO:

THAT'LL ABOUT DO IT....

P.O. BOX 555....

HERETOMYHOME, CA. , FOLLOWED BY MY ZIP CODE.

AND WE CAN THEN GUARANTEE YOU **THAT THAT**.... WILL BE THE END OF **THAT**.

❖   ❖   ❖

ANTHROPOLOGY
(FIRST USED: 680 AD)

Definition: The study of human behavior and interrelationships

Etymology: It is hard to undervalue the study of man and his early origins as a means of understanding current geopolitical climates. Pictographs were an inspired method of transmitting human thought and values to later generations. The Great Civilian Doubt, in 680, called into question the reasons for authority and governance by ruffians such as Visigoth kings.

In response, Wamba, a ne'er-do-well king of questionable judgment and intelligence, attempted to put down the rising calls for anarchy by having his poorly disciplined "army" enforce a levy of one goat per household, kingdom-wide. Outrage ensued! As a counter-offence, Wamba ordered his men to find ant nests, collect the insects in large leather pouches, and methodically visit every household in the kingdom and throw handful of ants into the living spaces of every horrified civilian.

That was the last straw for the citizens. They rose up as one and stormed the king in his castle. Just as they were about to throw Wamba into the Guadalquivir River, he shouted out a terrified apology for the abuses he had heaped upon both his subjects and the ants. Too little, too late—the watery execution was carried out.

The Cathedral of Seville (built in 1401), over the Grand Mosque of Seville, (constructed in the eighth Century), is sited alongside the once-wild Guadalquivir river. In the seventeenth century, when the Guadalquivir was dried up during the great drought of 1605, a tunnel was discovered that led from the riverbed to a sealed room beneath the cathedral. Ornate pictographs graced all four walls. They highlighted the vicious "ant throw" of 680 along with the "Apology of Wamba." They are studied even today.

A seventeenth-century apothecary named Ocho Nuevo, who enjoyed studying the ancient pictographs, as well as the aberrations in human behavior that they depicted, named the event THE **ANT-THROW APOLOGY**, and the phrase (*now referred to as* **ANTHROPOLOGY**) came to mean any investigation of human behavior.

BREAKABLE
(FIRST USED: 712 AD)

Definition: a thing that can be broken is said to be breakable

Etymology: Clearly, when one looks at the construction of this adjective, one sees the two words *break* and *able*, and one naturally concludes that the term **BREAKABLE** came from the indications that a thing (or person) was able to be broken. But one would be wrong to jump to that etymological conclusion. The term actually comes from Spain in the early days of bullfighting.

The first ten years of bull fighting looked a lot different than it does today. For example, a bull ring was not yet conceived, and the bullfighting events took place inside of any fenced field. Spectators found any available space on the outside of the fence to watch. Typically, the bull's owner was a farmer who was trying to raise some cash by taking bets on the winner of the event.

In those days, tight pants and red capes had not yet been introduced, and the bullfighter was usually dressed in his field hand clothes. It is also important to note that the only weapons allowed were the horns of the bull and the fists of the field hand. Typically, and of no particular surprise to anyone, the field hand might get in a few punches to the bull's jaw, but not much else. The punches served to rile the bull. It would end up either chasing the field hand to the nearest available exit, or it would skewer the poor guy. Everyone in the immediate vicinity knew when someone was gored because of the loud noise he would make as the horn passed into, and sometimes through, his body. This was also the inception of what we now refer to as the bullhorn.

In any event, whereas the original issue was the misguided attempt by the farmer to make some money betting on a fellow's ability to **break a bull** with his fists, it turned out that to **break a bull** was more likely to end up in the "breaking" of the field hand. And so the phrase **BREAK A BULL** came into common usage to mean "capable of being broken," or **BREAKABLE**.

PENCHANT
(FIRST USED: 745 AD)

Definition: strong inclination (to do something)

Etymology: Back in the olden days before the printing press (see "Gutenberg"—in a more reliable reference manual), the monks of old in the monasteries of old established a singing pattern referred to as Gregorian chant (which, by the way, was named after Greg of Old). With the addition of new chants to fill the quiet of the chapel, it became increasingly difficult for most monks to commit all of those songs and sequences of notes to memory. As a result, dissent developed in the ranks, and while most monks had committed to a vow of silence when they were not praying or singing, an underlying sound developed. It was the monks breaking their vow of silence and quietly demanding that the Gregorian chant be written down with pen and ink. You could hear: "**Pen chant…pen chant…pen chant…**" every time there was supposed to be silence.

It was a demand that the music be written down. It became a chant in itself. The father superior, once he understood what was going on, punished the outspoken offenders by having them sit and write all of the liturgical music down in multiple copies so that everyone would have his own music book. Thus did the word **PENCHANT** come into being and end up meaning "a strong inclination" (to do something).

EXCITED
(FIRST USED: 804 AD)

Definition: A physical state involving heightened alertness caused by an infusion of adrenalin as a response to positive or negative stimulus

Etymology: An alchemist in the early ninth century AD was confronted with his first experience with a patient whose vision had deteriorated over a period of three years. The patient was in a constant state of worry and stress. The alchemist knew of no salves or ointments that might remedy the situation, and the deterioration continued until the patient no longer had any vision. He was found screaming in distress as he fumbled about tripping over things that he could no longer see. In an extremely agitated state, he was brought to the alchemist one last time.

The alchemist, in an attempt to avoid losing the trust of his community of patients, declared that the loss of vision was a curse from God. After reading scripture, the alchemist (Manny) said that God revealed to him that henceforth, the malady would be referred to as **EX SIGHTED,** and without good hygiene and prayer, the same curse could befall anyone. None of the concerned community members believed that the loss of sight was a curse from God, and they banded together and issued a community decree that the alchemist could no longer **CITE** scripture. And from that day forward Manny was thereby **EX-CITED**.

If you read all of the thousands of books on etymological histories, you'll learn that no word was more horrifyingly influential in the establishment the new word **EXCITED** than the actual declaration that one is **EX-CITED**. You be the judge.

ORPHAN
(FIRST USED: 826 AD)

Definition: An individual without parents, typically referencing a child whose parents have passed on.

Etymology: As every child knows, parents are obstacles to fun. So there are two choices: either parents **or fun**, but not both at the same time. The reality, as we have grown up to learn, is somewhere in between the two. Not surprisingly, from that dichotomy (**Parents or Fun?**) arose the term we now refer to as "**Or Fun,**" though we spell it **Orphan**, which, as defined as a child without parents…

DEFY
(FIRST USED: 854 AD)

Definition: To not fall in line; to resist.

Etymology: **DEFY** is a complex word made up of four disparate letters. Without wading too deeply into the historical underpinnings, let it suffice it to say that the word's introduction into the lexicon came in 854 AD. As the history books describe it, a young boy, son of a poor widowed cow owner, took their only cow, Milky-White, to town to sell for food—or so they say. He got beans, and mom got mad. To make a long story short, the beans were tossed and grew overnight into a stalk that reached into the clouds. Everyone knows the story, right?

Except the Giant—who wasn't as bad a guy as the media would betray—was the first to utter the phrase that would make the word **DEFY** possible. It was during the encounter with Jack that the Giant rumbled his tirade: "FEE, **FI**, FOE, FUM!" I SMELL THE BLOOD…" etc. Many words in the Giant-land idiom begin with the letter *F* (as you may have noticed), and more importantly, this was the first time that the word "**FI**" was heard. Because of the circumstances, lingual experts tend to agree that the use of the term "**FI**" was intended to indicate a sense of ***shock and distaste***. I think that we can therefore assume that the Giant was not happy about the visitations from Jack, as would be evidenced by not only the giant's demeanor (the more Jack visited, demeanor the Giant got), but also by the fact that within a few days, he (the Giant), would lie dead at the feet of this young interloper. Historians still bicker over the tragic loss of an opportunity for the human race to ever again be able to interface with the race of giants that loom large over our heads. Nonetheless we do have the legacy of the Giant term "**FI**," which the same linguists have appropriated to the spelling selection of either **"FI"** or "**FY**."

In any event, the word, as we have stated, means **shock** and/or **distaste**. Some conservative linguists took umbrage at having a word to express "**shock and/or distaste**," feeling that if the word was made a part of the human language, then people would use it—potentially increasing "**shock and or distaste**" in general and thus lowering the enjoyment of an "all-positive" language. Those same linguists, in an attempt to de-emphasize the negativity of the term, developed a counter-assault and created a word to counter the impact of the "**Shock and Distaste**" approbation.

They did so by simply adding the "**de**"-to the Giant's word "**FI**." They began with the confluence of the prefix "**De**" (meaning essentially "undo what comes after) with the term "**FI**" changed to **FY** to create the new word **DEFY**. The word **DEFY**, therefore, means **to resist shock or distaste.**

*(In fairness it should be reported that the "counter-assault" by the conservative linguists began with a physical attack on the mainstream linguists. The "Conserves" physically chased the "Main-streamers" with broken and jagged slabs of granite countertops—until they figured out that with all of that extra weight, they couldn't catch up with their Main-streamers to do any serious bashing. Only then did they knuckle under and do the hard work necessary to find a counter-word that would undermine the negativity of the word **DEFY**.)*

SWEDISH
(FIRST USED: 887 AD)

Definition: A person or persons from Sweden are characterized as Swedish.

Etymology: In the pre-Middle Ages when the Goths and the Visigoths, the Huns and their Honeys wandered there and about pillaging and establishing ruin, it is said that when adequate pillage could not be found, they would occasionally resort to cannibalism until such time as proper game leaped into their encampment. One of those inglorious moments came as they swept through Scandinavia, and more specifically, what is now known as Sweden.

The marauding tribe found a group of tasty-looking victims cooking in a cave. They were busy boiling a concoction to be later cooled into dollops of what they called Chock-O-Let. The barbarians immediately seized the boiling vat and dumped the contents onto the ground in preparation for the boiling of limbs (several of the marauders severely burned their hands dumping the hot vat. *No one said that they were bright).* One of their group stuck a finger in the sticky paste from the vat, sniffed, and then tasted it, and declared it to be **SWEET-ISH**. Happily, everyone chowed down on the Chock-O-Let, and the Huns and their Honeys bid farewell to the tribe of candy makers without leaving the usual carnage. They dubbed the cave a **SWEET DEN** and declared the inhabitants of the cave to be **SWEET-ISH**, at the very place we now know as **Sweden**, and the very people we now refer to as **Swedish**.

CHRONOLOGY SEVEN:

THE PRETENTIOUS ERA

(FROM 900 AD THROUGH 1199 BC)

‹ THERE IS NO TOOT QUITE
LIKE AN ASTUTE... ›

IN SOME CIRCLES THE TERMS "NOBILITY" AND "NO ABILITY" ARE SYNONYMOUS.

MEDIEVAL
(FIRST USED: 962 AD)

Definition: This term typically refers to a period of time relating to the **Middle Ages** (and as such was located between the Dark Ages and the Age of Reason, or Renaissance). It can also refer to such "qualities" of man as mean-spirited, superstitious, and generally evil (sometimes to a fault).

Etymology: Somehow, after the **medieval** era was formally declared over, it was voted a 5—on a 1 to 10 scale—and (unless you were nobility) was not much fun to have been born into. The **Middle Ages** represented such negatives as the plague, the Spanish Inquisition, the rack, feudal governance, ignorance, and a general sense of despair. **Medieval** times occurred just before the invention of the gun (although gunpowder was still working its way east from China). Consequently, the weapons of choice were tools that sliced and diced, severed and scarred. Being impaled by a six-foot-long lance was something that every man of the era could potentially experience.

The period prior to the medieval times was commonly referred to as the Dark Ages. The predominance of superstition as the preferred and accepted form of "human intelligence" helped to define the time. During the Dark Ages, what you didn't know could kill you. During the Middle Ages, it didn't really matter what you knew. You either said "Yes, me Lord" to your lord, or baron, or marquise, or king…or you died shortly after partaking in some exquisite form of pain.

Given this unhappy scenario, when the ages and levels of evil were being identified and codified, it was decided that the eighth through the eleventh centuries were representative of the mid-range of evil, or, as translated **Mid-Evil**.

The **Three Stages of Evil,** as currently codified, are:

1.) **MAJOR EVIL:** Initially referred to as **Bowl We Evil** and later called **Bowel Evil**, referring to all of the things that are filled into the breakfast bowls, and thus the bowels of our children (and childlike adults). These are the break- fast bowls that are loaded with trans fats and sugars; bowls and bowels filled with "foods" that have no nutri- tive value. They led to such stunning horrors as diar- rhea, obesity, gaseous emanations, and demented sugar rushes.

2.) **Mid-Evil**: To this day, the post-Dark Age and pre- Renaissance age are listed among the three great evils (later misspelled in history and taboo related books as: **M-e-d-i-e-v-a-l**).

3.) **Minor Evil:** The least of the evils, this usually occurred when you were asleep and having a bad dreams from which you actually awoke.

NOBILITY
(FIRST USED: 1018 AD)

Definition: A person of note—due to his or her status in the community, based on family power and wealth.

Etymology: It constantly amazes me how common sense was frequently involved in the metamorphosis of words. The term at hand, **NOBILITY**, is an excellent example of that under**lying truth** (it's also curious how two words that are potentially opposite—i.e., under**lying** and **truth**—work so well together).

As everyone is aware, the term NOBLE as in nobleman (which itself is a contraction of "NO-BULL!"), was originally used as a chant to protest the consumption and control of all power by the upper class. The self-proclaimed nobleman had a tendency to leave the "great unwashed" unprotected and unable to fend for themselves in the hopes that they would stay subservient forever.

When the frustrated populace finally saw where they stood in the minds of their "superiors," they stopped chanting "NO BULL!" and began the new and more insulting chant: "**NO ABILITY**! **NO ABILITY**!" As generations crept out of the Dark Ages, the **HAVES**, over the protests of the **HAVE KNOTS**, dumped the *A* from **NO ABILITY** and began referring to themselves as **NOBILITY**.

ARCHITECT
(FIRST USED: 1063 AD)

Definition: *Referencing one who designs physical structures from homes to skyscrapers.*

Etymology: In the year 1063, in a small settlement that would become London, England, a man whose nickname was Howzit (because every time he passed someone along the lane, he would ask, "Howzit going?") was the first officially designated architect. He drew up plans and helped build the first known "cottage" for his friend Eddy. And he called it an **Eddy Face** because of the look of the windows, which resembled eyes, with the door a nose and the stoop a mouth, etc. Howzit began teaching how to design and build such edifices. He referred to his students as **art cadets**, and upon their graduation, they were raised from their designation as **ART CADET** to certification as an **ARCHITECT**.

CAPITOL
(FIRST USED: 1077 AD)

Definition: Domed building where representatives of government work

Etymology: The origins of the word **CAPITOL** are quite basic. After the construction of the first large domed "government" building, it became apparent to school children who visited the site of governance that the big domed building looked very much like a beanie, or cap, high up in the air. The most common comment from the children was that the "**Cap is tall**!" Government buildings came to be referred to as the "**Cap is tall**." Later (sometime during the twelfth century), the word was truncated to the now common appellation **CAPITOL.**

ASTUTE
(FIRST USED: 1112 AD)

Definition: A perceptive or incisive understanding

Etymology: This was one of the few words in our lexicon that can be specifically traced to the peasants of the Middle Ages. These poor fiefs were commonly called upon to meet every Sunday, after prayer, in the king's courtyard to listen to the king lecturing from his balcony. Each week's topic centered on "how good the commoner has it under the rule of this king." Each speech was long and bloated, expostulating on how dreadful life would be without the benefaction of His Majesty. The crowds were encouraged to interrupt with cheers and ovations.

It came to pass that some of the king's self-praise was so overstated that a contingent of the less decorous of the peasants would respond to such declarations with a passing of wind, or as was known in those less formal times, an **ass-toot**. The flatulent noises were greeted with glee from the surrounding peasants, and the term **ass-toot** came to mean someone who is perceptive or smart—i.e., "the guy knew the king was spouting a load of doo-doo." However, due to the vulgarity of the image that **ass-toot** generates, its spelling was changed to the more respectable version (**ASTUTE**) that it retains today.

CARBUNCLE
(FIRST USED: 1115 AD)

Definition: *Tumor or boil; an inflamed ulcer*

Etymology: Generations before the Atkins Diet, a little known food lover* who was the brother of the father of the plunder panther Genghis Khan, was the least likely of all of the Khans to go down in history for any reason other than the association to his nephew Genghis. Nonetheless, "Gaseous" Khan, as he was frequently referred to by his once-close friends, was, as mentioned, a lover of food. His devotion to all things chili ran a close second to the meat in his life. As if to mock the limitations of his own stomach, he was never seen (not even while asleep) without one of the following in his possession at any given time: bread, pasta, cakes, cookies, rice, pudding, rice pudding, custards, fruit drinks, juices, sodas, jams, jellies, and/or candy. The man was a walking carbohydrate incinerator.

His brother Gander (Genghis's father) made much ado about the constant passing of foul gasses that emanated from the churning innards of "Old Gassy," but despite the criticism, Gaseous bubbled and churned, farted and belched his way across China. He was always in a rear position when participating in the Marauding Horde—primarily because, frankly, none of the Mongol Mob could stand to ride behind him or the clouds of vapor that he produced. However, his contributions were that:

a) He was a one-man rear guard against sneak attacks from behind by virtue of his "biological emanations."**

b) Horde members who were not done pillaging and plundering when the army advanced were still able to find the advancing column by following the scent of Gaseous.

One slightly chilly evening, Gaseous, feeling more bloated than usual, excused himself from the evening pillage and went to lie down in his yurt. What followed was a scene out of a horror movie (although that particular genre hadn't yet been incorporated into the industry). Gaseous, who was lying on his back, began to experience pressure everywhere between his rib cage and his pelvic region. He called for a doctor, but as has been noted, the evening pillage had drawn all but Gaseous away from the encampment. Suddenly the pressure became too much to bear. Gaseous screamed in pain, and with a final enormous jolt, his overburdened middle ripped open with the sound of an explosion. His final breath was a gaseous exhalation of monumental proportions laying bare his internal organs and, most notably, his stomach, which was three times that of a normal human being. Inside the inner lining of his stomach were clearly visible sores that pulsated a full three hours after his death.

In the meantime, the horde began trickling back into camp and through the cloud of bacterial rot. All were horrified by the still-living, pulsating ulcers, and even more horrified by the fact that Gaseous, Uncle of Genghis, had eaten his last apple fritter. After the autopsy, the tribal coroner indicated that the stomach boils and tumors were in fact caused by overindulgence in a high-carb diet—something that until then had never been seen. As a final act of "remembrance" for Gaseous, the pus sores were named **Carb-Uncles** in honor of a man of tremendous proportions who both knew the value of a high-carb diet and who was the Uncle of Genghis Khan.

*euphemism

**that portion of the rear end from which gasses flow

❖   ❖   ❖

THRONE ROOM
(FIRST USED: 1152 AD)

Definition: As such, a **THRONE ROOM** refers to the room in the castle where the king or queen presides over the business of the realm.

Etymology: Everyone understands the concept of the **THRONE ROOM** as defined. In fact, up to and including "our time," the **THRONE ROOM** is still used as a place for pomp and ceremony. What most people do not know is the sad story and the chaotic buildup to the **THRONE ROOMS** of today. In Ye days of Olden, before kings had the time to sit and enjoy the power that came along with being the guy in-charge, they had a rough go. Most vassals, serfs, and other spawn of the Dark Ages were not inclined to worship at the foot of the first guy who came along and demanded obeisance. Frequently, the result of such attempts was insurrection. And though the fiefs were poorly armed (or in some cases, missing an arm), the battles raged all about the castle and its impeccably manicured gardens and lawns. It was not so rare for the battles to rage right into the great halls. Because of the ferocity of these battles, some of the less well-armed serfs found it prudent to defend themselves with the benches, tables, and chairs placed around the great halls. And more often than not, the furniture got thrown as the flashing sword blades got closer.

Typically the guys with the swords (All Yee King's Men) held forth... and the only "cleanup" issue was all of the splintered remnants of the thrown furniture and the twisted and torn limbs and egos of the vassal, serfs, and fiefs.

However—and not to put too fine a point on it—the phrase **THROWN ROOM** (where all of the furniture was thrown) came to mean the room that was symbolic of the great victory of the king and the room where he would sit in judgment and rule over his kingdom. The only problem was that scribes who wrote about these historical underpinnings decided to take the edge off of these battles and substituted the term **THRONE** for the rightful term T**HROWN**.

TURRET
(FIRST USED: 1160 AD)

Definition: A construction higher than the rooftop to allow a 360 degree view; an extension above an armored vehicle to allow gunners 360 degrees of visibility

Etymology: This is one of those words whose derivation came from the simplest of transferences. In the Middle Ages, in what we now know as Europe, kings and their ilk built castles on high promontories not only to show off their superiority, but also to be able to see their vast lands, as well as track an enemy advance should there be one (HA!). The addition of the tower looming into the sky, with its rounded shape and many windows, served to allow a 360 degree view. This device transferred nicely to tanks and other vehicles of war beginning with the age of the infernal combustion engine.

But back to the term **TURRET**. The kings of yore built these towers because they wanted to see all of their land. They wanted to **TOUR IT** without the inconvenience of having to mount a horse and clop all over the mud-infested hillsides. The use of the **TURRET,** which is Olden English for **Tour It**, worked well for the designers and gunners of **tour-ited** armored vehicles—and they too called their gunnery posts **TURRETS** because it gave them hindsight as well as side and foresight to determine which sites were infested with the enemy.

PURPLE
(FIRST USED: 1165 AD)

Definition: The color resulting from the combination of red and blue

Etymology: Purple is known as the color of royalty because of its deep, rich hue. It is both arresting and comforting. The term **PURPLE** came into being after alchemists in the twelfth century developed a pill to counter the aggressive behavior of the serfs of the manor(s). The kings and princes kept copious supplies of the medication and required that serfs take the pills at every meal. This simple pill, which had a stunningly calming effect on anyone who took it, was credited with subduing uncounted commoner uprisings throughout both the twelfth and thirteenth centuries. The pill became known as the Purr Pill, referring to the effects produced in the user—much like the purring of cats when they are sated and in complete harmony with their surroundings. The pill was also the color of red and blue combined—and was called **PURPLE** (from the root: **PURR-PILL**)—and became indicative of the control that royalty had over their serfs.

COLLAPSE
(FIRST USED: 1168 AD)

*(Again we are presented with the most common of etymological dilemmas. When scouring ancient papyrus, or manuscripts buried under years of neglect, the sudden discovery of evidence that a given word might have two separate histories is rare but exciting. The word **COLLAPSE** presents us with just such a dilemma. We leave it to the reader to determine which "history" this rich word springs from.)*

First Etymology: *COLLAPSE*

Definition: To give way, to fail, to break down

Etymology: The term **COLLAPSE** was first used to define those rare occasions when two parties who had mutually agreed to meet at a specific place at a specific time both completely forgot the agreement and both failed to show up for the appointment. It was said to be a **Co-lapse**. The term was later extended to mean any lapse or breakdown, up to and including the failure of a bridge or building.

Second Etymology: *COLLAPSE*

Definition: To give away; to fall; to break down.

Etymology: Any interested person can look up the definition of any term in the dictionary. (When you write an etymology of a word, you must look up every word in the dictionary to make sure you didn't misspell it. If, for instance, you are looking up the word **COLLAPSE**, you must look through all of the words that start with *A* and *B* before stumbling upon the *C* words—which is where you will eventually find the word **COLLAPSE**. This is a rule of etymology.)

As it happens, I was looking through the *A* words on my way to the *C* words when a little four-letter word caught my eye. The little word was **apse**, and it is described as a common architectural feature of the insides of many large churches and cathedrals. It is a domed or curved-roof projection, into the side-walls, or the front or back, of the church structure. It is usually a space set aside for personal prayer, and as such might be dedicated to a saint or a biblical event. It was sometimes a space paid for by an endowment from a family for their personal use.

In any event, I did some research on cathedrals and discovered that the majority of them were built between 1000 AD and 1600 AD. The cathedrals was based on the architecture of the older Roman basilica…and guess what? The basilicas also had apses. This information led me to some basic deductions, from which I was able to extrapolate the etymology of the term **COLLAPSE**.

First you have to posit that there were places in the Roman Empire that were cold—especially at night during the winter months. In those seasons, chunks of coal were stored in whatever spaces were available so that they could use them to heat up the basilicas and later the cathedrals. (Coal would also have made a great "chalk" if they had invented sidewalks by then—but sadly, sidewalks didn't come into common usage until expensive shoes were invented.)

In the early days, basilicas, and later, cathedrals were constructed with several spare apses. These "spares" were used to store coal to keep the "chill" off when it got cold. Apses, by nature, did not tower to the height of the basilica and cathedral ceilings, but they were pretty high. A lot of coal could be stacked up in these forty- to sixty-foot-high projections that bubbled out from the church. The obvious problem that developed was that coal cannot be stacked uniformly, like bricks. Coal can only be loosely stacked—and loosely stacked things tend to eventually fall apart. It was almost with weekly regularity that some church's coal storage would come tumbling down, blackening the faces of all who were worshiping.

These disaster apses were referred to as **COAL APSES** and may well have been the historical underpinning of the etymology of the term **COLLAPSE**.

DISEASE
(FIRST USED: 1172 AD)

Definition: The result of malicious organisms attacking the human body

Etymology: You either feel good or you don't. If you don't, it is either a result of a mental or a physical aberration. If it is mental, then you can be said to be sick in the head. If it is physical, you can be said to feel ill (sick in the body). In either case, one would not feel **ease** but rather **DIS-EASE**, meaning lack of ease due to a physical or mental dis-order. Therefore the opposite of a feeling of ease is a feeling of **DISEASE**, which is never a good thing.

Further study of the etymology of this term indicates that during the thirteenth century, when the expansion of trade routes was under-way via ships at sea, many of the early and newly conscripted sailors came to believe that the sea was an evil place and that it was out to get them. Seasickness was all the rage, and sailors who were ill and angry about being subjected to the constant motion were heard to shout out: "**DIE SEAS!** DIE!" And from the plea to: "**DIE SEAS!**" ultimately came the term **DISEASE.**

HIMSELF
(FIRST USED: 1199 AD)

Definition: From the Irish and English: a man of importance, the master of the house

Etymology: In a dimension such as Middle Earth wherein reside elfin creatures, trolls, fairies, hobbits, orcs, pixies, and gnomes, the hierarchy within the society is ruled by an elf called **H.I.M.-S.ELF**. While the title is impressive, it is wholly an acronym within an acronym and has its own separate etymology in its title. It stands for: **H**is **I**mperial **M**ajesty and **S**upreme **ELF** (the E.L.F. standing for: **Earnest Little Fellow**). All of this Middle Earth intelligence was passed on through and to our dimension by way of leprechaun to some lucky Irishman, and from there became a part of the Irish lexicon and, of course, a part of our permanent language.

CHRONOLOGY EIGHT:

(FROM 1200 AD THROUGH 1499 AD)

THE TENACIOUS ERA

< MESQUITOES ARE BETTER THAN NO TOES AT ALL! >

"IT SMELLS OF DUNG AND OTHER FORMS OF CAMEL ROT..."

MAGNA CARTA
(FIRST USED: 1215 AD)

Definition: A document that established the rule of law for freemen who lived under the rule of King John in 1215.

Etymology: In the year 1215, King John of England had been "bumping heads" with the barons and other non-king people of the realm. The argument was about rights and wrongs with respect to the rule of law. The king increasingly found himself cornered by the fact that it was the barons and other nobles that supplied him with the soldiers he needed to keep the realm safe.

Scholars rarely discuss the here-noted assumption that on June 14 of that year, the ground shook and **Mount Carta**, which loomed above the castle and keep, bellowed smoke and ash—and then the magma began to flow. One of the magma streams was within a few hectares of the castle. The barons met with the king and issued a warning. If the king did not accede to the demands of the barons (on behalf of the freemen), then said barons would employ many of the freemen to load up wheelbarrows full of the magma in the middle of the night and fill the king's moat with the sulfurous liquid heat.

The king understood immediately that any such action would kill all of the mosquito fish he had breeding in the moat. Any decrease in mosquito fish breeding, in turn, would make for a miserable summer of mosquito-filled afternoons in a castle with large view window cutouts. There would then be nothing to prevent the winged biting machines from entering the castle and commencing dining at will.

On the very next day, as the magma from **Mt. Carta** continued to flow, King John acceded to the demands of the barons and signed a document so stipulating. And thus was "the Rule of Law" restored to the kingdom. The document was known as the **Magma Carta** well into the thirteenth century, when scribes copied it incorrectly as the **Magna Carta.**

(It is unclear why a man as smart as King John would not have seen through the ruse and realized that all of the wheelbarrows of the realm were made of wood and would have burned up before the magma could have been transferred to the moat.)

QUESTION
(FIRST USED: 1216 AD)

Definition: An inquiry; an interrogative; from the Latin *Questus Shunoribus.*

Etymology: In the early twenty-first century, it seems that even though a large number of people are blessed with the latest electronics, including PCs, pods, and pads, there are still people out there who are looking for answers to all manner of inquiry. We even have electronic search engines to assist. We have Wikipedia, Ask.com, Google, and Ad Nauseam.net. The fact is, we have more questions now than we had in the Middle Ages (sometimes referred to as the Muddled Ages). Apparently, despite our sense of entitlement and all of our personal computer apps, we all still have, right alongside the known's, many daily unknowns to deal with.

In the days of yore, it wasn't all that different. People needed to know things to survive. Everyone had information gaps. "Who left the bloodstains all over my good sword?" "Why do I have to walk through pig slop every time I'm trying to enjoy a sunny day?" "What gives you the right to appropriate my only bushel of hay?"

The people of higher status were not immune to the puzzles of everyday life. In fact, we still, to this day, talk of the Quest for the Holy Grail, the tribulations of Don Quixote, and of the better-than-average rule of King Arthur. All of the Grand Quests of those days were handled by the Grand People…the kings, the knights, the dreamers. To be honest, those jobs were dangerous, but it was understood that if you wanted answers, you had to risk personal safety.

Over the years we have become more and more risk-aversion inclined. So much so that if someone suggests a quest, we tend to shun it and them until the actual quest has been completed and the answers are available. This particular type of risk aversion became known as the "**Quest-Shun,**" and later the more convenient **QUESTION.**

So—simplified: in Ye Olden Days, if you needed an answer, you either:

a.) went on a quest to get it, or in the typical "survival of the fittest mode," you:

b.) waited until someone else, via **a quest**, came up with the answer—or with a method of getting answers.

In effect—and for the sake of the survival of the unmotivated—your plan to stay alive by shunning the quest was a success. Hence, we have the origin of the **QUEST-SHUN**—which we currently referred to as the **QUESTION.**

CAMELOT
(FIRST USED: 1237 AD)

Definition: A mythical place where dreams come true.

Etymology: The first whispers of a **CAMELOT** came with the ascension of the enigmatic Cleopatra to the throne of Egypt. In addition to all of her grand plans to improve the conditions that the Egyptian people lived under, she was determined to have replacement camels at every oasis throughout the great deserts that stretched for a thousand miles into the interior of Africa. But Cleopatra's dream was not to be. The expense to water and feed hundreds of the animals in remote spots throughout the kingdom (in the unlikely event that a caravan needed to "retire" one of its camels) was not economically feasible—and Cleopatra's camel lots were not to be.

However, the term was pre-empted by the fiction of the thirteenth-century **Camel-lot** of King Arthur and his Round Table Knights—a fiction that lasted well into the twenty-first century. But it is a story without a single camel. Therefore, be well advised: if it is truly a **Camel Lot**, it will smell of dung and other forms of camel rot.

FOREMAN
(FIRST USED: 1308 AD)

Definition: The person in charge—on the job or on the jury

Etymology: Because mankind only has five fingers on each of his hands, and   because prior to the invention of colleges, he needed one of his hands to count the number of fingers on the other of his hands—for many years, mankind could only count to five. Most men in those precollege days worked for someone else. Most bosses, in order to guarantee that each of his men was working on whatever job was assigned, promoted the smartest guy in each group of five guys to be responsible for the productivity of the other four guys. This ingenious method of dividing up the workforce allowed the guy who was promoted to crew boss to match a worker to each of his free fingers on one hand. He used the other hand to count with. The guy who was promoted generally saved one digit, usually the thumb, to represent himself. Each crew boss was named **THE FOREMAN**, obviously, because he had four men to keep track of. The reason that they spelled it **FOREMAN** instead of **FOUR-MEN** was because, as previously noted, college hadn't been invented yet.

BACHELOR
(FIRST USED: 1315 AD)

Definition: An unmarried man; a knight's knight.

Etymology: It might surprise you to know that the term **BACHELOR** derives from the Middle Ages. In feudal times, knights had the responsibility of protecting the kingdom, slaying one another for religious purposes, and in general making sure that nobody "clocked" the king. It could then be said that the knight's job was to service the king and to make sure that the new recruits were properly trained to step up and fill in during vacations, sick leave, or for the sudden onslaught* of death.

Knights were quite proud of the young (trainee) knights assigned to them and were forbidden from using these eager lads to polish shoes, scrub backs, or otherwise detract from the main goal of preparing their charges for future life-and-death struggles. Each knight of the realm had up to twelve knight trainees to prepare for war (and yes, in answer to your next question: that included twelve days).

Each group of young knight trainees was given a **batch** number, and each trainer knight was required to report to the king on the quality of his young charges, or **batch**. This, obviously, led to friendly rivalries and contests, and is, in fact, where the whole concept of jousting tournaments came from. You may also recognize the phrase "May the best **batch** win...," again a turn of phrase from the training of knights, at night, even if they might not want to do it. Some of these young knight **batches** were especially heroic, and their tales of battle became the stuff of legend. Thus the term **Batch-Lore**, later truncated to **Bachelor**, referred to a knight in training, who was single but who would use his Batch-Lore to attract a date, in an attempt to win the Battle of the Sexes

> * *Slaught <from slaughter> is the past pluperfect of the verb: To slay, to be slain, and to have had to kill a bunch of people (as in slew).*

AILING
(FIRST USED: 1348 AD)

Definition: Not feeling well; "under the weather"; sick

Etymology: Situational awareness of how words actually become an integral part of the lexicon is, to some, a gift. To others, it can shake the very foundations of their being. As an example, if you were afflicted with the black death during the Middle Ages, you would be well aware that the only consequence was a "black" "death." Black because the primary external sign of the disease was the spewing (from both ends) of a black, foul-smelling liquid (which no healthy person wanted to be anywhere near, let alone have to clean up). The secondary external sign was, of course, death itself—which most people hoped to avoid, and of course, which none did.

The passing of the plague in Europe was met with stunned disbelief on the part of those who never contracted the disease. After months of cleanup work, including torching anything and anyone who came in touch with the victims or their possessions, it was determined that a celebration for the survivors was due. Plans were made, calendars were cleared, and a date was set. It was to be a simple celebration—considering all of the sadness from the recent loss—but nevertheless, a celebration. People scraped together what shekels they could find and bought ale by the barrel load. The day of the celebration, they started early—the first mugs were quaffed before ten bells. By ten bells that evening, people were lying in the streets in alcoholic stupors. The people who could still stand, sat—for fear of falling—and everyone slept for a good twelve hours.

When the celebrants awoke, they awoke into one of the largest mass hangovers in recorded history. Heads swelled up to the size of beach balls. People had wet heaves and dry heaves, and there was much weeping and gnashing of teeth. Most of the ex-celebrants believed that they had been overoptimistic and that actually, the plague was still with them. It wasn't until two days later that they could say with some authority that they had survived the plague. They also realized that the excesses of polishing off barrels of ale could make people feel as if they were dying. And so it began—then, in the post-celebratory days of the end of the black plague—that the irresponsible act of over quaffing **ALE** became known as **AILING** and has since come to refer to anyone that is feeling "out of sorts."

METRONOME
(FIRST USED: 1349 AD)

Definition: **A device used to count the beats of musical time**

Etymology: Every large city has its dark little secrets, its crevices and warrens. They may be the dark sides of alleys, the abandoned tunnels of once-proud subway infrastructure, or the many boarded-up dilapidations that were once the homes of families who have long since relocated to the suburbs. These dark, forbidding, boarded-up, pestilence-ridded urban crevices frequently became the shelters of the nether-people (beings that live between this world and the last). They are known to inhabit no other places than vastly populated cities and only come "out to play" during the darkest of nights. Only in the dimmest of lights do these creatures slink and slide along the shadows and gutters, hiding even from the pale of the moon. They do not eat, but rather absorb and assimilate any stray cats or lost and wandering pets that have the misfortune to cross their paths. They do not sleep, but rather in the daylight fade to invisibility in the shadow places. Sometimes, during the night they have been known to wander into the bedrooms of the living—but only those of us who are in deepest slumber. They keep track of the night hours and are ever aware of the placement of the sun by counting the steady beats of their hearts— the sound of which is remarkably similar to the tick-tock of a wind-up clock. They know exactly when to retreat into their "safe-places" before sunrise only because of an unnatural ability to internally count all 43,200 seconds of that unceasing heart-tick—which determine when the night is about to end.

It was in the Middle Ages, in only the largest cities during the plague of the black death, when the condition of the incurable teetered on the brink of death, that the dark gnomes would gleefully show themselves. Generally they would sing a dark song, keeping time with the tick-tock of their beating hearts. It is through reports from those sorry souls that we have learned of the existence of the so-called **metro-gnomes**.

It was only after the black death had passed and the Renaissance had ripened into full swing that the term **metro-gnome** was finally used to describe the new device that imitated the tick-tock of the gnome's heart. It was a major breakthrough in music and the training of musicians and writers of musical compositions. It was first used during orchestra practice in the cold winter of Nome, Alaska, where the spelling was suitably changed to the current **METRO-NOME** (which in that one instance could also refer to the city center of Nome, Alaska).

❖   ❖   ❖

TAPESTRY
(FIRST USED: 1352 AD)

Definition: Thick woven wall hanging used for decoration and warmth.

Etymology: If you have ever traveled through medieval Europe, you may have noticed that castles have few, if any, windows. This is because glass panes had yet to be invented. Often, the few windows available in a castle had a form of thin bark material curtain that rolled down in inclement weather—and then were rolled up in good weather. To help with the insulation value, the curtains were made of thin woven strips of bark from the dreaded sycamore, or "pest tree." There was so much pollen blowing from the European tree that the owners of castles literally had their help strip the bark from the trees and weave it into window coverings to reduce the pollen plagues. The very name **sycamore (sick of more)** is derived from the dissatisfaction of the people who lived near them. They were also referred to as the "**pest trees**" because the bark being harvested was generally full of tiny insects that made their homes on the inside of the bark. Consequently, if one was not careful, one could end up with a bucket load of these tiny pesticles roaming the corridors of the rich and famous.

The "bark harvesters" had to shake and/or tap the strips of bark before loading them onto the wagons to be delivered to the weavers.

The result of this new rule for harvesting—the process of shaking off the bugs—became known as **TAP PEST TREES**.

Shortly after the pest tree issue was resolved, sheep were invented. Sheep were a cross breeding of goats and a Bishon Frise. The result was an animal the size of the modern goat but covered with puffy, curly white fur. Once the Weavers Council got wind of the new furry creature, they began, at the insistence of the Castle Owners Council of 1337, to raise these creatures. They were named **sheep** (a common misspelling of the term **cheap**) as a reflection of how inexpensive the fur was to obtain.

Once the weaving Industry was fully converted to wool, they began weaving pictures into the window coverings. The most popular picture was the landscape. Castle owners became enamored of the large curtains with pictures. They soon began ordering even larger hangings with pictures of any trees that were not sycamores. Big bodies of water, or their favorite horses were also frequent subjects. They used these larger hangings to decorate the vast, cold castle walls. Soon, however, the limited subject matter for the hangings became boring and overly repetitive. In 1352, a joint meeting of the Weavers Council and the Castle Owners Council got together in Geneva to discuss ways and means to modernize the hangings.

The result was so simple it was elegant. A wise old weaver had only a two-word recommendation to solve the problem. He said: "**TAP HISTORY!**"

And so was born the modern **TAPESTRY**—now depicting events as simple as a family sitting down to dinner and as complex as a battle scene. To this very day, we have not run out of subjects for the weaving of any **"TAPESTRY."**

ARTHRITIS
(FIRST USED: 1449 AD)

Definition: A debilitating pain caused by the swelling of tissue around the joints.

Etymology: Gutenberg invented the printing press in 1450. Prior to that time, if you were going to read something, you would have to pick from what was available in the libraries of the era, which were typically attached to monasteries. And though the printing press was not invented in the monasteries, arthritis was.

The many monks sequestered in religious houses spent their entire lives handwriting all of that which was written. The Bible was the most frequently reproduced book. Those of us who have picked up a Bible know that it is composed of hundreds of thousands of tiny little words. Each of those words came from the quill of a pen prior to 1450. Some of the monks, as they got older, experienced extreme pain in the joints of their hands. That made the meticulous job of hand dupli-cating books difficult at best. A connection was made between the terrible pain and the task at "hand" (printing entire tomes). The syn-drome was named **Author Write Us**, which was a Latin term for the painful hand-bone syndrome common to each and every author of a hand-written book—not to mention the thousands of monks hand writing readable copies of those books. Today we refer to the blight simply as **ARTHRITIS.**

AMBITION
(FIRST USED: 1476 AD)

Definition: An overwhelming need to excel or master some specific human function.

Etymology: We all seem to associate the term AMBITION with politics, whether it is in the halls of government or the back rooms at work. But this term, in fact, came into being as a reference specific to a young man in fifteenth-century Ireland attempting to win election to high school senior class president. Young Will Yam, the son of Farmer Yam (who, not surprisingly, farmed yams) and twin brother to Shawn Yam, yearned with a fiery intensity to be popular (which he was not) and to be elected senior class president (which was never going to happen). Young Will's brother, Shawn, with his eager and generous disposition, was the class favorite, and the polls indicated that he would win the position an easy 30% ahead of his brother and only rival, Will. Will Yam, being somewhat sullen and given to quirky behavior, assessed the situation for what it was and determined to win the position by subterfuge.

On the morning of the election, September 17, 1476, Will kept a close watch on his brother and, in fact, followed him into the hen house for the morning chicken feeding. When they were both inside the hen house, Will grabbed Shawn and, without a word, cold cocked him with a left hook. Shawn went down like a wet sack of chicken feed. Will exchanged clothes with Shawn before taping up Shawn's mouth and binding his hands and feet. As you may recall from your own high school history, the senior class elected Shawn in a landslide and when Will, disguised as Shawn, walked up to the podium to accept the honor, the entire student body began booing and protesting the obvious ruse. (Obvious because Will and Shawn were fraternal twins and did not particularly look alike, although Will had always believed that twins are twins and therefore would always be able to fool people into thinking one was the other). When it was discovered that Will Yam had surprised, assaulted, and detained his brother, he was charged with attempting to ambush Shawn. The next day the leading newspaper headlines read: Will Yam Attempts to Ambush Sean. From that day forward, the words AMBUSH SEAN (contracted to AMBITION) were synonymous with a consuming need to attain a desired outcome. (*For further reference materials on this historical event, please refer to the etymology of the word* **POSITION**.)

SINCERE
(FIRST USED: 1483 AD)

Definition: Without affectation; that which is presented is true.

Etymology: It wasn't until the Spanish Inquisition and the increased exhortation by the church that **failure** to confess your sins was an invitation to lodge with the devil. It was then that the church came to the realization that they had the power to make those **failures** relate directly to the Everlasting Fires of Hell. They decided that as an example to all who might be contemplating sinning and/or not confessing, evil-doers would be punished by death. The feeling was that since you would be going straight to the everlasting fires of hell, it would be cool to burn you at the stake as a sort of "intro" to hell—and it would set a righteous example to other potential sinners.

The fire squads of the Inquisition were vassals (slaves) who prepared the wood and the stake. The stake was anchored so that the evil-doer could be tied to it. When the fire was lit, death of the person being burned would, by example, mean something to the witnesses who might be contemplating evil themselves. The image of someone searing to death was not easy to shake off. The term **SINCERE** was a conjunction of the terms: **SIN** and **SEAR**—and somehow it sounds nicer than it really was. But it will always be a reminder that unless you were honest and forthright, your only option was a dance with a very hot devil. The term **SINCERE** still reflects both sides of this moral choice.

UNCOMFORTABLE
(FIRST USED: 1493 AD)

Definition: anxious or uneasy; not physically relaxed

Etymology: The term "uncomfortable" came into being as a contraction of two words: **UNCOMFORT** and **TABLE**—which, in turn, referred to the Spanish Inquisition confession device known as the rack. The public relations team of Killjoy, Karnage, and Kullusion persuaded the Inquisition Committee to soften the public perception of their philosophic and interrogation processes by referring to the new "stretching machine" as the "**UNCOMFORT TABLE**."

MIGRATING BIRDS
(FIRST USED: 1497)

Definition: Flocks of birds, in flight, on their way somewhere

Etymology: I read somewhere that in the year 1497, in a run-down castle in Italy, an eccentric uncle of Christopher Columbus nurtured a hobby that folks in the surrounding countryside found a "bit odd." Faustus Vivian Columbus loved the idea of being able to corral ducks and geese and keep them indoors until such time as he needed to relieve them of their delicious fatty livers. In essence, one could call Faustus a liver lover.

He began this "liver hording" adventure in early spring of '97 when the geese and ducks were laying their eggs and settling in to raise their young. Faustus had purchased copious quantities of bird netting and used the netting to cover all of the windows and doors of his dilapidated "palace." He kept some of the netting in his pockets and used it to snare birds anywhere that he might run into three of four at a time.

Once back home, Faustus would release his catch into the cavernous rooms of his home, where they would live among the other unfortunates until selected as a liver donor. By early summer, Faustus, from all reports, had netted a handsome flock of three hundred or so birds when he determined himself to be out of space. In all likelihood the inside of the castle must have been a mess. In fact, bird droppings, plumage feathers aflutter, loud screeching, and throat-scratching dander apparently served to disavow Faustus of his desire to continue with his "food storage" project. Among other things, it had made his precious home unsuitable for human "consumption." But mostly it was the noise generated by all of the captive creatures. He told one young man whom he had employed to keep the cages clean that "I can no longer stand the noise!" He said that "the grating noise is getting on my last nerve." "The feathers," he moaned. "The slippery whitewash of poop! And the noise! The NOISE! I HAVE GOT TO GET RID OF **MY GRATING BIRDS!"** And with that, Faustus raced into the castle ripping and tearing down all of the protective netting he had covered the exits with. The birds, to a feather, swept out through the windows squawking and squealing all of the way.

Faustus, sadly, slipped on the white coating of poop covering the floor, cracked his head, and never recovered.

At his wake, which was attended by hundreds of locals, a young nephew told of Faustus and his last wish: "to get rid of "**MY GRATING BIRDS!"** Henceforth, any time a flock of geese or ducks was seen flying overhead, the image of Faustus and the "**MY GRATING BIRDS"** came to mind. In Italian, the phrase "**MY GRATING BIRDS"** came to mean noisy flocks flying. The English for "**MY GRATING BIRDS"** is, of course, **MIGRATING BIRDS** and has the same meaning.

CHRONOLOGY NINE:

(FROM 1500 AD THROUGH 1599 AD)

THE SEMI-MALICIOUS PERIOD

< *OFF WITH THEIR HEADS-UP* >

THE NOTION OF "THE UNWED MOTHER" IS A MISS CONCEPTION

CIVILIAN(S) / CIVIL SERVANT(S)
(FIRST USED: 1515 AD)

Definition: Persons who make up the majority of society, and persons who are functionaries (policemen, judges, or kings, etc.) of society

Etymology: Civilian is truly a fascinating word—and a word that witnesses (if you will) the transition of Western society from the burdens of the dark and feudal ages to the enlightenment era that we refer to as the Renaissance. In the early sixteenth century, Spain had spun out of the grips of the dark ages and feudal vestiges, as had much of Italy and Portugal. The Britons had yet to come to grips with the chauvinism of Henry VIII or the Reformation.

In Spain, King Charlie, who ruled from Valladolid, had a special place in his heart for the city of Seville, Spain's center of commerce and learning. King Charles, in an earnest attempt to change the way "society thinks," ruled that the servants who did extraordinary work enforcing the king's mandates, such as sweeping the streets or firefighting or helping to protect the streets from flagrants and vagrants and who were, in general, in the king's direct employ, should henceforth be referred to as **Seville Servants**.

The edict was met with great alarm from the general population, insofar as they were attempting to get away from the concept of "slave," "serf," and "servant." King Charlie, ever the benevolent ruler—and to allay any misgivings of his loyal subjects—declared that an amendment to the edict would, from that day, state that all persons under his protection, whether in Valencia, Madrid, or the Andalusia countryside, would heretofore be referred to as Seville-ians. It is from this edict that the terms (**Sevillians**) **CIVILIAN(S)** and **(Seville Servants) CIVIL SERVANTS** became a part of our language.

LEVER
(FIRST USED: 1533 AD)

Definition: A rigid device used to provide the force needed to lift or move heavy object; a rod or bar used to reduce the amount of energy needed to lift an object

Etymology: The word **LEVER** is pronounced just as it is written in the United States. However, the Brits, using the same language, somehow pronounce the term "lever" remarkable different. Their pronounce-ment sounds out as **"leave her."** Since etymology is not the "science of pronouncement," we will leave it to the "scientists of enunciation" to bicker about how the word sounds as it passes through our lips. However, it is now a good time to make the point that Brits were around and developing the English language well before America was "discovered." The liberties we Americans took with the English language became known worldwide as "Ameri-speak" (sometime between the beginning and the ending of the Revolutionary War).

The term **LEVER** (pronounced "**leave her**," or in the Cockney, "**leave'ah**") was recorded as used in England during the reign of King Henry the VIII. It came into the lexicon as a direct result of his use and misuse of his many wives. Every time King Henry cashed in an old wife for a new, he was said to announce to the court that he was about to "**leave her**" (wasn't he?) and that "it will be a great day in England when that happens because it will be like an enormous weight lifted from my chest" (wouldn't it?). And then all roundabout would clap and nod gaily now that their troubled ruler could again "walk as if on air"—or at the very least, without the encumbrance of that "she-burden." The heavy, emotional, stress-laden load would be lifted. The device for such a "heavy life" was the sudden breaking with Rome and the subsequent authority to "divorce" at will. That is how the word **LEVER** (pronounced "**leave her**" in Britain) became known as "a heavy burden being lifted." As to how the word came to be pronounced **LEVER** in the colonies will remain for others to determine.

SATIATED
(FIRST USED: 1536 AD)

Definition: Having your fill of something; more than enough

Etymology: Sadly, Anne Boleyn never made friends easily, although she did get the attention of the king. As a function of being Henry VIII's mistress, Anne got pregnant in 1532. Because King Henry was an honorable man, he married Anne shortly thereafter. Unfortunately, for Queen Catherine, Henry's other wife, things got a little dicey. The king's court was awash with gossip and disquietude regarding all of the problems that Anne Boleyn was causing. By midsummer of 1533, and as a result of the pressure put upon him by the king, Cardinal Wolsey annulled the marriage between Catherine and Henry. This marriage/annulment process further disturbed the court and country. In addition, it was the cause of much grief in international circles, not to mention the Vatican.

Both the court and the nation were in turmoil over Anne's reign as queen during the next three years. While the king turned a blind eye to the commotion, Anne was making enemies at every turn. It is rumored that Thomas Cromwell, who was one of the king's most trusted ministers and confidants, decided that Anne must go. To facilitate this imperative, Cromwell devised a plot as devious as it was historical.

The king loved lemon meringue pie. He was so fond of the confection that he instructed his kitchen staff that under pain of death, they were to provide him with his own (not to be shared) pie at each dinner. The king never failed to eat the entire pie, which, on a nightly basis, more than astonished everyone in his court. More importantly, no one else at any of the tables was allowed to have anything that faintly resembled the Royal Pie.

On the evening of May 2, 1536, Cromwell had the entire court, except for the king and queen, assemble in an anteroom next to the main dining room. This was thirty minutes earlier then the scheduled grand entrance of the royal couple to the dining room for the evening's dinner and entertainment. They all sat and listened attentively as Cromwell ticked off all of the ways that the devious queen had changed all of their lives and had corrupted their confidence in the king to do the right thing. Cromwell's plan, as he somberly advised, was to remove the Royal Pie from the Royal Pie Plate and dump it into a sack that could be later disposed of. When the king noticed the missing dessert, everyone was to point to the queen and say she had eaten it.

The plan worked beautifully. When the king heard everyone accusing Ann of eating his pie, he began his infamous rage: "Off with her head!" The incident was later documented in history books as "The Great Pie Lie" and of course, **"The Pie-Lie Massacre."** The phrase: "**SAY SHE ATE IT**" morphed into the term **SATIATED** and now refers to anyone whose **ROYAL PIE EYE** is bigger than his or her stomach.

BOWLING
(FIRST USED: 1536 AD)

Definition: Typically defined as a game played with a large, heavy ball that is rolled down a wooden alley at the end of which stand the target, ten upright pins.

Etymology: The origins of this game have been disputed for over four hundred years. The root cause of these disputes seems to be grounded in the code of honor sworn to by every serious bowler, even into the twenty-first century. However, most wholly independent and nonjudgmental historians, in the fog of medical marijuana, insist that some of the more-than-craven acts of King Henry the VIII squarely connect the dots between a hearty game and the evil antics of a king.

Some scholars suggest that every gesture of the king was directly associated with a political motivation of one kind or another. These motivations even crept into his personal and family life. Some of the trademark acts of the king were his highly volatile relationships with a number of his wives. When Henry's first wife, Catherine of Aragón, failed to provide the king with a son, she was banished, with a few servants, to a cold and damp castle in the north. That was a minor inconvenience compared to what the king had in store for his second (non male-offspring producing) wife.

Because Anne Boleyn was having her own affairs with several men right under the king's nose, it is said that he devised a special punishment for both her and her consorts. Ann's head was the first to experience the king's "No Head Policy" because of the **Great Pie Deception**. Immediately following, he had all of the men who participated in the deception, including those who only knew about it, beheaded. Then he had the heads of those unfortunate men lined up in a triangle format at the end of the castle ballroom. He referred to them as "**Pin-Heads**." Using the hair of Anne's head as a grip, he stood at the opposite end of the **Ballroom** and rolled her head into the heads of his now bodiless competitors to attempt to get them all rolling. He became so enamored with the game that he sent out invitations to all of his friends promising "**Pizza and Boleyn**," which, as we all know, became **Pizza and Bowling.**

(Some historians, while not contesting the actual beheading incident, do advocate for evidence they have found to indicate that an incident they refer to as the Pie-Lie Massacre was in fact the trigger that led to the slaughter of Anne and her cohorts.)

PALISADES
(FIRST USED: 1541 AD)

Definition: A fence or moat full of pointed stakes often used in medieval times as a method of defense; a row of high cliffs rising sharply from the ground; a high and defensible place

Etymology: Henry VIII (1509–1547) was known primarily for his many wives (eight at last count) but was, in fact, known for many other things, not the least of which was his physical status. He was small of stature, and frequently when it was said that he was "known" for this or that, it was typically an underground attack on the king and a slur of the first order because the intention was to say "He was gnome." But we digress.

It is hypothesized that Henry was, in fact, known for the extraordinary number of aides he went through during his reign as king of England, and that is where the term **PALISADES** comes to life. It was said that Henry had the entire moat around his residences planted with a thick nest of pointy stakes aimed at heaven and extending generally fifteen feet from the palace walls toward the outer edge of each moat.

To the casual observer, it would appear that the king was a forward-thinking battle architect and had very much a military siege mentality. In fact, however, Henry had more in mind than the next attack on his fortress castles and fortress. The fence of stakes served another very useful purpose.

But before we address the stakes, let us here point out the very term "defense" came directly from Henry's Moat Stake Fences, which were to become known and copied worldwide. They were commonly referred to as **the Fence**, which later, as we know, came into the lexicon as the term **De-fense.**

Henry, however, had, as we mentioned, another use for **the Fence**. Domestic and business help was never hard to find for a king who had the whole country for his fiefdom. He could conscript help from anyone at any time. Frequently the serf conscripted was not up to the task, and that was where **the Fence** became an offensive weapon when defense was not needed. Henry would punish any palace aide for any infraction, real or imagined, by simply throwing him or her out of any convenient palace window. Within the palace, the array of stakes around the moat was referred to as the **PALACE AIDES** (may they rest in peace), which was later morphed into **PALISADES**.

CORSET
(FIRST USED: 1556 AD)

Definition: a female undergarment made of bone or baleen, and fabric, shaped to sculpt the form into an hourglass figure

Etymology: A garment predating the "modern" corset was worn by both Minoan women and men as far back as 2000 BC, but the modern corset, worn as early as the 1500s and all through the 1900s, was a garment meant to shape, stretch, pad, puff up, and generally present the wearer as a lady of exquisite proportions. The phrase "hourglass figure" was an offshoot of the invention of the corset. Sometimes it inflated the chest or puffed out the hips, or choked the waist into a spine-like width—all to emulate the beautifully crafted carvings of the Greek goddesses.

The term **CORSET** came into common usage in the mid-sixteenth century when the French craftsman Pierre Pomposette decided to find a way to return his wife, Marie Allete Pomposette, to her former girlish figure. Marie, after birthing two beautiful children, had discovered that age and beauty were, at least in her case, mutually exclusive, and as a result had asked Pierre to fashion a garment that would return her to the 22" waist that, in her youth, had made her the object of desire for the men of her childhood village of Soupcon—a waist that had transformed into a "waste" over the years.

Pierre decided to use whale bones because of their curved shapes and facile nature, which allowed for easy carving and shaping. He used a tough but tanned goatskin to stretch between the bones and had it decorated with lace and sewn-on bows and gems. With grommets and lacings, he fashioned the back in such a way as to allow a chambermaid to tighten or loosen the garment to suit the fancy of the lady he loved: Marie Allette.

The garment, heretofore unnamed, got its name on the first fitting.

Marie's chambermaid, Millie Fyenellie, with one knee braced into the small of Marie's back, was tightening the laces to pull Marie's "waste" into a proper "waist" when Pierre, who was helping with the fitting, asked his beloved Marie: "Does it hurt, dear?" To which, through her grimace, she snapped rather irritably, "Of **course it** hurts!" From that day forward the garment was referred to as the **COURSE IT** (later truncated to **CORSET).**

BOTCHED ROBBERIES
(FIRST USED: 1566 AD)

Definition: A robbery is the taking the possessions of others by force

Etymology: The very first recorded occurrence of the taking of a printing press by force was in the year 1566, near Wittenberg in Germany. It was 116 years after Johannes Gutenberg had invented the printing press and the year that the German Lutheran Church changed the function of the Monastery of Faint Praise from a place of solitude and worship to an apparent home for the disturbed.

Aside from the time-consuming functions of eating, sleeping, praying, and making printing copies of the Bible by hand, the monks had just barely enough time during the day to meditate on their sore and blistered writing hands. The process was: Each monk was assigned a book, or books, of the Bible to copy—over and over and over. The repetition was as mind boggling as was the soreness of their ink-stained fingers.

When the monks heard that an old printing press was being stored in a shed at the nearby Gutenberg household, the monks (without the consent of the prior) left the priory after lights out and shuffled in their long, dark robes across the valley to the Gutenberg estate. They jumped the wall, found the press in the storage shed, and wrestled the press outside. The monks had appropriated the old buckboard wagon sitting next to the shed. They underestimated the weight of the old press and lost control of it as they were struggling to lift it from the shed floor to the bed of the wagon. The press fell off of the almost-upended wagon and crashed to the ground with a loud clank.

The story, which has been suppressed for all of these years and has yet to be confirmed, indicates that the Gutenberg heirs were light sleepers and came running at the sound of the press falling off of the wagon. The three monks grabbed makeshift weapons (a leather lead from the wagon, a stout wooden rod that had broken off of the press, and a metal crank). The robed monks, in their desperation, advanced on the Gutenbergs with their cowls cinched tightly around their noses so that they would not be recognized. They yelled obscure phrases in Latin, waving their weapons. They terrified the Gutenbergs, who turned and fled. The monks then quickly loaded the wagon with the much-damaged pile of wood and metal that had once been a working printing press. They skulked away pulling and pushing the purloined press back up to the priory.

The prior was beside himself when he discovered what had happened. He personally visited the Gutenberg household the next morning to return the stolen property and beg for forgiveness. The Gutenbergs settled for a signed guarantee from the archbishop stating that they would be guaranteed an entry into heaven (when the appropriate time came). They also stipulated that the monks were to be locked in the monastery and the public locked out for the rest of their days. The crime was referred to as a "**Botched Besiegement with Larcenous Intent**" because there was no established word for the larcenous act that had been committed.

Seven years later to the day, in the midst of a severe drought, Baron Thebotem, along with Prince Fredrick the Wise-as-Canbe (who held political sway over the region), contacted the prior with a special request. They had word that a farmer two valleys over was hoarding strawberries—and they wanted them. They offered the monastery its very own printing press in exchange for a wagonload of strawberries. The prior jumped at the opportunity to legitimately own a printing press and immediately agreed. He sent his three robed "sinner" monks to commit the **Besiegement**.

At the bottom of the hill, in the moonlight, one could clearly see the strawberry fields and a small barn wherein one might find a strawberry bonanza. The monks, with their one donkey and rickety wagon, slowly and quietly approached the barn. They removed the latch on the door and opened it wide. After the one loud creak, there was silence. They lit several lanterns, and the bonanza lay before them. In portable but poorly constructed wooden totes, strawberries were stacked two and three boxes high. They were in rows as deep as the barn and across the entire width.

The three robed villains established a "Bee Line" and piled the strawberries onto the wagon, in some spots six and seven crates high.

The monks closed the barn door with a loud creak and a bang. They began the trek back to the monastery. One monk held the reins and walked with the donkey at his side. Much to the donkey's dismay, the other two monks got behind to push the wagon. Just as they were starting up the incline, the peaceful night was interrupted by the sounds a man shouting. And then, out of the night behind them, he rounded the corner, looked into the empty barn, and howled like an enraged bull. And he came running. There was a confrontation, but it was three against one. Ultimately, the farmer was directed to return from whence he came lest there be unnecessary bloodletting.

The lead monk strapped the donkey on the rump and yelled for it to gallop. The donkey rose up on its hind legs and then jumped forward—a maneuver that jostled the wagon enough to upend all of the crates of poorly stacked strawberries, which in turn slid off of the back end of the wagon and onto the ground. At the same time, the donkey dislodged from his poorly put-together harness, and the wagon rolled backward and over the strawberries before upending itself in a ditch, disengaging a wheel in the process. The two monks bringing up the rear were pummeled by the dislodged strawberries, which turned their robes from brown to red. They tried to jump out of the way but only succeeded in getting meshed and flattened in a muck of something resembling a huge strawberry jam smeared across the road.

Within the hour, just as the monks had cleaned themselves off and rehitched the wagon and donkey, the farmer returned with the constable and some of his poker-playing buddies. The monks were detained in Prince Fredrick's dungeon. The prince disavowed any connection to the assault and theft and declared the prisoners Felonious Monks. Because the court felt that the term "Besiegement" was a charge that was not specific enough, the monks were officially accused having **BOTCHED STRAWBERRIES**.

Generally the population thought that as a criminal act, **BOTCHED STRAWBERRIES** sounded a bit goofy. So they successfully petitioned to have the charge changed to reflect the monks' participation. They came up with **BOTCHED ROBE–BERRIES**, which was rejected**.** As time passed, that which was once called **BOTCHED STRAWBERRIES** morphed into the current **BOTCHED ROBBERIES** (which is pronounced pretty much the same as the aforementioned **Botched Strawberries**).

ACCRUE
(FIRST USED: 1577 AD)

Definition: To gather, collect, to add to

Etymology: The sixteenth, seventeenth, and early eighteenth centuries were ones of revolution and expedition. It was during this era that piracy on the high seas became an extremely deadly fact of life. But piracy did not occur only on the high seas. The seaport town of Shanghai in China developed a reputation for a form of piracy on land.

Everyone has read or seen the movies: the accounts of men having too much to drink in a bar and being grabbed from behind or dropped through a trap door—and then taken to a ship anchored in the harbor. There they were conscripted, against their will, to be members of the ship's crew until they escaped, died, or (adding insult to injury) more often than not, were thrown overboard when they were "all used up."

So the term **"Shanghaied"** refers to the unlawful taking of a person or persons. The term **ACCRUED** originally referred to the building of a ship's crew through the "Shanghai" process (as in: "Captain, the ship is, **uh**…**crewed**, sir!"). The term later morphed into the all-encompassing concept that the accumulation of anything is to **ACCRUE**.

CHRONOLOGY TEN:

(FROM 1600 AD THROUGH 1699 AD)

THE CAPRICIOUS ERA

< DON'T CALL ME "PERRY" UNLESS YOU SEE TWO OF ME... >

"MOST PEOPLE HAVE PROBLEMS LEARNING A FOREIGN LANGUAGE BECAUSE OF IRRECON-SYLLABLE DIFFERENCES."

MOAN
(FIRST USED: 1603 AD)

Definition: a sound made by living beings to express discomfort or pain

Etymology: After the discipline of horticulture was accepted as a valid form of knowledge, it was determined that plants were living things. One of the first, and to date most important, steps in the development of that science took place on June 13, 1603. On that date, by order of the king's own minister of pronouncements, plants were proclaimed to have life. Since that eventful day, we have come to discover that as such, plants may indeed be sentient. Shakespeare himself chimed in on the matter and was quoted to say that "if you prick them, do they not bleed?"

While naysayers continued to munch on celery, sympathizers marched on the produce markets and demanded an end to the slaughter. Ultimately it was decided that without consuming plants of one form or another, mankind would perish. And so the cry of **"Stop the Madness"** was quelled while all parties digested the implications.

In the interim, the early-Pleistocene invention called **lawn mowers***
was rediscovered, igniting outrage once again. The wanton slaughter
of massive quantities of grass blades was memorialized in the universally recognized description of a freshly-cut lawn. It was said by non-
believers that newly trimmed lawns were mown. However, the faith-
ful sympathizers of the mangled blades of grass said that the blades
of the mower drowned out the anguished cries of living, breathing
blades of grass, and those awful lamentations thus became memorialized in the new, compromised term that we now refer to as **MOAN,**
a word we now use to help eradicate the horrors of a grass lawn being
MOWN.

*See Etymology: Lawnmower

COURTESY
(FIRST USED: 1611 AD)

Definition: The act of extending kindness or politeness to someone

Etymology: In the dark ages just before knights became famous,
codes of behavior were specific to specific groups of people. The Huns
were considered barbarians. To the non-Christians, the Christians
were considered arrogant. The vassals and serfs were considered
meek and lowly.

As the Dark Age was overcome by the dawn of the Middle Ages and
the Renaissance, a knight in the army of the English King noticed that
even the nobility had a specific code of behavior. That behavioral code
included deep bows from visitors to the king's court, the polite holding of hands with the fairer sex, and the opening of doors for persons
of the female persuasion. Most men would engage in the spreading
of their waistcoats* across puddles to prevent "her ladyship's" feet

from becoming soiled. In the opinion of the masses, they perpetrated all manner of exquisite behavior that lent them an air of kindness and gentleness that was to be admired. (In fact, the oft-used phrase "Good Night" is a hand-me-down from that very era.)

One of the king's knights (Sir V. Toode) had a young son by the name of Curtis. Sir V. Toode was most anxious to train Curtis in not only the arts of battle and defense, but additionally his ultimate purpose was to teach Curtis the noble behaviors of kindness and politeness. To this end, and whenever he was home and had the chance, Sir V. would bring Curtis into the room and emulate one of the "noble" behaviors—such as the "waist-coat toss" or the gracious sweep of a deep bow in "my lady's" presence.

Each time he demonstrated the behavior he would say to his son: **Curtis! See!** And thus was born the term **COURTESY**.

> *It should here be noted that the "waistcoat" was so named as "homage" to the flinging of the heretofore-named "waistcoat" into the mud to prevent "m'lady" from soiling her shoes as she stepped from portico to the waiting carriage. The coat became a "throwaway" or "waste coat" due to its condition upon being flung into the mud. The "waste" was changed back to "waist" once cobbles paved the way for mudless streets.*

BEHOOVE
(FIRST USED: 1637 AD)

Definition: To be appropriate; designating the proper tack; the right thing to do or way to behave

Etymology: Several nearly fatal blows to both the etymological and entomological communities occurred when it was discovered that both of these groups had signed off on a questionable definition of the term **BEHOOVE**. At the time, **Bee Hoove** was a term to signify the feet of bees, or, more specifically, the hoofs of bees.

First was the blow to the entomological society when it was discovered that bees did not have hoofs (hooves) as such, but rather—it was thought—paws. During that period (1637 AD), it was difficult to determine the makeup of the smaller appendages and extensions of insects due to the fact that magnifying devices were still in a primitive developmental stage. Consequently, identification was mainly visual. The bee hoof theory came about because of one Dr. Arthur Manfred, who was hosting, at his home, an entomologist during the annual Insect Focus Group (IFG) held in London. Bees were the primary topic of study at the time, and the entomologist, one Miss Sallie Delia-Fourth Higganbottom, was, unbeknownst to the study group, terrified of insects—especially the stinging kind.

Sallie was staying in a room that faced onto a city street. The first evening of her stay at Dr. Manfred's house, she dropped a jar holding an angry bee, and the bee flew directly to the window. It wandered around on the glass hoping for a way out, and during that event, the passing of horses on the cobbles outside sounded to Sally, in her panicked state, as if the escaped bee was making the clopping noises as it stomped across the window pane. Sally included this event in her presentation to the society the following day, citing empirical "evidence" to conclude that the clopping sounds could only be explained by the fact that bees had "hooves" (hoofs). These "results" were also accepted by the etymological community, which then signed off on the development of the word **Bee Hoove**.

The second blow was when independent study groups could not confirm the hoof (hoove) theory—and in fact concluded that not only did no clopping sound occur with the bees that they were observing, but that in fact there was no sound at all emanating from the footfalls of the bees under study. It was commented that the new studies indicated that "for all we know, bees could have paws for feet based on the softness of their treading". When the results were published by the prestigious publication *BUG* ("Bees Under Glass"), the word "could" was edited out of the article and the quote was changed to "…bees have paws."

At the time, no one in the IFG or the etymologic world took issue with the deduction, reasoning that every living thing "had a pa—as well as a ma." and this additional grievous error (along with several others) led to a complete dismantling and reconstruction of the IFG and etymology training centers worldwide.

Some of the additional "insights" that caused the demise of the IFG as well as etymologists worldwide were:

Bee Little (belittle) referred to the size of the average bee.

Bee Come (become) was a beekeeper command.

Bee Came (became) was the result of the command Bee Come.

Bee Con (beacon) was a rogue bee.

Bee Gun (begun) was a weapon used to bring down a rogue bee.

Bee Fall (befall) was what happened when you shot a rogue bee with a bee gun.

Bee Get (beget), before its use in the Bible, was just another bee keeper's command.

Bee Gale (beagle) was a female bee named Gale.

Bee Eat (Beet) was a beekeeper command at feeding times.

Bee Four (before) was the number of bees that is larger than three but less than five.

Bee Friend (befriend) was a bee pal.

Bee Head (behead) was the head of a bee.

Bee Held (beheld) was having treated the emotional needs of a bee.

Bee Labor (belabor) was a working farm of bees—what you need on a honey ranch.

Bee Leave (believe) was a bee keeper command.

Bee Long (belong) was the horizontal measurement of bees after torture on the rack.

Bee Loved (beloved) was one's favorite bee.

Bee Low (below) was the emotional state of a bee that is not bee loved.

Bee Nine (benign) was a pre-adolescent bee.

Bee Rate (berate) was the going cost of bees at any given time.

Bee Siege (besiege) was an angry swarm.

Bee Ware (beware) was a bee shopkeeper's goods.

Bee Witch (bewitch) was the female version of a bee shaman.

TEE SHIRTS
(FIRST USED: 1639 AD)

Definition: A lightweight shirt made in the shape of the letter *T*.

Etymology: Connoisseurs of **Tea** had shirts made out of dried tea leaves, only to find out that the tea "leaves" when the **Tea Shirts** got wet. So they switched to lightweight cotton and called them **TEE SHIRTS**.

AMAZING
(FIRST USED: 1650 AD)

Definition: Something causing wonder or surprise

Etymology: It should not "amaze" anyone that the term **AMAZE** (**AMAZING**) derived from "**the Maze**," which was a common garden attribute of royalty in England, most of whom lived in great houses called manors. The garden maze brought a sense of wonder and astonishment to the rich and famous of that period. The garden game consisted of sending couples into a **maze** of tall hedges, and then timing their ability to solve the puzzle and eventually egress at the other end. The activity was called was called **AMAZING** (just as initiating Plebs is called a hazing), and as a result of this popular amusement, the term **AMAZE**, or **AMAZING**, came to mean anything that causes wonder or surprise.

And speaking of surprise, it was truly **AMAZING** that half a world away, in the terraced mountains of Peru, the Incas grew corn (**maize**) to use in the brewing of beer. The process was referred to as **Maizing**, and the resulting taste tests drew breathless whispers of "**AMAIZING**"—which became the Incan term for "truly wonderful—yum!"

BUFFALO
(FIRST USED: 1660 AD)

Definition: A four-legged grazing herd animal found wandering the plains of the North America.

Etymology: The great tribes of Native Americans who were referred to as the Plains Indians had an ongoing love affair with the noble buffalo of the American plains. Of course, in those days, the tribes and their lands were not referred to as the Plains. That appellation was not bestowed upon the people or the lands they occupied until the early 1920s, when the fledgling city of Des Moines was selected for a new regional "hub" airport. The mayor of Des Moines was asked to come up with a name for the facility. Mayor Crawford, a spirited man with a Cajun background and vocabulary said: "Well! We just gonna go and call it De Planes Air-Port because dis is where de planes will port."

Several weeks later a committee of "concerned citizens" overruled the mayor and renamed the airfield the Plains Airport ("Because we are in the middle of the Great American plains.")

But I digress. North America was re-settled by the Europeans, who were prone to migrate west. They encountered Native Americans at every turn. As the story was told, friction existed between the Native Americans and the newcomers, primarily based on the fact that if the settlers found an area they considered "charming," they would simply appropriate it, build fences, and in general assume it was their right to settle any which-where that they were inclined.

As history documents, the main thing that kept these settlers awake at night was the fact that the Native Americans did not have the same philosophy as they did regarding the topic of land ownership. The next biggest concern was that the "Indians" (a name given to the indigenous people by Columbus and his minions because he, Columbus, thought that he had reached India.) who seemed inappropriately hostile, fierce, and very strong physically.

The "very strong physically" terminology came about because depending on the weather, the "Indians" (and especially the warrior "Indians") were prone to ride around during the day with no shirts on. This relaxed dress code tended to show off the muscled physiques (which in those days were referred to as "ripped physiques") of these native peoples.

History records that a man named Samuel Snortdown was befriended by an Indian shaman named Cachoo Horse Feathers. They would get together once a week and spend an afternoon sitting, smoking, and sharing insights from each other's culture. One of the key historical lynchpins of these discussions was the derivation of the term **BUFFALO**—which was the Indian name for the North American bison. The first time the two were together talking, several bison grazed by, and the subject of the majestic creature came up. As it turns out, and based on the revelations from Cachoo Horse Feathers, the "bison"* was considered a deity to most Indian tribes. This great muscled creature was considered a god of ripped physiques, and the warrior Indians strove throughout their lives to diet and exercise in an attempt to emulate these four-legged "gods of the plains." They would pray to these creatures each and every time they encountered one. They, however, did not call these creatures by any other name than what they were—and that was "**buff fellows**." And so, five centuries later, the name of this impressive creature, despite its near extinction, has remained as named by the Native American Warriors: **BUFFALO**.

*It is interesting to herein note that the term **BISON** was a frequent comment from father to son as Dad rode off to shoot some four-legged dinner. Ultimately the audible wave morphed into "Bye, Son."*

HABERDASHERY
(FIRST USED: 1665 AD)

Definition: A store, usually a small business that caters to men's clothing and fixtures

Etymology: In the year 1665, in the village of New Amsterdam (now known as New York City), a Dutch man called Bjorn Svenson opened a tiny Shoppe above his garage (*barn*) dedicated to the sale of men's fixtures and clothing. Bjorn was an A-type personality and was constantly rushing from one chore to another in order to keep up with his many projects.

Bjorn kept a few cattle and chickens, a couple of goats, and a pig. His barn was also his blacksmith Shoppe—located just under the loft that he had walled in to accommodate his men's store. His house was at the front of the property—the last one along the Broadway and right on the edge of the city (*village*) limits. Bjorn opened the gate to his property every morning after breakfast and shut down his business every evening just before dinner. During the average workday, he was in a constant rush to finish projects and deal with his customers.

When a customer for the men's store opened the gate to his property, it would trip a bell, and Bjorn would drop what he was doing wherever he was and scurry over to the customer. Because the men's store was upstairs, Bjorn would rush about trying to speed up the transaction. He would respond to each request with a breathy whisper: "**Have'ta dash....hurry!**" "**Have'ta dash....hurry!**" Then he would race up the stairs, grab the appropriate garments or hats, and race back down before the customer had a chance to finish his sentence. Bjorn became known region-wide as the "**Havetadash/hurry**" guy, and the term was ultimately invited into the lexicon in its original Dutch form: **HABERDASHERY**.

ALP
(FIRST USED: 1669 AD)

Definition: One of about 180 mountains that comprise the mountain range spread across eastern, central, and western Europe.

Etymology: When the Britons (Brits) first discovered their ability to speak, they began the process of creating a language (approximately 1657 AD). As the process moved forward, they found the letter *H* to be somewhat "h"aughty and unmanageable. Among other things, they decided to omit the *H* from the "known" alphabet in an attempt at lingually distinguishing themselves from other nations. Secondarily they were seeking ways to "button down" the alphabet so that there wouldn't be so many letters to remember.

Once the alphabet was completed and everyone was speaking properly, they turned their attention to mountaineering. Climbing had not yet been established as a sport or a lifestyle with the Brits because there were no mountain ranges in Britain. Scores of volunteers were recruited and assembled near the White Cliffs, where they were provided with mountain climbing gear and then "H"ustled (*boarded*) onto newly constructed rafts upon which they would cross the channel. Over nine hundred budding mountaineers and 360 men and women medical specialists began the channel crossing with "eye" expectations (**Eye** was the new spelling for the old word **"H"igh**).

It had been predetermined that the European mountain range consisted of some 180 individual mountains, each identified by a pre-assigned number up to 180. The Brits were going to climb and then name each one of the mountains as a service to all of the peoples of the great European continent. The group was divided into 180 teams of five climbers each. At the adjoining base camp for each group of mountains, there were first aid teams of two waiting to be "H"ailed" (*called upon*) should any of the mountaineers get into trouble.

The process agreed upon was that any climber who got stuck or hurt would call out for "H"ELP" as loudly as possible.

And so, on September 15 in the year 1669, the climbing began. Within two days problems surfaced. The first problem was that the inexperienced mountaineers had unexpected difficulties figuring out how to overcome obstacles. There were lots of falls, missteps, and broken bones. However, the biggest problem turned out to be the unexpected "Eco-o" (formerly: *Echo*) factor. Every time a trapped climber called out for "**elp**," the call was bounced off of every mountain within earshot. Every call for **"elp"** sounded like: "**ALP!**" Those "**elpers**," listening to the Ec(h)o chaos, could not determine which mountains the pleas were coming from.

After a month of this unfortunate pandemonium, Swiss, French, German, and Spanish elders got together to discuss how to rid the continent of these shouting Brits. It is said that this meeting was the beginning of the European Union. However, the real story is that the weather turned, and with each day getting colder, the Ec(h)o diminished and the calls for **ELP** got swallowed up with the winds and snows. Everyone went home to think up some new substitute for mountain climbing. The new term **ELP** was transformed to **ALP** and came to mean any one of the many mountains in Europe. Nonetheless, Britons everywhere continued to drop their *H*s at every opportunity.

EXPIRE
(FIRST USED: 1692 AD)

Definition: The end of someone or something—example: death

Etymology: It was not unusual for "Justice" to be at the colorful end of a match in reference to the so-called Dark Ages, the Middle Ages, the

Spanish Inquisition, or the Witch Hunts of Salem, Massachusetts. The "match," as such, was not perfected as an invention until the "Lucifer" of 1826—however, fire had been invented, so that if you met your fate at the end of a matchstick, you were said to have been **Pyred** (died on a pile of activated firewood).* When it was all said and done and there was nothing to show for your life except a pile of ashes, you were said to be: **EX-PYRED**. We still understand the word **EXPIRE** as a reference to death.

*If you were **Pyred**, it was a given that you also lost your job **(Fired)**.

WATCH
(FIRST USED: 1698 AD)

Definition: A personal timepiece carried, hung, or worn on the neck, wrist, or clothes

Etymology: Life was difficult and complex up to and slightly after the beginning of the sixteenth century. Up until that time, if you wanted to know what time it was, you needed to either ask someone; own a bulky pendulum clock and be able to carry it with you; or using the mastery of the ancients, hope for a sunny day, and with a calibrated eyeball, calculate what the shadows said on miniature sundials that could be carried in your pocket.

In short, if you wanted to know the time, you had to **WATCH** for signs. A few of the common examples might be the rising or setting sun, the lack or length of shadows, or the clock placed in the shoppe window.

People were so relieved when the fob and wrist timepieces were invented that they unanimously proclaimed the dangling timepieces the **WATCH**—a name that explains all that went before.

OFFICIAL
(FIRST USED 1699 AD)

Definition: An event that verifies or finalizes an act

Etymology: A fish yells by blowing water through his gills, which causes his entire body to jerk around. Fishes yell for various reasons (stubbed toe, warning a friend of a looming predator, low back pain, etc.), but the most frequent reason for a fish to yell is when a hook on a fishing line pierces its upper lip whilst it is feeding. Above the water line, each time a fish yells it is manifested in a jerking of the pole tip, to which the line (and thereby the hook) is attached. The jerking of the line (caused by the fish yelling) notifies the fisherman that he has caught an unsuspecting fish—that is to say, that he knows it is "**a fish yell,**" or simply put – "It is **OFFICIAL**". He caught a fish.

CHRONOLOGY ELEVEN:

(1700 AD THROUGH 1799 AD)

THE EPIC LITIGIOUS ERA

‹ *THE BRITISH ARE CUNNING...THE BRITISH ARE CUNNING!!* ›

CORRALS THAT HOLD GROUPS OF HORSES ARE KNOWN AS "NEIGHBORHOODS."

PAINFUL
(FIRST USED: 1755 AD)

Definition: Full of pain; the opposite of painless

Etymology: There are thousands of ways to experience pain, not the least of which is slamming into a brick wall. Related painful acts such as falling from an airplane or falling from a tall building have a similar effect (although technically the actual pain comes from hitting the ground at a high rate of speed). They can be said to be **full of pain**.

While we could consume hour after hour listing painful events both likely and unlikely to befall the average citizen, it is not our function to create a sense of dread. The whole reason for discussing the word **PAINFUL** is to understand how and why the word came into being.

Most everyone agrees that the experience of pain is less than optimal. No rational person lives with pain by choice. In fact, there wasn't always a word to express pain. If one suffered some form of discomfort, such as intersecting with an enraged bull in one's matador outfit, one's first impulse would be to run from that madness to the nearest door. (This, in fact, is where the phrase "MAD! A DOOR?" actually came from.)

Before the invention of the term PAIN, various civil and uncivil exclamations were used to describe the notion of pain. Some examples: Ouch, Ow-Ow, Yikes, Zowie, and the ever popular Argggg! The truth is that the term **PAINFUL** came into full use and fruition with the discovery of glass. As anyone who has encountered glass in any of its forms knows, it can elicit discomfort of a special glass class, including the dreaded dismemberment.

Glass was discovered in its original form by two cavewomen who were excavating to create a sewing room. The small pieces of shiny glass that they discovered had been formed by the extreme temperatures required to create a planet. Originally, glass was considered a jewel.

When men began to "mess" with nature, they discovered the process to "man-make" their own glass. They changed the configuration so that they could have sheets of the opaque stuff—which they incorporated into their outer walls to let in more light. Somewhere during the 1600s AD, tinkerers figured out how to create a clear glass sheet. This, of course, revolutionized the use and abuse of glass, and was, in fact, the beginning of the employment of the term **PAINFUL**.

In 1756 Pastor Perry Paine, possibly the uncle of our own Thomas Paine, was the first man in recorded history to feel the full effect of breaking through a large plate of window glass. He was directing the unloading of an order of plain and stained glass from a ship in Boston harbor when a gust of wind blew the glass loose from the grips of the longshoremen. The sheet slammed directly into the pastor, plastering him to the side of the dock warehouse. The glass shattered; Pastor Paine was knocked senseless. However, (glory be) he escaped with only minor injuries, and because for years most of his parishioners generally referred to him as "senseless" anyway, no lasting harm was done.

The general population thereafter referred to Pastor Paine as "Window Paine." Curiously, the window industry, to distance themselves from the Pastor Paine imbroglio, renamed their sheets of glass Window Pane. Not to be outdone, the Paine family had their name changed to **Payne** in an attempt to save face. The name Paine (later shortened to **PAIN**) has since come to mean anything that physically hurts (such as walking through a "pain" of glass). The more it hurts, the more **PAIN FULL** (**PAINFUL**) the experience.

VICTIM
(FIRST USED: 1761 AD)

Definition: One that is subjected to oppression, hardship, or mistreatment

Etymology: Victor Timothy Dupe' was the unluckiest man alive, and all was never well wherever Victor traveled in mid-eighteenth century New York City. If a pocket was going to be picked, it would be Victor's pocket. If a mugging was to occur, Victor took the first blow. If there were people who got trampled underfoot in a stampede, Victor became the first layer of "man" trampled. At the age of twenty-one, Victor had been in seventeen different hospitals around the New York boroughs a total of fifty-seven times. He had more broken bones than the actual number of bones in his body—some of which had been fractured several times. Every doctor and nurse working within twenty-five miles of New York City knew Victor by name and began referring to him as **Vic Tim** in conversations (short for Victor Timothy). Aside from his many injuries, he was the root (canal) of our present-day term **VICTIM.**

MALICIOUS
(FIRST USED: 1775 AD)

Definition: intent to do harm

Etymology: The Dark Ages began around the fall of the Roman Empire and lasted into the sixteenth century with the Protestant

Revolution. In the beginning of the Dark Ages, the Goths, Visigoths, and Huns became the scourge of Europe. What has not been known until this time is that this so-called scourge was nothing more than organized groups of civilian "military" who were out of control. Nonetheless, they were only doing what they needed to do to put food on the table and a roof over their heads. What was "over the top" were the simple but fun experiments with pyromania, torture, pillaging, and plunder—none of which was out of line, considering the times and the impending gene-pool purge that was soon to be named the black death.

However, and to be fair to all sides, it was a problem for the poor serfs and peasants who lived in their own form of slavery. These were people who were totally beholden to the barons, lords, and kings whose lands they tilled and whose crops they watered with their own sweat and blood. From the serfs' point of view, the horrid groups of armed men that swept through and destroyed everything that they had worked for were hated with an intensity that begs description. These were the malicious marauders who maimed and destroyed everything before them.

But things changed in the sixteenth century.

The formation of a citizen army by the countrymen of the newly settled colonies in North America changed and adjusted the spelling and intent of the word used to reference bands of marauders bound on doing harm to others.

The British were well schooled in "traditional" battle and had little doubt that the colonists would be begging for mercy once the real fighting began. But the colonists had a surprise for these well-dressed and armed regiments who lined up on the battlefield and fired and reloaded by the "regimented" command of the squad leaders. The colonists hid behind trees and rocks and fired at will—decimating the rigid regiments. The British were horrified at the undisciplined and sneaky attacks and took to calling the colonists **MALICIOUS**.

Because of the noble quest for freedom and the negative implications of the term, and out of respect for their cause (seeking freedom from the monarchy in England and independence from all), a new term was penned into the constitution. The old term **MALICIOUS** was replaced with a new term: **MILITIAS**, which had a more formal military sound then the old term. It was introduced into the US Constitution and has remained in our dictionaries since its introduction in 1775.

WARRANTY
(FIRST USED: 1775 AD)

Definition: Assurances; a thing that is guaranteed

Etymology: The Boston Tea Party, the Minute Men, and the ride of Paul Revere were all events that led to frequent demonstrations against the British in 1775 and 1776. The chant "**War and Tea! War and Tea!**" became the rallying cry prior to the outbreak of the Revolutionary War. The threat, which subsequently developed into armed conflict, was, in its way, a **guarantee** that war would follow any attempts by the British to tax any more imported products. As we all know, the Revolutionary **War** was instigated by the dumping of five shiploads of **Tea** into Boston Harbor in 1775. The rallying cry "**WAR AND TEA!**" has since been contracted to **"WARRANTY"** to indicate assurance that the British would now rethink their plan and go home. The term remains in use today to indicate a guarantee for goods and or services.

PHOBIA
(FIRST USED: 1776 AD)

Definition: Aversion, fear

Etymology: One of the lesser-known pirates, marauding the southern Atlantic coast of the emerging United States of America in the year 1776, was Beauford Adam Danforth, better known as "Bad Dan." It was, in fact, Beauford who made famous the oft-plagiarized pirate term "Yar!" which even today is included in the dialogue of any self-respecting pirate story or movie. Interestingly enough, Beauford is also responsible for the term **PHOBIA** becoming a part of the lexicon of the English language.

Beauford had captured a British supply ship in the summer of '76 and, at the point of a sword, had directed all of the crew into lifeboats. While the officers watched with trepidation and dismay, the pirates plundered the ship's stores and armaments. The ship's captain, Sir Reggie Slipshod III, expressed his outrage by crying out that the British were engaged in a war against the rebels and that his government would pay good money—not including the "booty" that could be plundered—if only Bad Dan would join in the king's struggle.

Bad Dan, who was the son of an immigrant himself, proclaimed: "**Yar! Foe be yeah, Yar, Yar!**," and with a wave of his sword, moved Captain Reggie backward, up against the rail, and head over heels into the ocean. Captain Reggie struggled into a lifeboat and was rowed off by members of his crew as they watched Bad Dan clear the ship of plunder and set it afire. Captain Reggie would later retell this tale, relaying his fear for his life and the terrifying words of Bad Dan forever seared into his memory: **"FOE BE YEAH!...YAR!"** The word **PHOBIA** still symbolizes the fear and aversion experienced when coming into contact with a pirate.

WEATHER
(FIRST USED: 1777 AD)

Definition: The local condition of meteorological forces that determine temperature, wind direction, wind velocity, and the moisture content of the air.

Etymology: The question has always been: Is it going to rain, is it going to be hot, or is the wind going to try to rip off my hat? The question of meteorological forces has always been the need to know whether "this" or "that" will happen. And this question of **"whether"** is what prompted the Congress of 1777 to officially mandate that a term be created to reference **whether** or not it was going to be safe to plow the fields, or sow the seeds. Congress determined that the new word should be differentiated from the old word **whether** and yet be the same. Thus was the term **WEATHER** created to ask the oft-repeated interrogative as to **whether the weather could be weathered** without confusion.

TAKING TURNS
(FIRST USED: 1778 AD)

Definition: groups of people sharing equally by engaging in orderly participation—one at a time

Etymology: Early and unsubstantiated folklore tells us that in the fog of the morning of January 20, 1778, Captain Jaimes Cook (aka Jimmy "the Sea") and his crew turned a fateful corner and discovered the Hawaiian Islands. Captain Cook was an English explorer who was traveling the Pacific looking for just such places. The reason the discovery was "fateful" was that had he not found the Hawaiian Islands just when he did, the entire population of the island of Hawaii itself may have become extinct.

It was the middle of typhoon season. It was only a month prior that an enormous storm had swept in from the sea and, with the exception of about fifty survivors, killed and or carried every living thing (except the palm trees) out to sea. The small group of men, women, and children who survived had done so by lashing themselves to palm trees using the reeds made from the fronds of the palm, which they had fashioned into lengths of thin "rope."

As Captain Cook approached the first navigable bay that he could find, he and his crew were amazed with the spectacle that unfolded before their eyes. An enormous flock of heretofore undiscovered seabirds had been working the sand and shallows of the bay—harvesting small sea slugs and shallow-swimming bait fish. Suddenly, from out of the tree line onshore, came all fifty nearly naked, brown-skinned natives running and yelling at the top of their lungs. Their obvious goal, as it appeared from the forecastle of the ship, was the flock of birds—a flock that knew a threat when it saw one (running and yelling at them). It was a flock that, without further consideration, flapped its wings as one and rose up and out of reach of the screaming natives.

It was only then that the natives notice the frigate bobbing, just shy of the shallows. As one, their attention shifted from the birds circling overhead to the men on the ship. The captain ordered a skiff lowered, and he and his first mate, with five other men armed for protection, rowed to shore. When they reached the shallows, they left one man with the boat while the rest of the party made its way to the natives.

Upon closer inspection, Captain Cook was shocked to find that these people were on the verge of starvation. Though communication had to be filtered through hand signs and stick pictures in the sand, he determined that food was nonexistent on this island and the natives were trying to find a way of sneaking up on the circling birds in the hopes of having something to eat.

Captain Cook and his crew devised a fairly simple "stick net" using materials readily available from the surrounding underbrush. The net was in the shape of a large square that was interlaced with hundreds of strands of the thin palm "rope" that the Hawaiians had used to save their lives a week earlier during the typhoon.

In a trial run, the captain and his crew helped the natives carry this large "net" to the edge of the bay and let it drift a few feet offshore, where they anchored it to keep it from floating away. Through hand signs, Captain Cook admonished the natives to come away from the net with him and to watch from the shelter of the surrounding flora. Within minutes of the beach being cleared, the flock of birds descended and immediately began investigating the new floating curiosity. And once again the natives sprang into action and ran screaming, en masse, toward their prize. This time, as the birds panicked and initiated flight, several of them became enmeshed in the net and in their struggle to free themselves - instead drowned or broke their wings, legs, or any and all of the above.

The injuries were compounded when the half-starved natives hit the water at full gallop. They lunged at the trapped birds in desperation and then got themselves tangled in their own net. With all fifty "aboard," the net promptly disintegrated. Although the natives got some food that day, it was a disappointing catch, and Captain Cook promised to return the following day to help them finesse their next hunt.

As promised and noted in the history books, the captain returned the following day. The natives built the new net in half of the time. After installing it, they followed Captain Cook into the cover of the jungle. With the birds happily exploring the new net, Cook began this day's instruction by lining the natives up one after the other. He then had one of his crew fire a pistol into the air. Not only did he get the attention of the natives, but the birds as well. The birds took to the sky, as expected, and about half of them became hopelessly entangled in the net. Now, with a firm hand, Captain Cook took the first person in line and led him to the net while the crew kept the remainder in a quiet line in the trees. The first native was allowed to select one of the trapped birds and retreat from the beach while the next in line was escorted to the net to select his or her dinner. The lesson was a total success, and each of the fifty natives left with a bird of his or her own. The captain called the lesson **TAKING TERNS,** which was the first recorded use of these two words as a phrase. It is now widely held by at least three people that this single event saved the population of Hawaii in 1778.

It is somewhat ironic to note that Captain Cook took the carcasses of several of the birds back to England, where the remains were documented. At that time it was noted that these birds were a new species to the Royal Ornithological Society and as such were held to be "protected" until the flock could be studied in depth. When the ROS identified the birds as terns and learned of the slaughter of the birds at the hands of Captain Cook, they immediately censured him for the **TAKING TERNS** episode. Nonetheless, they named the birds **Cook's Terns**. Histories written about the incident referred to the (one at a time) hunting technique as **TAKING TERNS**, but historians made corrections when they realized that the birds were named after, not during, the events of 1778. Nonetheless, the new concept of **TAKING TURNS,** one at a time, became a basic foundation for social behavior.

FOR CRYING OUT LOUD
(FIRST USED: 1782 AD)

Definition: Exclamation of frustration

Etymology: Eighteenth-century folklore scholars, who sometimes hit the jug a bit too often, claim that it was not until the 1780s and the discovery of the "other" Hawaiian Islands by Captain Jaimes Cook, that anyone other than the natives took notice of the abundance of undocumented species of birds and animals that the islands har-bored. Not the least among them was the strange bird with the orchid plumage that inhabited and infuriated the natives of one of the northernmost island of the chain. This bird, which the natives named Naw-Willie-Willie, was similar to the annoying rooster or peacock of larger landmasses. It would screech out an irritating song both day and night during the eight month mating season. It was also hard to admire the beautiful orchid plumage of the odd bird because of the strange facial feature upon which no man could look without staring in disbelief: the bird had only one eye, centered in the middle of its face. It was enormous and looked exactly like the eyes of the domesti-cated bovine that roamed the prairies and hillsides of the continents. Because of that similarity, the bird was commonly referred to by the natives as the cow-eye. Simply put, the Naw-Willie-Willie had the sin-gle eye of a cow, and no one could see past that odd feature.

Additionally, the bird would sing out in a harsh, rasping voice some-thing that sounded like "**COW-EYE**...**COW-EYE**," singing it over and over until the natives would shout out, "Shut up already, **FOR COW-EYE-ING OUT LOUD!**" The birds, of course, did not shut up and were summarily executed by the irritated seamen who stopped at the island to load up on breadfruit and sugar cane. The infuriating bird, however, did get the last laugh, **FOR CRYING OUT LOUD**, because the island where it was wiped off of the planet was named after its **COW-EYE**—and to this day is still referred to in Hawaiian as **COW-EYE,** or translated into the English: **KAUAI**.

THEORY
(FIRST USED: 1782 AD)

Definition: Philosophical explanation of moral or physical phenomena

Etymology: (See **THEORETICALLY**)

THEORETICALLY
(FIRST USED: 1782 AD)

Definition: an explanation by, or in the manner of

Etymology: This term came about due to the behavior of a man named **Theodore Riddick Lee**, who was, by all accounts, a know-it-all. It was said that if you had a question, he had an answer—not a few of which were demonstrably inaccurate. As a child he was coddled by his family, who called him **Theo**. His mother called him her "little **Theo'ry**," and his father, who often got angry and upset, addressed him by his almost full name: **Theo Riddick Lee**.

In any event, in his village it came to be known that if you needed an answer to a question—any question—Theo was your man. His quick mind allowed him to posit explanations for all sorts of phenomena. All of the explanations and answers he came up with made sense at the time. His now infamous answer to the question "What is the world?" was assailed as "just another **Theo'ry**." He, of course, had responded that "The world is flat," which had, in turn, discouraged exploration of the seas for fear of falling off of the "edge of the world." In addition to being a false **Theo'ry**, the answer was also the first major failing of his "intellect." The questioner claimed that he was asking a philosophical question—not a physical one. That, of course, as we all have come to know, was the pivotal point in Theo's life and reputation. From that point forward, all explanations of the known and unknown world were referred to as "just a **Theo'ry**" until they were proven correct, and all references to such explanations by **Theo Riddick**

Lee were prefaced by the now-useful contraction of his name: **Theoretically**.

WEEKEND
(FIRST USED: 1787 AD)

Definition: A term used to describe the two days following the end of the traditional workweek—specifically, Saturday followed by Sunday.

Etymology: During and after the Industrial Age, woes were equally shared by the workers (pre-union) and employers. While labor was cheap, manufacturing was slow. It was not uncommon for an employee to expect to have to work six and sometimes seven days per week for as little as $3.00 to $5.00 a month in wages. To lay railroads across the continent, Chinese "Coolies" were brought into the West from across the Pacific Ocean to work for "slave wages". As technology slowly progressed and worker protestations were whispered, unions of likeminded laborers began to stand up for their heretofore unestablished rights in the workplace. Slowly, painfully, and grudgingly, management conceded some issues to labor and the labor movement was off to a shaky start.

One of the first major accomplishments made by fledgling labor was to secure Saturdays and Sundays as days of rest. It was during those negotiations that management would frequently and vociferously claim that anything less than a seven-day workweek severely **weakened** their ability to survive and thrive. While complaints were many, it was labor forces that ultimately decided that the two consecutive days off per week were a right. Management again claimed that they would be severely **weakened**. They threatened to fire any man who did not work a minimum of seven days a week. A long and bitter struggle ensued amid threats and counter-threats. In the end, labor won the issue, and from that day forward, from labor's point of view, the two-day break every five days was subsequently referred to as **WEAKENED.** Several years later the term **WEAKENED** was changed to **WEEKEND** as a concession to management.

CRUISE—CRUISE SHIP
(FIRST USED: 1789 AD)

Definition: A passenger ship used for the sole purpose of providing vacation escapes for tourists.

Etymology: In 1789, as is well documented, His Majesty's Ship the *Bounty*, after taking on a load of breadfruit from Tahiti, was commandeered by Masters Mate Fletcher Christian with the majority of the crew. They put Captain Bligh and his eighteen loyal crew members into a longboat and set them adrift near Tonga. The remaining crew then sailed off to the east—able now to do as they pleased (sleep till noon, lie about in the sunshine, drop anchor in a beautiful South Pacific cove to swim, frolic, meet the natives, buy souvenirs, and generally "have it all," as they say).

The fact is that despite the current disputes among etymologists, it was, as here documented, that the mutinied HMS *Bounty* became the first **CREW'S SHIP**—and indeed, the cruise industry had the spelling changed from **CREWS** to the current **CRUISE** in order to avoid the negative connotations engendered by a relationship between the armed takeover of the HMS *Bounty* and the modern-day **CRUISE** and **CRUISE SHIP** experience.

RESTAURANT
(FIRST USED: 1789 AD)

Definition: A business that serves meals to make a profit

Etymology: Just after the French Revolution, the new citizens of Paris (who, prior to the siege of the Bastille, were simple peasants) would meet in what were called Rant Houses on the streets of Paris. These Rant Houses were a platform for anyone who wanted to expostulate vehemently about whatever grieved him or her. In short, they were places to rant, to listen to rants, or to rest between rants. (The very same type of activity was taking place in Philadelphia when it was considered the capital of the newly formed American Republic. In Philadelphia the rant houses were called places "to Philly-buster.")

Over time, the "rant audiences" suggested that the house make food and drink available while they rested and listened to the daily rants. Food service became an essential part of the venue, and the Rant signs were replaced with signs that said **Rest 'o Rant**, which, as every kindergartener knows, was the inception of the modern-day concept of the **RESTAURANT** (still spelled as you can see, in the original French).

SEVER
(FIRST USED: 1789 AD)

Definition: To remove, or lop off

Etymology: This term comes from the word **severe** and is a result of the beheadings of the French Revolution. To have one's head chopped off was, at the time, the best of punishments and the worst of punishments. In order to have a word that described the very act of beheading, it was determined that the final letter **e** would be **lopped off** of the word **severe** in order to illustrate to how the guillotine was the most serious punishment available, and the drop of the e emulated the drop of the severely offending head into the basket. Thus the origins of the word **SEVER**.

ANIMATED
(FIRST USED: 1792 AD)

Definition: a full-of-life infusion of spirit

Etymology: Victor Hugo said it all when he said, "It's not about the man! It's about his hump."* Nor was it about Quasimodo, nor about Esmeralda, nor about the bells, the tower, the parapets, or the gargoyles. Rather, it was about the hidden story behind Quasimodo (*The Hunchback of Notre Dame*) and his wife, the former Mademoiselle Annabelle Ringer.

Annabelle was a striking apparition, especially when she was walking beside her unfortunately shaped husband, who lurched along, hunched over with that great mound to the rear of his shoulders. He looked more like one of the gargoyles precipitately poised on the narrow cathedral ledges high above the street. But Anna loved her husband and took it as a personal insult when someone mocked the frequently unhappy man.

Annabelle's demeanor, however, was generally quiet but friendly, withdrawn but attentive—and she was known and beloved by all of Paris.

The attention was unseemly in her mind, and she had no illusions about why there was so much attention and so little privacy, being married to one of the strangest little men in France at the time.

Annabelle and Quasimodo had five children—a fact that increased the curiosity and gossip among Parisians. They whispered among themselves in wonderment, trying to understand how anyone (referring, of course, to Annabelle) would be able to have children with the little "toad" of a man called Quasimodo. For her part, each time Anna got pregnant, she underwent a profound personality change. Her eyes brightened, her skin tone glowed, and her smile became temporarily permanent. She chatted with anyone who had the time. She was more generous, more thoughtful, more heartfelt and endearing to all those with whom she came in contact. After each pregnancy, Annabelle's personality returned to the quiet, withdrawn but friendly woman that she was known to be.

There was a rumor among Parisians at the time that Annabelle had a "thing" for humps—that she so loved being pregnant that even the sight of Quasimodo's hump excited her obviously due to its similarity to her own belly when gestation was nearly complete. And so it was that in 1792, the revelation that there was a sixth pregnancy spread from mouth to ear all across Paris. It was told that Anna once again had undergone the metamorphosis to the bright-eyed, smiling, engaging, soon-to-be mother. Every Parisian knew that Anna had mated and was with child. And it was in that year that the phrase **ANNA MATED** (later contracted to **ANIMATED** was permanently added to the lexicon) and came to mean a show of extra energy, or a full-of-life infusion of spirit.

Not to be confused with the Victor Hugo of literary fame. Our Victor Hugo was a charlatan who cheaply capitalized on the name similarity. Our guy's complete name was Victor Hugo Knot.

CHOO-CHOO TRAIN
(FIRST USED: 1797 AD)

Definition: Affectionate name given to a steam-powered locomotive pulling rail cars. The **CHOO-CHOO** sound approximated the noise the pistons produced as the bursts of steam and smoke exhausted through the smoke stacks.

Etymology: Anyone born between 1780 and 1954 is familiar with the iconic sound of a steam-powered locomotive. It might come as a surprise to some that the original name, **Choo-Choo Train**, did not come from the sounds made by the mechanical components of the engine. Additionally, the very term **Train** had a completely different meaning.

When the steam train became the workhorse of the great American Industrial Revolution, there was a serious shortage of experienced engineers (the etymology of the term **Engineer** is discussed at length under that heading). The railroad barons hired raw recruits to train as captains of these rail cruisers. Each novice was enrolled in elaborate training seminars and in hands-on railroad boot camps to become familiar with every task involved in operating these steam powered freight-hauling systems. Because steam engines were under production in only a few factories, it was a difficult task to train the future pilots of these great land ships on actual working vehicles.

Consequently, it was decided to take a lesson from the pages of the ancient Mediterranean galley ships. Full-sized mock-ups of steam engines were constructed out of plywood and 2X4s. These "**Train**"ing vehicles were mounted on rail-wheel carriages, which in turn were placed on actual rails extending from the training facilities for a distance of three to five miles out and back.

Judging from casual outside appearances, these mock-ups could be mistaken for the actual "iron horses." But once you climbed into the cockpits and looked down where the boilers should have been, you would have found what appeared to be ancient oarsmen seats with metal rowing bars attached to piston-like devices. Pushing and pulling the fake oars turned the six or eight sets of wheels that the "engine" rolled on. Originally trainees would sit at the oars and attempt to move the vehicle forward by timing the pulls and pushes so that they were in unison. Those attempts were complete failures, so the railroad bosses devised a method similar to the ancient Roman "slave propulsion" system.

Instead of having someone with a whip shouting out "PUSH! PULL!", the rail master would hand out very tough saltwater taffy for each of the trainees. They would place large globs of the taffy into their mouths. The rail master would then shout out: "**CHEW…CHEW**," and with each "**CHEW,**" the trainees would clamp down on their taffy-filled jaws and transfer the exertion through their arms to push or pull the "row" bars like a piston. Amazingly, the vehicle would move forward or backward as smoothly on the track as if there were strained blasts of steam moving the behemoth.

When the trainees mastered the piston propulsion concept through precision chewing, they would be moved into the classes on braking (as opposed to breaking). And so it went until all aspects of the running of a steam engine were covered. This extensive hands-on training is, in fact, why we now refer to these vehicles as **TRAINS**—and, of course, the "**CHEW! CHEW!**" aspect of the training was fondly referred to as the **CHOO-CHOO TRAIN (ing).**

SEAL
(FIRST USED: 1798 AD)

Definition: an aquatic slug-like creature that barks a lot and sported whiskers; the ability to prevent liquid seeping, or prevent the advance of moisture

Etymology: Prior to assigning a name to this ambulatory gelatinous mass, it was commonly referred to as **"OH MY GOD!"** Or sometimes "**WHAT THE #&%@!!**"

As scientists calmed down and realized that it was just another sea creature, they became less repulsed and actually snared one for further study. Making notes as they cut through the layers, they found to their amazement that the creature was not filled with water (as suspected), but rather with blubber. While they did find several interesting organs, they calculated upon completing their investigation that 90 percent of the mass was as stated: "just blubber." None of this inspired a name for the creature, and it was not until 204 years later that while dissecting another of these creatures, the eminent scientist Sir Juan Twono, a noted seaologist and gourmand, discovered that the fur and blubber that covered the creature's body was so dense as to create a perfect closure, protecting the inner layer of skin from the cold ocean waters. It was only then that the creature was named the fur **SEAL**, and while not very original, it communicated. As every third-grader knows, there are several types of this sea creature—all of which, it should be noted, have had the term **SEAL** incorporated in their name because of the ability of their coats to **SEAL** out undesirable elements.

TREASON
(FIRST USED: 1798 AD)

Definition: An act which by its nature indicates a lack of allegiance to one's country.

Etymology: This term came into common use during the recruiting in France for the Napoleonic Wars. Conscription of soldiers was done by teams of regulars who would go into town and country and physically take possession of any young men they came across. Being forewarned was forearmed. So fathers would gather the sons together prior to these army raids and ask each boy if he was willing to fight for the emperor. If the boy said yes, he was told to gather his things together so as to be ready when the recruiters came. If the boy said no, then, oft times the father would advise the boy with the words: "Then go into the woods and hide in a **TREE, SON**." Some of the boys who were caught among the branches were accused of the act of **"TREE SON"**—later contracted to **TREASON.**

CHRONOLOGY TWELVE:

(FROM 1800 AD THROUGH 1849 AD)

THE OBSTREPEROUS ERA

< CAN YOU EAT YOURSELF OUT OF A JAM? >

THE FRENCH REVOLUTION WAS AN ATTEMPT BY FRENCH CITIZENS TO GET A HEAD.

SEAMSTRESS
(FIRST USED: 1803 AD)

Definition: a person (female) who sews

Etymology: As everyone who has been through a kindergarten social studies class knows, complex sets of problems arise in conjunction with the convergence of two or more languages. A clear example would be the naming of that infamous architectural blunder masking as a restaurant on stilts that the French, in a misguided attempt at mockery of our language, named **The Eye Full Tower**. Why won't they stick to naming the architectural disasters in French words so that the world community does not cast aspersions on the English language? Another insulting example was the horrifically criminal **MAD MAN O'SELLE**, who had been convicted of outrages on the hapless village of Guard-Ann Grove. The French, apparently with nothing better to do, confounded linguists world-wide when they co-opted the name of that horrendous villain (Mad Man O'Selle) and changed his name to mean the equivalent of our word **Miss** (as in unmarried woman, or maiden), which morphed into Mademoiselle. With outrages like these, it is clear that each and every word in the language should have specific and definitive copyright protection if we are to sleep soundly at night.

The beauty and purity of our own language is illustrated in a term like **SEAMSTRESS**. As is well documented, the Industrial Revolution (unlike the French Revolution) was the apex of an age of commerce in the USA. All the while, "protection agencies" were established to police manufacturers and insure the rights and safety of the workers. Specifically, and to the point, the garment industry was frequently singled out as an industry that was "less than optimally" inclined to look out for the welfare of its workers. To that end, workers organized and formed the first garment Union (**GRIM:** Garment Retail/Industrial Members).

GRIM seized the opportunity to publish a book called *Sew What*, which in effect was a listing of garment manufacturers along with ratings on how they treated their employees. **GRIM** applied three (3) rankings for each facility and sent undercover employees to assess the working conditions. The rankings were as follows:

1) *(A-)* **generally good** conditions, flush toilets, break room with coffee machine

2) *(B-)* **somewhat harried**, outhouses, padded chairs

3) *(C-)* **seem stressed**, no facilities, standing room only.

To everyone's horror and revulsion, 98% of the factories that were surveyed scored a **C** (pronounced: SEE, or, SEA, or CEE). It was with that report, and the resultant national headlines (followed by the national disgrace), that the term **SEEM STRESSED** became a household word(s). Over time the phrase morphed into **SEAMSTRESS,** which was meant to reference all sewing persons—because that is what they did best (or *sew* it would *seam*). On the other hand, naysayers conjectured that the phrase **SEAM STRESS** referred to nothing more than the amount of stress a good seam would withstand before ripping out on a hapless garment wearer. Studies were pursued under the guidance of the "**Burst" Underwriters Tautness Testers**, or **BUTT**, who exposed the un**seam**ly underside of the industry.

ENGINEER
(FIRST USED: 1804 AD)

Definition: A person who operates an engine

Etymology: With the turn of the twenty-first century, the language we both love and cherish—due to its ability to allow us to communicate—has changed subtly, and sometimes without our notice. The term **ENGINEER** is a case in point. It has become the term to identify someone who uses scientific principles and logic to plan or manage the construction of equipment, buildings, or computer structure and operation.

For those of us who grew up in the mid-twentieth century, the term **ENGINEER** is a reference to the guy in the coveralls who operates the trains on tracks that crisscross our nation and the world (oceans excluded—sorry, oceans!). In any event, we are attempting to peer into the past to determine how the term **ENGINEER** came about and then evolved.

To begin with, the root of **ENGINEER** is **engine**. As we know it, the **engine** is the thing that powers the train (or the boat, or the car, or the truck). Let's start there. The engine is simple but complex, in that it is more than a bunch of ropes and pulleys but less than the Theory of Relativity. Because of the enormous loads it must bear, the engine requires constant attention. The attendant, in this case, is, of course, the **ENGINEER.**

The **ENGINEER** (In this case, the Railroad **ENGINEER**) must know every inch of the engine he is controlling. He must be able to guide the train along the tracks—slow down the engine on curves and speed it up on straight runs - to maximize its potential. The only way one man can understand and control an engine the size of a locomotive is to listen to the sounds of the engine. If a gasket blows, he feels and hears it.

If the pistons don't pist properly, the engine guy hears it and gears it. This term, at its inception, referred to someone who could interpret each sound from the engine. The word **ENGINEER** was the person with the **Engine Ear**.

HIGH SCHOOL
(FIRST USED: 1804 AD)

Definition: A place of learning where we send our teenage children to prepare for college and life.

Etymology: As children, we have all heard the stories of how much worse our parents suffered as teens than we did—much worse than *our* spoiled teen years could ever be. There was talk of horses and buggies, blizzards, one-room schoolhouses, jobs before the school day began, and jobs after it ended. And then to add insult to our need to get outside and play, the lecture would end with them telling the tale of having to do homework by candlelight.

As we grew up, most of us who married and generated a new crop of teen-agers fell into the trap of repeating much of the history stolen from our own parent's so-called rough schooling experiences. One of the main claims, going back to the early 1800s and hopefully ending with us, was that **"we had to trek barefoot, five miles uphill each way, in the blowing snow, to get to school."**

It was that claim, "uphill to school," that was actually used to catego-rize the type of school we were attending. **Kindergarten** was used to warn people away from rooms full of active toddlers. **Grammar Schools** were designed to teach how to construct sentences and ultimately learn to speak and write correctly. Schools for teenagers got their name as a direct result of the oft-told fable about the barefoot trudges to these institutions five miles **uphill** in each direction, whence came the term **HIGH SCHOOL.**

COOPERATE
(FIRST USED: 1807 AD)

Definition: To work together, in consort, as a team

Etymology: At one time fledgling doctors operated on patients without any assistance—so that no one would be witness to any of the gross errors that they might make. That system was flawed because it was easy for the public to take measure of the "body count" (i.e., failures) that could be observed leaving the facilities in body bags.

In the beginning of the nineteenth century, it was only after several years of what history referred to as "the white-coat massacre" that the public demanded that something be done to "stop the bleeding." Hospitals took the first step. They created "surgical theaters" so that there would be an audience (or witnesses) to the events unfolding under the flaps of skin. Secondarily, these surgeries were staffed with a pool of people (the suction guy, the nurse anesthetist, the jumpstart guy who keeps yelling **CLEAR** and scaring the beejesus out of the surgeon)—all of them, in a sense, **CO-OPERATING** with the chief surgeon. Since then, the term **COOPERATE** has been co-opted to also refer to any teamwork effort.

WHO'S 'UR DADDY?
(FIRST USED: 1816 AD)

Definition: a colloquial expression meant to instill confidence and prolong a potentially dead-end relationship.

Etymology: This colloquial phrase is derived from the root phrase **Hoosier Daddy**, which was a common courtroom interrogative directed at any child from Indiana whose parents are involved in any given palimony suit.

SEINE (RIVER)
(FIRST USED: 1818 AD)

Definition: the river that runs through the first district of Paris, France

Etymology: In the days of Louis IV (1638—1715), there were frequent emergency calls to rescue some poor fool who had fallen into the river that courses through Paris. The river, in those days, was the waste dump for the fiefdoms of what was to become the nation of France. There were no plumbing systems, no trash pick-up, nor waste disposal sites of any kind. In lieu of toilets, holes were dug into the ground and human waste was allowed to seep into the creeks and rivers along with the rainwater. This was an age with no pesticides, so actual pests, be they human or otherwise, were thrown into the rivers for disposal. Additionally, the Paris River covered many hundreds of miles before it coursed through the city and onward. It served as the digestive system of a country. It carried the effluvia of a nation through its golden city of Paris.

This river, as noted, like most rivers in the Age of Enlighten, was primarily a vehicle for flushing the effluvia of tosspots and most other human waste thereabouts and for miles upstream. Many men who fell into the river were never seen again. Some were lucky enough to have heroic friends who would rescue them with a rope or a long pole before they floated away with the rest of the "floaters."

Unfortunately, most of the poor souls who were rescued were inexorably altered. Even with a good hosing down and a thorough brush scrubbing, they would never again be accused of being "normal" in the head. Though it was possible to bring their physical appearances back to normal, they tended to drool, they walked with the gait of a one-legged sewer rat, and there was only babble where once there was speech. No matter where they were placed, no matter what the circumstances, they never really got over the smell of the horrid river of waste. In effect, most became as mad as hatters and were consigned to the asylums for the mentally estranged.

As their numbers compounded, the river was increasingly seen as a hazard to the health and welfare of all who traveled around, by, or through it. As a way to warn people of the dangers of walking too close, or falling into the river, in May of 1702, the king was prompted to place large signs along the entire river, claiming it to be "The River That Induced Insanity." Each sign proclaimed: **Danger! Do Not Enter! INSANE RIVER AHEAD!**

The signs seemed to do the trick. Fewer people fell in, and therefore fewer of them were committed to the asylums. The king set about finding ways to clean up the river. It wasn't until the reign of Napoleon Bonaparte that the river was no longer considered a menace. It was only then that Napoleon himself proclaimed that the river no longer caused insanity. He had all of the **INSANE** signs removed and in the summer of 1818 sponsored a three-day festival during which the River was renamed **the Sane River**—which, in French, is spelled **SEINE**.

AWED
(FIRST USED: 1820 AD)

Definition: Something that inspired awe; a thing so out of the ordinary that it evokes a sense of reverence or dread

Etymology: The English language was not always as complicated as it is today. During a simpler time, fewer words were required for expression. Normal days and normal things were described, or thought of, in normal terms. Things that were out of the ordinary, like a two-headed wasp, or a cow that was utterly out of milk, were considered to be a bit "odd" but not remarkable. As mankind spread from his humble beginnings hanging from trees limbs to more suitable endeavors such as building a space station for us to flee to when green house gases destroy the planet, terms to describe events tended to become more complex.

The bearded lady in the carnival, while odd, can't hold a candle to the Eye of Hubble taking pictures of the rings of Saturn more than eighty-one million miles from our sun. Cataclysmic tsunamis and force 5 hurricanes stand in bold relief to the odd amusements of the seven-foot-tall circus clown. The jaw droppers of modern experience have supplanted the old **ODD** for a new, more complex term, which we spell **AWED.** With this term we can finally say with the approbation of our peers:"I am **AWED!**" and not suffer the humiliation associated with the old phrase "I am **ODD.**"

"BATTEN DOWN THE HATCHES"
(FIRST USED: 1823 AD)

Definition: Generally understood to reference the need to secure the ship's hatches prior to the onset of an impending storm.

Etymology: The nineteenth century was the pinnacle of the Age of Seafaring. Not coincidentally, it followed closely upon the pinnacle of pillow making. However, when pillow making was in its infancy, research indicates that it was somewhat poorly thought out.

The primary element in pillow making in the late eighteenth century was the raising of enough goslings to produce enough "baby" feathers (down) to fill cloth bags that could then be sold as pillows. Mass producers of pillows maintained large farms where they bred and raised the young goslings so that the young, soft feathers (down) could be harvested. The farms were surrounded by acres of fine netting to capture any wayward feathers that might blow out of the reach of the pillow fillers. When severe weather swept in from the north, the winds would often overpower the goslings' ability to stay securely attached to the ground. Even though they could not yet fly, even the mildest of gusts would send the almost lighter-than-air creatures blowing in the wind. Under such conditions, the farm foreman was often heard to shout to all of the farm hands to quickly begin swinging sticks, or nets, or whatever they could lay hands on and to bat down, out of the sky, any of the young chicks that they could reach. All hands would grab whatever was available and commence to "smack down" the little chicks to save them from blowing away in the wind. When each little bird that could be reached hit the ground, many of their fine golden feathers would disengage from their bodies and be swept back into the wind. Some of the prized feathers from the chicks would be caught in the netting, and after each windstorm, the workers would collect the feathers and fill the pillows. The feathers retained the name **DOWN**, in honor of the life-saving order to grab nets and sticks to bring our young feathered friends **DOWN**.

Sea captains would echo the call out to begin **"Batting down the hatchlings"** when storms were brewing, and the shout outs across the decks became **Batten down the Hatches** ("tie everything down before it blows away") which is now the famous "squall call" of sailing lore.

JAM
(FIRST USED: 1831 AD)

Definition: a pasty concoction made of sugar added to crushed fruit

Etymology: It should come as no surprise to anyone that **JAM** was an accident. In fact, early on, fruit pickers disdained the very sight of what we now know as **JAM**. Actually, **JAM** was only detected as a point of irritation for the people who had to clean out the bottom of the picker barrels once all of the usable fruit was sold or moved into smaller containers.

Fruitologists tell us of a young man with questionable hygiene habits who was told to scour out the crushed fruit remnants at the bottom of the fruit barrels. And he, as the story goes, having missed lunch, swiped a finger across the mashed layer of fruit and put it into his mouth, only to discover that the taste was quite good. When the fruit farmer came to inspect the barrels, he found his young charge bloated and sleepy, with a fruit smeared smile across his face. The young man, named James Arnold Manfred, explained his discovery, and the farmer, who loved the taste of apple and peach pie, took it upon himself to experiment with mashed fruit and sugar in the kitchen. He called the concoction **JAM**, which was short for **James Arnold Manfred** out of deference to the young man who actually discovered the treat (but was to share none of the profits).

Because the treat was discovered as something crushed under the weight of all the fruit in the barrel, the term **JAM** also became synonymous with getting into trouble (**in a JAM**), with forcing a thing into a tight spot (**jamming it in**)**,** as well as with the musical term **JAM session** (trying to jam too many notes into too few air molecules).

PROPERTY
(FIRST USED: 1831 AD)

Definition: A piece of land or real estate

Etymology: England in the Victorian Era was a place of stark contrasts. The gap between the classes was highlighted by posturing and pretension. In the corridors of societies so-called "greats," it was customary to build your domiciles with a rooms designed specifically to host others at 4:00 tea.

The room was generally labeled as the parlor (*parlors are herein discussed under that heading*) or the tea room. If you could not afford the luxury of tea-specific rooms in your home, you were not listed in the *Who's Whom* of society. Oh, you could have tea in your kitchen or on the front porch, but it was not considered "proper," and you would not be welcomed into the homes of those who had such tea-specific rooms. Obviously, one needed to have the wealth to buy and build a grand house with a tea room. The room was essential. From the concept of a **PROPER TEA** came the need for **PROPERTY**. And so was born a new term, adapted to mean land or real estate that was originally required to add a parlor to your home.

FERTILE
(FIRST USED: 1836 AD)

Definition: Something or someone that reproduces frequently.

Etymology: It is commonly suggested that to better understand the etymological underpinnings of this word, one should pronounce it syllabically in a slow manner—thus the phonic pronunciation Fur Tile, which itself takes us one step closer to the origin of the union of the two words FUR and TILE and leads us to an etymological discovery.

The first damp basement with tile floors produced the descriptive **Fur Tile** because of the fur-like substance found to grow on and between the tiles in the dark and damp basement. The tiles were referred to as furry when it was discovered that the conditions promoted growth resembling an experimental Petri dish of slimy organic and fur-like materials. Consequently and subsequently, **Fur Tile** (later spelled **FERTILE**) came to refer to something reproductive, or the abundant production thereof.

KANSAS AND ARKANSAS
(FIRST USED: 1836 AD)

Definition: The current names of the states of Kansas and Arkansas.

Etymology: There are 63,900 entries in Google to explain how we got and kept the names of the states **KANSAS** and **ARKANSAS**. Rather than subject you to the complicated process of reading and discarding each entry, I will here give a truncated mythical version of how these two states became so similar in name.

As a territory, the area we now know as **ARKANSAS** was originally referred to as "the territory **WAY OUT WEST**," or **"WOW"** (usually followed by some pointing). Established in 1861, it was well known, nationwide, and even prior to statehood it was hailed as a territory in which the growing and exporting of the famous black apples helped to feed half of a continent. Black apples (which were actually red) were the backbone of the **WOW** apple exporting business.

Backing up twenty-five years, the territory to be known as **KANSAS** had been established in 1836 and had been named the Great State of **Hood**, or **State Hood** for short. **Hood** was also in the apple-producing business and had been into doing apples for twenty-five years longer than the Great State of **WOW.** By 1861 **WOW** had begun a fledging canning business so that the apples would stay fresher for a longer selling season. That is where push came to shove between these two great states.

Shortly thereafter, **canned** applesauce had begun showing up on store shelves in the Great State of **Hood**. More importantly, they were coming by stagecoach all the way from the Great State of **WOW. HOOD**, in an effort to maintain a market advantage, jumped feet first into their own canning operations. **WOW,** wanting their own potential marketing advantage, petitioned the federal government to incorporate its territory as a new state and to call it **OUR CANNED SAUCE.** Obviously that wasn't going to pass the federal government muster. However, Washington did approve what it felt was a good compromise and declared the new state be named **ARKANSAS** (which phonetically sounds like the same thing). The State of **Hood** protested loudly as an issue of unfair government-assisted marketing. **Hood** declared that it too should have a phonetic advantage. Washington, in its role as Great Appeaser, assented and changed the name of the State of **Hood** to **CANNED SAUCE,** which remains its phonetic enunciation. However, **KANSAS** became its new spelling.

PURSUIT
(FIRST USED: 1837 AD)

Definition: The act of striving for something; attempting to catch someone or something

Etymology: As the Victorian Era began in England and strict codes of ethics and mores were being developed, there was an underground movement to counteract the snobbery and rigidity of the Queen's haughty and imperial social caste. Within this underground movement were the first indications of a science developing, and it had as its thesis that the psyche of the human being was the key to individual happiness.

It was within this context that certain groups of people would meet to discuss what made them happy and what made them sad. It examined what things could be done, or experimented with, to expand the "happiness quotient" and dissipate the sadness.

One of the first experiments involved the concept of petting. Since petting seemed to be favored by the domestic cats that abounded in households everywhere, that was where experimentation started. All had the common experience of finding that the act of petting an animal seemed to elicit contentment in the animal that was enviable for most humans.

The experiment involved a hand-sewn suit of fur that was pleasing to the touch and similar to the soft velvety coats of cats. Volunteers were fitted with the suits and sent home in the evenings to invite family members and strangers alike to treat them as if they were the household cat, petting them at will. The reports were all very optimistic. It seems that the petters and the petties, one and all, reported an increase in their sense of well-being.

The excitement regarding the experiment engendered a spurt of entrepreneurs who made custom petting suits to order. The suits were called **the Purr Suits of Happiness**. Sadly, with the "Victor" Rhian crackdown on all things happy, most municipalities outlawed the **Purr Suits**, and the first experiment in psychology became no more than a footnote in the history books. However, because all human endeavor since then is about the **Purr Suit** of Happiness, we are left with the reminder of that noble experiment each time we use the term **PURSUIT** (a contraction of Purr Suit).

POEM
(FIRST USED: 1840 AD)

Definition: A group of words composed to evoke emotion while describing in rhyme or evocative prose an event or imaginative state.

Etymology: As is taught in every third-grade classroom but denied by most reputable scholars, Edgar Allan Poe was the "inventor," if you will, of the modern-day **POEM**. It has been said that while great strides have been made since the mid 1800s to enhance the style and quality of **POEMS**, the first years were quite traumatic, and it is gratifying to aficionados that the literary form did not die an early and tragic death.

POEMS, in those early days, were terrible renderings of the English language and drew the ire and ridicule of all but the heaviest drinkers. The very term **POEM** was a contraction of the man's name (**POE**) and the dubious monocled grunt—**HMMMM** that led to the modern day term **POE-HMMM**! Nonetheless, at the time, the **POE-HMMM** was a hideous aberration of language. It has even been said that the term **POETRY** was an injunction beseeching the master of the horror story (**POE**), to **TRY** (**POE-TRY**) harder to rhyme his way out of trouble with

the new medium. But despite the mortification, Edgar Allen continued to use the new literary form to create such famous icons as "The
Craven." He later attempted to break the art form into other classifications—one of which was called the **ODE,** which by all reckoning
was a term derived from the word "**ODIOUS.**"

To drive the point home that **POEMS** were an early aberration among
the followers of Edgar Allen Poe, please find below an example of
how deep the pit was dug that could, and to some, should, have buried this newest form of expression:

A LEGEND TO REST

Disembodied legs

Came "wandering" 'round the bend.

They had no sense of purpose,

They left a sense of dread—

('Cuz disembodied legs can't "wonder"

With no head)

It may not now surprise you

That several legs, it's said,

"Belonged to EDGAR ALLAN,"

With POE knees that had bled,

And dribbled on the carpet,

And somehow turned it red.

The rest of EDGAR ALLAN

Was hanging from a limb.

A branch had skewered organs

And become a part of him.

A RAVEN flying over

Was never more happy –

When Seeing EDGAR ALLEN,

POE...

A TREE.

❖   ❖   ❖

BUTTOCKS
(FIRST USED: 1841 AD)

Definition: The fleshy rounded end where the hipbones meet

Etymology: If the year was 1842 and you were a settler moving west across the wild plains of Nebraska or Colorado with plans to claim the free land in California or Oregon, you would, of course, be one of hundreds of thousands other families seeking a new life as far to the west as the land would carry them. Emigrants used mules, horses, or oxen to pull their covered wagons on the typically two-thousand-mile journey. Oxen were the easiest to handle because they were more deliberate. They could also be used for food in an emergency, as well as being easy to feed on the open range, and they were essential for plowing when they arrived in California or Oregon. Additionally, the Native American Indians were less tempted to steal a bunch of oxen. If they were going to raid a wagon or train of wagons, they would much rather return home with all of the available horses.

The primary problem with oxen was that they took years to train. They were bulls before they were castrated. After that, it took five years before they would be considered oxen. The problem: they tended to forget what they were doing. If you hitched them in pairs and made the lead oxen the youngest pair and the hind two the oxen with the most experience, you had a more efficient and effective overall team. This was true because the lead team, the youngest, tended to forget what the mission was and would periodically slow down and even stop to just look around and munch their cuds. The rear team, based on innate oxen experience and status, felt that they should be in the lead. They simply could not abide all of the slowing down and stopping. They would simply head-butt the younger lead oxen in the rumps until they were back up to speed*. And so it would go: "Giddy-up!" Strain, pull, slow, stop! Butt, Butt, pull, slow, butt, pull, etc. Eventually the older teams of oxen were tagged with the appellation "The Butt Ox." (You now can understand why it took five months or more for the migrating settlers to finally reach the coastal states). The term, of course, has since morphed into our current-day spelling of **BUTTOCKS** but still references that fleshy flank.

The average distance transversed in a Calistoga Wagon pulled by Butt Oxen was 16 miles per day (assuming you were traveling on the flat lands). Do the math.

PHILOSOPHER
(FIRST USED: 1842 AD)

Definition: One who requires an armchair from which to spout philosophical* notions.

Etymology: Those who have read the etymology of the word **HUMAN** will have a bit of an advantage trying to understand the word **PHILOSOPHER**. All of the advances in archeology involve painstaking onsite digging, sorting, identifying, and classifying tiny bone fragments, broken tools, and other implements of life. Once the digs are complete and all of the samples are collected, large crews proceed to the site to backfill areas where holes were dug and where harvesting is complete. Because the sites are sometimes not completely scoured, it is not untypical for the archeologist-in-charge to appoint one of his staff to oversee and fill in the blanks regarding the importance of the site. Whenever possible, the archeologist-in-charge will typically ask the member of the team with the most experience to take on this responsibility. It is usually the team member with the talent and thoughtful ability to pull all of the data together and extrapolate how all of these finds will impact life going forward. He is typically referred to as the **FILL OFFICER**—that is, the one who, before the site is refilled, is able to **Fill** in the blanks regarding missing data and significant implications of the finds. **FILL OFFICER**** is the title that we now use to describe one who spouts Fill-osophic notions— that is, the **FILLOFFICER with a spelling correction of: PHILOSOPHER**

(Refer to etymology of the term PHILOSOPHY)

**(It is particularly poignant when the man selected to be the FILL OFFICER is himself named Phil.)*

VICTORIAN ERA
(FIRST USED: 1843 AD)

Definition: The historic period from 1837 to 1901, which non-coincidently was the period in which Victoria, Queen of England, reigned.

Etymology: There was a CPA who worked directly with and for the queen of England. He was obsessive compulsive and was the first bureaucrat to be so identified. He was officious, suspicious, and scrupulous in an overbearing way. He was fastidious to a fault and given to extravagance only regarding upholding the letter of the law. He loved the finest detail and was awed by minutia. He thrived on excessive displays of formality interwoven with garish and gaudy displays of heavily laden, repetitious wall, window, and floor coverings. He also was endowed with an innate sense of the timing of mundane daily events and was offended by any break in the accepted norms of time spent in washrooms or time spent alone with people of the opposite sex. He was the consummate consensus builder when it came to the minute managing of things that should have been no more than a passing and unimportant function—whether it be personal or interpersonal. Yet through his mannerisms and interdicts, he was the unheard answer to the phrase, "who cares, and why should they!" With all of these foibles and the ear of the English queen, he was the designer of the era that would forever be known as the **VICTOR RHEIN** Era.

MINER
(FIRST USED: 1849 AD)

Definition: One who excavates the earth to extract minerals, precious stones, etc.

Etymology: With the discovery of gold in the mid-1800s, a migration began that would rival any in history. People came to California by any means available to reach the gold fields of the Sierra Nevada. The majority of gold was panned in streams and rivers, but to some men, the real fortune lay buried in the earth—and by digging, they planned to amass great wealth. Of all of the gold seekers, there were approximately forty men who felt that the shovel was the pathway to riches. They became a specifically identifiable group even though they were from different walks of life. They felt that if they could tap into a vein, then working together, they could change their lives forever—which, in fact, they did.

Historical notes indicate that these men were of a single-minded purpose. They would only entertain sharing their potential discoveries
with one another. That meant no partners, no family, no collabora-
tors except each other. When an ordinary citizen would come upon
them deep in the hole that this group of fellows was digging, he or
she would be run off by the irate shovel jockey with rabid threats and
exclamations such as "**Go away, It's Mine! All Mine**!" Such exclamations have morphed over the years into the term **MINING**. All forty of
the miners generated such bad reputations for their self-obsession
that they needed one another just to protect themselves from local
citizens who claimed that the mines were no one's personal property
and that the gold was lying at the bottom of those holes for anyone
to take. This band of men is referenced in the history books as the
Forty-Miners, and they created for themselves not only a place in
history, but in the hearts of the citizens of the city of San Francisco.
For when the "mines" played out, they returned to their port city and
formed the city's first major league football team, known to this day
as the San Francisco Forty Miners.

CHRONOLOGY: THIRTEEN

(FROM 1850 AD THROUGH 1862 AD)

THE CHLAMYDIAN EPOCH

< *ITCHING TO SCRATCH* >

"THE TERM "JURASSIC" IS THE EARLIEST KNOWN REFERENCE TO DIARRHEA."

CANOPIES
(FIRST USED: 1850 AD)

Definition: Decorative (or otherwise, as dictated by taste) covers above such things as beds and thrones.

Etymology: It must be mentioned here that the one exception to the above definition is that canopies cannot be considered a cover over certain vegetables. Again: WARNING: Not to be confused with a can of peas. But we digress! Actually, if you were a pea, being inside a can of peas would be considered the ultimate in warmth and comfort, bundled up with 127 of your closest friends, locked in a friendly group hug with a fine roof over your head and no worries. Thus, because of the fact that CANOPIES came before the **can of peas**, and that the words sound identical phonically, we are compelled to ignore the scientific evidence. We are unequivocally persuaded that **can of peas** was the forerunner of the **CANOPIES**, in concept if not execution. And to quote certain **can of peas**: "We are unanimous in that decision."

ELLIPTICAL
(FIRST USED: 1851 AD)

Definition: **Ellipse** is defined by Webster as "one of the sections of a cone"—i.e., "the elliptical orbit of a planet," which in itself is the description of a shape outlined.

Etymology: What Webster doesn't tell you is that the *E* in elliptical is an abbreviation for **E**lephant. Way back when, during the founding days of zoos (not to be confused with Zeus), an animal trainer named Numbly tried, using some ostrich feathers (still attached to the terrified bird), to tickle the lips of an elephant named Brutus (who was new to captivity). This activity so startled and alarmed Brutus that he swung his huge trunk from the ground in an orbital fashion, all the way around, and on the downswing, slammed it into Numbly so hard that we now use the word numb to describe the aftereffect. The poor ostrich's head was also slammed into the soft ground, burying it—leaving its neck and body dancing wildly about above ground. Once the zoo people cleaned the carnage up and talked about the incident—the term **E** (for elephant) **lip tickle**, or, **ELLIPTICAL**, came to refer to the arc of the trunk (like the orbit of a planet) and was highly discouraged among elephant handlers. Residually, the term **numb** came into common use, and we are all familiar with the references to an ostrich burying his head prior to some impending unfortunate event.

NUMB
(FIRST USED: 1851 AD)

Definition: The feeling that you get when an elephant trunk slams into you.

Etymology: (See **ELLIPTICAL**)

EXPENSIVE
(FIRST USED: 1852 AD)

Definition: **EXPENSIVE*** usually refers to an item or items that are generally listed as having a high cost to purchase or own. Example: *I drive an expensive car.*

Etymology: The etymology of the term **EXPENSIVE** is relatively easy to understand, especially to people for whom the acquisition of money is difficult. The term ultimately is derived from two combined terms: **expense** and **sieve**.

As everyone knows, a **sieve** is any contraption that filters out various bits of matter, leaving only the desired product. For example, the process of panning for gold was a basic process in sifting, with the gold being the product left in the pan. A colander is basically a sieve or sifter, allowing for water and any undesirable particulate to filter through the holes, leaving only the cleaned lettuce or pasta.

Now that we understand **sieve**, let's explore the concept of **expense**. Simply put, **expense** is anything that costs you money (generally with the silent word **unnecessary** proceeding the term **expense**). So, for example, the movie called *The Money Pit*, about a house purchased for a song and ending up costing a fortune in upgrades and repairs, could be said to be a reprehensible expense. Another example might be joining a book club in which the first five choices are a dollar each, but the ensuing contract (notice how the similarity of the word **ensuing** is to the words **in suing**) **requires** you to purchase two books per month for the remainder of your life at a special editor's cost of twenty-five dollars per copy (subject to terms of inflation, taxes and license extra, void where prohibited by law…).

So now we can combine the two words **expense** and **sieve** and fully understand the subtle reality of the "word combo" and the **expense**

sieve nature of many of the products we buy (be it our car, our house, gas for our car, gas for our house, or the little brown pills we take to eliminate the need to produce our own gas).

*Expensive can also be referred to as a person who once was "thoughtful" but now is not. Example: He is no longer pensive. He is EX-PENSIVE.

ABSOLUTE
(FIRST USED: 1853 AD)

Definition: Complete and total assurance; the best, the greatest of a thing

Etymology: In the mid 1800s, because of newspaper articles that tracked competitions across the country, body building became a vicarious experience for the common man. The competitions culminated in the grandest of the conceits, known as **the National Bodybuilding Championships**.

One of the most popular events was the presentation of the trophies for the best abdominals. The winner was traditionally awarded with not only a bronze sculpture of the "**Abs** of Adonis" but also with a standing ovation and salute from the spectators. This honor was referred to as the **Abdominal**, or **Ab Salute,** and was the root and derivation of the term **ABSOLUTE**, which came to mean Complete / Perfection / Pure/ et al.

FILIBUSTER
(FIRST USED: 1853 AD)

Definition: An obstruction tactic (prolonged reading from various sources) to block a bill from being passed into law

Etymology: In the mid-1850s, the use of the **FILIBUSTER** was introduced into session by an inordinate number of senators who, being in the minority and having washed out of clown college, wanted nonetheless to control legislation. They decided to stall and obfuscate by taking to the lectern with a Bible and a phone book and reading out loud until a motion to adjourn was heard.

The opposition, in an effort to stop the madness, would signal to their pages and aides by shouting "**FILL A BUSTER**" (a **Buster** was a large water balloon that had the capacity to hold one gallon of water). The pages and aides would wheel large tubs down the aisle filled with **Busters.** The senators would then commence throwing the **Busters** at the "readers." Typically after five or six direct hits, the senator at the lectern would retreat from the chamber, saturated; with a phone book that was also waterlogged and no longer readable, proclaiming that he would "**Yield the Floor**" so that the business of the country could continue. **FILIBUSTER** is how we now articulate the term, a term that was once a raucous free-for-all called **FILL–A–BUSTER**.

PORTABLE
(FIRST USED: 1854 AD)

Definition: A thing that is easily moved from one place to another

Etymology: The first recorded abuse of the table was during the Victor Rhein Era. In the British motherland, as in all of the colonies, it was a time of rest and a time of unrest. The kingdom was divided into the Traditionalist faction (who proclaimed a strict adherence to a principle of maintaining the status quo) and the so-called Enlightened faction (who favored radical departures from the staid conservatives and opined that any change at all was good). The first inkling of the unrest to come was when the Marquise de Munchas persuaded the Queen to move her spring and summer Queen's Gala from the ornate palace ballroom to the ornate palace gardens. This sudden change in the traditional gala format was taken as a direct assault on the loyalties of the Traditionalists. They argued, first and foremost, that the palace tables should not be used for any outdoor festivities. They were of great historical value, and to move them from their positions in the great ballroom would be an affront to decency, an act of thoughtless wanton destruction, and a symbolic casting of aspersions upon the loyal Traditionalists, who, as anyone could guess, were the bedrock of the kingdom.

This affronted segment of the population began a populist uprising to protest the transport of such antique furniture from the safety of the palace dining and ballrooms to the unforgiving tempest that was the outdoor environment of the great gardens. Large groups of these intrepid souls would gather at the gates of the palace on each day of the queen's gala, carrying signboards and chanting the now-famous phrase "**POOR TABLES**! ALAS! THE **POOR TABLES**!"

After many months of such protests, the queen relented, and in her finite wisdom, she commissioned Sir Emory Bored to develop new types of tables and chairs that could be used in any environment and that could be folded, stored compactly, and stacked in strategically placed storage rooms for quick and efficient access. Once the new storable furniture was built, it was, at the queen's behest, named **the Poor Tables** in a noble gesture to the forthright Traditionalists. Over the years the term has remained a part of the English language and still describes the reason for the invention of things that are easily moved. The only change is that a letter *O* has been misplaced, and now the phrase has become the single word **PORTABLES**.

SEWING BEE
(FIRST USED: 1854 AD)

Definition: The phrase generally refers to the activity(s) of a group of people considered to be "as busy as bees." In this example we refer to a ladies' sewing group.

Etymology: Historians, entomologists, fiction writers, and philosophers all gave reference to the huge and beautiful swarms of golden bees that delighted people of all lands worldwide. It was with the so-called Industrial Revolution that the sightings became rare. Sadly, nearly two centuries later, it has been determined that the golden bee, along with so many other species, will have to be classified as extinct.

These were some of the few known insects that were capable of "farming." They accomplished this by transferring the plant seeds (that stuck to their pollen-laden feet) to the earth as they alit and walked to their hives, which were built to resemble large rocks in the dirt. As the bees traveled between the flowering shrubs and their hive, the seeds would drop to the ground, thus laying the foundation for the next flower crop. These bees were referred to as golden **sowing** bees. They were originally discovered during exploration of the Spice Islands in the late fourteenth century. Word spread of their **bee-havior**, and everyone in the Western world was astonished. The **SOWING BEES** became the topic of conversation and a source of amazement for the good part of the next four hundred years.

Eventually people tired of the subject. When others brought up the topic of the **SOWING BEES** in conversation, the common retort became "Sow what!" And with that, the "shine was officially off the shoe." Beginning in the nineteenth century, the golden **SOWING BEE** population began a rapid decline. As billions of golden **SOWING BEES** died off, ladies would collect them and string them into necklaces. In fact, the etymology of the term **Bead** came from this practice—that is, if you were given a necklace of bees, you were said to have been **Bee dead** (later changed to **Beaded**). The ladies became famous for the **SOWING BEE'D** jewelry, and during the mid-nineteenth century, they formed more groups to make the special necklaces. When the extinct bees were no longer to be found, the ladies, who wanted to forever remember their association with the little golden **SOWING BEES**, honored them by calling their stitching groups **SEWING BEES**.

PARASITE
(FIRST USED: 1856 AD)

Definition: a thing that lives off of other things

Etymology: Conventional wisdom about the origin of the term **PARASITE** came into question when the British Word Police (BWP) made a determination that the term **PAIR-A-SITE**, in essence, was an oxymoron (as distinguished from the two-legged and the four-legged types). As such, the term **PAIR-A-SITE** should not be used in the already-established constraints of the accepted definition—that is, an organism or thing that survives off of other things—primarily because one could not have a **pair** (plural) of **site** (singular).

It was further ruled that the term **PAIR-A-SITE**S was clearly a word that referred to two identical places, as in a **pair of sites,** and consequently, the word would have to undergo a change from singular to plural in all contexts. A hue and cry arose from the masses, and as a compromise, final word came down from the BWP. It stated that given the fact that two blood-sucking organisms could, in fact, live off of a single individual in separate places, or **sites**, thereon, then as a result, the term **PAIR-A-SITE**S could therefore be stretched to reflect the original intent of the word. A **pair of sites (PAIR-A-SITES)** was restored to its near-original meaning and original spelling, and while still allowed, the use of the singular **PARASITE** was to be discouraged*—all of this to the great relief of the general public.**

*<Author's Note:>

The BWP were disbanded shortly after that ruling when it was discovered that all past meetings of the commissioners on the committee had been held in McTaggart's Pub on the Strand.

** Some still contend that the origins of this word are directly related to the decision to build the city of Paris in the specific area of France upon which it now sits—i.e., the **Paris Site**.

FOR ALL INTENTS AND PURPOSES
(FIRST USED: 1857 AD)

Definition: Generally analogous to "For all practical purposes," referencing things "as they now stand."

Etymology: Toward the end of the nineteenth century, there were many copycats trying to duplicate the successes of the famous Phineas Taylor (P. T.) Barnum. Few succeeded. However, one circus copy-cat did manage to make his mark on the history of language. His name, familiar to every third grader, was Ebenezer Zachariah Barnone (shortened to E. Z. Barnone).

EZ's "circus" consisted of one large tent wherein were displayed such oddities as a man who could write limericks on his belly with nothing more than the pressure from his finger (an ability that the medical profession later named Dermographism), and a "lady" who could blow out candles from poofs of air that she launched through her eye sockets. Aside from these two "headliners" in the large tent, E. Z. also had a smaller outdoor enclosure with two portable vinyl blow-up pools. In these pools he housed two marine mammals commonly known as porpoises.

It should be here noted that in the larger circus community, E. Z. was somewhat of a joke. And to add ignominy to the mix, prior to his arrival in any given town, he would typically be mocked not only by his own community but also by articles in the local newspapers about the upcoming "goofy" show. Nonetheless, he always filled the tent with paying customers, though most were there to get a chuckle from his attempt to emulate the "real" circuses.

E. Z. was not to be deterred, and he was a good businessman and a swell gaffer (manager). He met with his crew at the beginning of each day. He always brought coffee and donuts (for himself) and began each meeting with the same phrase: "For all (of you) in **TENTS**, and **PORPOISES**, let's run through what needs to be done today." While his meetings tended to last until he had consumed the very last crumb of his four donuts, his instructions never varied, and most of his staff (consisting of a porpoise handler and the two circus acts, along with one pool/tent expert) typically would spend the hour-long meeting doodling his opening words. Those words were repeated so often verbally, and scribbled so many times on paper, that they eventually wormed their way into the *American Book of Phrases* from their birth form, **"FOR ALL IN TENTS, AND PORPOISES..." to their** adjusted form, **"FOR ALL INTENTS AND PURPOSES..."**

OFFICER
(FIRST USED: 1858 AD)

Definition: A person of rank in a military or any other organization

Etymology: Much is still unknown of Victor Rhein England's highly developed and complex military organization, but the stuff that we know* provides us with a bright tapestry of etymological development.

It is clear that Queen Victoria had a complex indoor and complex outdoor command and control of all branches of her **Monolithic Military Machine** (MMM). We do know that the **Indoor Command and Control** was typically referred to as **ICC** and that the **Outdoor Command and Control** was commonly referred to as simply the **Outdoor Command and Control**. All of the **Monolithic Military Machine** of Great Britain was divided into four separate services at the time. Rank, from private through colonel, captain through commander, and all organizational structure in each service, were mirror images of each other:

First: The forces guarding the castle gates (one of the least-sought-after gigs) was called **GUARDS AT GATES**, or **GAG** for short, and sometime referred to as **Gag Gig**

Second: The divisions patrolling the deserts of Arabia were called **DIVISIONS OF ARABIA**, or **DOA** for short.

Third: The Navy of the Unconquerable and Mighty Britain was called **NAVY OF THE UNCONQUERABLE AND MIGHTY BRITAIN,** or **NUMB** for short; and finally,

Fourth: The **HEADQUARTER OFFICE MAZE EDIFICE** was called **HEADQUARTER OFFICE MAZE EDIFICE,** or **HOME** for short. The latter was ultimately changed to **HQ COMPLEX** or simply **HQ** because it sounded so much more "British."

Within the HQ, any man of high rank was referred to by all of those of lesser rank as **an Office-Sir** because he or she worked in the **office** (HQ)! (This is apparently where the term **OFFICER** originated.) When those **Officer-Sirs** who worked the night shift received their commissions for that assignment, they were said to be **NIGHTED** (this, apparently is where the term [badly misspelled] **knighted** originated). Because they were **Office-Sirs**, or "those who worked in the offices," they tended to be less testosterone laden than their cousins in the battlefields and thus they were considered to be **Gentler men**, as it were. (This, of course, is where the term **Gentlemen** first originated.)

As indicated, the toughest duty at HQ was said to be that of a **Nighted Office-Sir**. It was tough primarily due to the fact that they were required to move in stealth, observing all of the entries and exits. They kept tabs on their fellow **Office Sirs**. They reported any indiscretions to **Her AUSPICIOUS ROYAL MAJESTY (HARM).** Most importantly, it was considered the toughest duty due to the fact that they had to stay up all night doing it. Because of the need for discretion, these **Nighted Office-Sirs** were referred to not as **Office Sirs and Gentlemen** but simply as **Gents,** or as in the singular, **A-Gent.** This is apparently where the term **Agent** originated—which referred to the **Nighted Office-Sir** as an **A Gent** (-tleman) of the queen.

Therefore, and in summation, there were three distinct classes of military servants working at the Queen Victoria Military Head Quarters (QVMHQ). The first was the **Office-Sir and Gentlemen,** the second the **Nighted Office Sirs**, and the third, and more clandestine, were the **Nighted Office-Sirs and AGents.** This then should leave us with a greater appreciation of Victor Rein England as a virtual **cornucopia of etymological profundity** (CEP) and hotbed of bureaucratic redundancy.

*is pretty much all fabricated

CEREAL
(FIRST USED: 1861 AD)

Definition: A breakfast food, typically grain based.

Etymology: One of the causes of the American Civil War was a series of unsolved murders. It was suspected that a Chinese acrobatic troupe that was wandering the Atlantic Coast, performing in cities and villages, making friends as they went, was somehow involved. Detectives and private eyes alike were following the trail of the Tzu Wongz Troupe because after each performance and a night of rest, they would move to the next venue, and with each move, one or two people would be found, typically slumped over the kitchen counter, dead. Suspicions were rife.

One night after the troupe crossed from Virginia to Maryland, there was some sort of dustup at Fort Sumner. It was April 13, 1861, and law enforcement from all over Virginia was fed up with the fact that they were not advancing their case against Tzu Wongz. Virginia Law Enforcement decided to just get on with it. They crossed the border into Maryland and seized the troupe until such time as they could determine if the troupe was, indeed, the problem.

Tzu Wongz was a favorite of the Maryland bunch, and the disregard for territorial sovereignty along with the arrest of the troupe on Maryland soil was more than they could bear. Within hours, the war broke out. The South, in a skirmish on the Fields of Disdane, was able to capture the troupe and bring them back across the Potomac for questioning.

Most people were quick to note that after the Tzu Wongz Troupe was detained, the mysterious deaths stopped. Tzu Wongz, who pleaded innocence, explained that while the deaths involved the same people invited to breakfast with the troupe before they got on the road, these were all people whom Tzu Wongz respected—people with whom the troupe wanted to establish an ongoing friendship. Further questioning revealed that Tzu Wongz received a weekly mailing of the troupe's favorite breakfast grains from his maid in China, and which he had shared with all of the victims. (In China, it was considered a matter of respect to serve your guests your best foods while you sat behind them [and a bit to the right] engaging the guest in conversation but not participating in the enjoyment of the food).

All of the newspapers on the East Coast raged about the "serial" killer. Detectives went to China to visit JuJit Sue, Tzu Wongz's maid. It was then that the story unfolded. JuJit Sue, in an attempt to keep the special grains for herself, bought severely inferior grains and coated them with copper sulfate and benzene to give them the appearance of the highly prized grains requested by Tzu Wongz. She wasn't aware of the toxicity of the ruse, and upon hearing of the deaths, despaired. JuJit Sue committed Seppuku (the reverse of the Japanese version of the ancient Chinese tradition of ASIAS*, which amounted to self-snuffing) to maintain her honor. Tzu Wongz and his troupe were released from custody. The newspapers reported that since there was no "intent," there were, then, no **serial** killings. They did concede, however, that the word **serial** could be adjusted to reflect the fact that there were, however, CEREAL killings.

It would be twenty to forty years before Americans got over the Break-Fast **Cereal** Killings and before **CEREAL** could get a fresh start. The key was to switch to less caustic grains. John Kellogg and C. W. Post took up the reins around the turn of the century, and since then, the term **CEREAL** has come to be known as a respected breakfast food.

ASIAS refers to a pre-ancient day practice of "eliminating" the person that you have unintentionally dishonored so that you would not have to feel remorse every time you passed that person in the hallway, et al. **ASIAS** stands for "**A S**nuff **I**s **A S**nuff." The practice fell out of favor before the *establishment of the First Dynasty, primarily because the population levels in Asia were in decline.*

CHAMPAGNE
(FIRST USED: 1862 AD)

Definition: A cousin of the wine family primarily differentiated by the infusion of effervescence, or carbonation

Etymology: From the mid-eighteenth century until the early nineteenth century, medical remedies were hard to find for the average American, who might be feeling poorly but could not or would not pay for the assistance of a physician. However, "for every need there is a greed," and with the new world and its wide-open frontier came shysters and hucksters who, for a couple of quarters, were ready to cure every upset, undigested, and/or peptic stomach. This then was the age of the elixirs, and they were the wonder cures that would soothe every pain and salve every ache. Elixirs usually contained a small amount of rough alcoholic spirits to give the illusion of pharmaceutical effect. The peddlers of these elixirs preyed on the common man and his family to the benefit of naught but the peddler's whim.

Not to be outdone, and understanding that the upper class clearly shunned the fake marketing attempts as well as the company of scoundrels peddling the fake "physical-forgiveness," a clever snake-oil salesman with the unlikely moniker of Sir Dane Lee came up with an astonishing plan to cater to the upper classes and the barons of wealth and power.

Sir Dane's epiphany came about when he realized that only the rich could afford to pour the finest of wines at their (sometimes breakfast), lunch, and dinner tables. Additionally they found the need to nurse an aperitif or two in the evenings to stave off the lumbago. Sir Dane was the first to introduce a new kind of wine that sold itself to the rich and famous based on its combined ingredients of wine and a bit of carbonation. Sir Dane expounded on its curative value and the "fact" that it would relieve pain, soothe frayed nerves, and send its imbiber to a sound and deep slumber where dreams were sweet and the new dawn was bright and cheerful.

All of this madness may have worked, had Sir Dane Lee understood that the only people supporting the medical community in those times were the well-to-do. The Medical Community (MC) had no intention of letting Sir Dane and his carbonated elixir stand between them and a profit, and as a result launched a campaign against what they described as "**Sham Pain-Relief.**" While the Medical Community campaign worked against the middle-class, it backfired when the curious and rich taste tested the **Sham Pain-Relief**, and the elixir "turned a head" or two among the moneyed mighty. As a result, it became the tickle wine of the time. The wealthy continued seeing their doctors, and they continued sipping their "**Sham Pain**." The name of the new wine was "tidied up" a bit and became the **Champagne** that we all have grown to know and chug love.

CHRONOLOGY: FOURTEEN

THE LOQUACIOUS ERA

(1863 AD THROUGH 1899 AD)

‹WHEN WAS YOUR
LAST STAND?›

I WASN'T
FLIPPING YOU "THE BIRD"!
I WAS SENDING YOU MY "EGRETS."

ANARCHY
(FIRST USED: 1863 AD)

Definition: Lawlessness, confusion, without governing rules

Etymology: In England, during the period that found Charles Dickens in his top form, a child was born to Thomas and Annabelle Key, a child who was to inspire the definition of the worst form of communal human behavior. She was named in honor of her mother and so was called Anna Regina Key. She was Thomas and Annabel's only child, and some would later claim that little Anna was a warning to Anna's parents, not to have any more children. The problem, as it was later determined by one S. Freud, was that little Anna was not happy if she did not get her way at every turn. Her parents, who were somewhat progressive, were of the opinion that a child should "earn" her way in life through activities that contributed to society in some measure. Little Anna thought differently and screamed and raged her way from the toddler stage, through young childhood, straight to her teen years, and then into young adulthood. Rules did not apply, in her mind, and when push came to shove, Anna Regina Key shoved so hard that things broke—including the spirit of her parents who, after failing to have her committed to a school for wayward children, put a contract out on her life. As it turned out, there were a number of people, including her grandparents, who tried to do the deed without benefit of remuneration.

In the long run, chaos was the order of the day in Anna's life. Her parents and grandparents were incarcerated for "attempted," and the local constabulary spent 13.4 percent of their manpower and time refereeing around Anna issues. If it had not been for the fact that Anna fell off of London Bridge and drowned while being charged by an irate horse pulling a carriage—a horse that Anna had used as a target for her new slingshot—there would be no telling what sorts of disasters may have occurred. Ultimately Anna Regina Key's legacy became her name—which was shortened to **ANN R. KEY (ANARCHY)** and referred to lawlessness, confusion, etc.

MILITARY SECRETS
(FIRST USED: 1863 AD)

Definition: Information that the branches of the military reserve for only the highest-ranking officers; usually specific to the conduct of the enemy or the current war.

Etymology: The phrase Military Secrets first came into use during the Civil War and was specific to the navy until the concept was further developed and became useful to the other branches of the US military. It was during the Civil War that the US Navy was developed. This newest branch of the military was responsible for protecting and defending against any and all incursions from the sea. The newly built warships (including the ironclads) became effective vehicles to establish blockades, patrol the coastlines, and venture up major rivers such as the Mississippi.

Since the concept of sailing was new to the majority of the military, the finer points—such as providing adequate food and water supplies for long voyages—was an experiment in progress during this time. One of the mistakes that the planners ultimately learned from was with regard to food storage and food supplies. The most horrific teachable moment regarded grits made from millet.

Millet was harvested as the primary grain to bake breads and whip up loads of pancakes for the hungry crews. The millet was stored in gunnysacks in the bowels of the ship and brought to the galley each morning to prepare meals for the day.

The problem that developed was that the bowels (if you will excuse the expression) of ships were always damp, and the millet that was stored the longest tended to fester in the moisture. Molds and funguses grew in the damp millet. (See: **etymology: FERTILE)**

On one occasion the entire crew of the the USS *Whoolyhull*, including the captain, got so violently ill that the ship drifted virtually unmanned for close to thirty-six hours. Fortunately no one died, and the ship did not encounter the enemy during that period. But when the captain was able to confirm the cause of the illness by scrutinizing the contents of the bags of millet that the grits had been made from, he sent a special messenger overland from St. Augustine, Florida to headquarters in Washington, DC.

As you may imagine, there was considerable alarm once the information reached the hands of the military leadership. For fear of the possibility of poisoning of entire ship's crew, and of the enemy making good use of such information, measures to resolve the potentially devastating issue were undertaken in ultra-secrecy. A naval committee was formed to address the issue immediately without causing or spreading alarm. The committee was named the **N**aval **S**ecurity **A**gency and became the forerunner of the current **N**ational **S**ecurity **A**gency (NSA) of today.

Their first responsibility was to review the file labeled **TOP SECRET:** *Millet—Hairy Sea Grits* and come up with a plan to resolve the problem. The name of that very first secret file ultimately morphed into what we know today as MILITARY SECRETS.

GETTYSBURG ADDRESS (THE)
(FIRST USED: 1863 AD)

Definition: An historic speech given by President Abraham Lincoln in November of 1863 to inspire and focus the Union.

Etymology: It has been alleged that for several weeks there had been capitol whisperings of "behind the scenes" dramas playing out within the Lincoln family in preparation for a speech to be given at Gettysburg. The first alleged whispering was that Mary Todd Lincoln was frustrated in her efforts to decide on an appropriate wardrobe to pack and a new dress to wear during the short excursion to the battlefield speech with her husband on November 19. Secondarily, whisperings have suggested in the politest of ways that Mary was horrified at the thought of being seen in any place that had a name with "**BURG**" as the suffix. She was allegedly "overheard" to say that such a place as anything **BURG**" would beneath her dignity to visit! Additionally, it is said that she thought that referring to Gettysburg simply as "**GETTY**" sounded so much more refined, and even gracious.

So the story goes that once Mary Todd decided on a dress (found on a trip to the New York shop of a world-class seamstress), she had it made to her specifications, to be shipped during the second week of November. Tragically, the stagecoach that was delivering the dress overturned in New Jersey. And when it was finally righted, it was, in fact, pointed back toward New York (a detail that completely escaped the driver until he found himself crossing the Hudson River…again). By then, it was impossible to deliver the dress on time.

They say that when Mary Todd realized that the dress was going to be late, she went into a mild state of shock—and in an attempt to communicate her horror to the president, she could only stammer: **"GETTY'S...BURG! A DRESS?"** The president, who loved his wife despite some misgivings of "possible vanity," assured Mary that he understood and did not expect her to accompany him to the speech under the circumstances. Mary was put under the care of a doctor, who referred to the incident as **the GETTYSBURG DURESS**. So the inspiring speech given by the president, despite the drama of: **"GETTY'S BURG! A DRESS!,"** would be forever known as the **"GETTYSBURG ADDRESS."**

CACOPHONY
(FIRST USED: 1864 AD)

Definition: A loud discordant sound

Etymology: Though currently unverifiable, it was said that Annie Oakley had whooping cough as a young girl. Her mother, who was hard of hearing, claimed that Annie's cough was the only sound she could easily recognize, so she urged Annie to cough frequently, as it was a pleasing for her to hear any sound, even though the cough was a nasty and upsetting percussive for most people. Annie's mom, it is said, also suffered from a stuttering disorder (poor dear), so when she wanted to experience "hearing," she would say to her daughter: **"Ca-cough**, Annie." As Annie grew into adulthood and became famous, the story of her childhood "**ca-cough**" became the talk of the West, and the phrase "**Ca-cough Annie**," later spelled **CACOPHONY**, came to be known as any loud, abrasive, or discordant sound.

FREQUENTLY
(FIRST USED: 1868 AD)

Definition: A reference to something that happens repeatedly

Etymology: Jedidiah Quentin Lee grew up in Savannah, Georgia, but lived as a southern gentleman in the nineteenth century in New York City and was one of the first serious political activists. He was beloved by the common man. But, it was said, he was hated by Tammany Hall and Boss Tweed. The problem was that he spent his time pointing out, for all to see, the corruption and massive thefts from the public coffers that the organized swindling machine of Boss Tweed was orchestrating. Tweed was the leader of the Democratic Party and the Grand Sachem of the Tammany Club, which had originally been formed as the Society of Saint Tammany back in 1789. The society began as a patriotic and fraternal club but had morphed into a political machine that controlled New York City.

At every opportunity Quentin would organize protests and march on Tammany Hall, and each and every time, Boss Tweed would have the corrupt police chief arrest Quentin. With each arrest, Quentin would get the publicity he barnstormed for—and thirty days in the slammer. After the first twenty arrests, Quentin's admirers began a grassroots protest of their own. Each time Quentin was incarcerated, they would form in large groups outside of the Tammany Hall, holding signs and chanting **"Free Quentin, Free Quent Lee."** This cycle was repeated so often that a new word was added to the lexicon. Yes, the term **FREE QUENT LEE** was a contraction of the chant heard so often in the streets of 1865 New York and became the term **FREQUENTLY**.

CRIBBAGE
(FIRST USED: 1871 AD)

Definition: A game using cards and a pegged counting board for scoring

Etymology: Champs were started young. Boards were rested on the side panels of two opposing cribs. The game was so competitive that babies were trained from infancy. As they became more proficient (and grew older), much like the ancient Chinese practice of wrapping women's feet to fit into tiny shoes, the **CRIBBAGE** parents would stuff the growing cribbage players into tiny toddler outfits to stunt their growth. The term **CRIBBAGE** came in the lexicon as a result of the attempt at modifying the occupants' **CRIB AGE**.

❖   ❖   ❖

PURLOIN
(FIRST USED: 1872 AD)

Definition: to take without permission of the owner.

Etymology: This is a term that was frequently used in the silent movie era, and it was copiously used by Messers Gilbert and Sullivan in their nineteenth-century operettas. The word originally came to life as a description of the actions of big cats in the wilds of Africa and India. Scientific observation determined that big cats were happiest when they were engaged in the consumption of the fruits of the hunt. Scientists observed the cats eating a giselle, or wildebeest—or any other form of captured meat—and purring loudly, as cats will when they are at their happiest. Their favorite "cut," if you will, was the loin. Chowing down on the loin would always be accompanied by a loud, satisfied purring noise. Technically, the **LOIN** does not belong to the big cat, but rather to the animal to which it is (or was) attached and is rarely given up freely. Consequently the term **PUR(R) LOIN** came to mean stealing meat—and subsequently came to mean taking anything without permission.

CUSTER'S LAST STAND
(*FIRST USED: 1876 AD*)

Definition: Commonly refers to the Battle of the Little Big Horn in 1876

Etymology: It is time to separate fact from fiction regarding this unfortunate incident. Rumor has it that the Indians (specifically the Lakota tribe) had some negative feelings for a US army general named George. The same rumor has it that General George was of small stature but a bellicose fellow, cussing, swearing, shouting orders, and offending the sensibilities of the local Indian population who loved the peace and serenity of the tranquil valleys and mountains. They referred to General George as "**CUSSED" HEARD** and **The Little Big Horn**.

For his part, General George was rumored to be somewhat vain and felt that it was of the greatest importance that: A) He looked good!, and 2) He got lots of promotions. In line with the rumor that "he looked good," the story goes that the phrase **CUSTER'S LAST STAND** actually was referring to the last day that **"CUSSED HEARD" LAST TANNED.**

In a misguided attempt to develop a respectable tan while visiting the region with his Seventh Calvary, General George was completely unaware of the proximity of a large band of Lakota warriors just around the next bend. To add insult to injury (and certainly, this rumor has yet to be verified by other accounts), the Lakota felt that the "white man" with "the tan" was attempting to disguise himself as an Indigenous American, and that, as such, was an action frowned upon—so much so, as a matter of fact, that the offending party was subject to death at the hands of any Native Americans who might catch him in the act of "tanning."

Finally, should the rumors be verified, General George was not caught unaware, but rather caught in his underwear while tanning. Attempts to deny this aspect of the story are suspect and could be construed as a cover-up. Over the years animosity waned, and historians changed the name of the incident from **CUSSED HEARD LAST TANNED** to **CUSTER'S LAST STAND** (unless, of course, the entire story is a fabrication).

MAXIMUM
(FIRST USED: 1876 AD)

Definition: The greatest quantity, the most attainable

Etymology: As translated directly from the British, **Maxi Mum**, or biggest Mom. Usually reserved for plus-sized mothers, the term came to represent the greatest or biggest of a thing in general.

MINIMUM
(FIRST USED: 1876 AD)

Definition: The least quantity, the smallest amount

Etymology: Translated literally from the British to mean the smallest mom, as derived from the standard: to measure no more that 5'2" tall. This little mother generally weighed in at less than 44.78 Kilograms, or 120 lbs. The term **MINI-MUM** came to represent the least quantity of a thing in general.

PETRI DISH
(FIRST USED: 1879 AD)

Definition: A dish, sometimes with cover, to grow bacteria and other microorganisms.

Etymology: Ethyl and Peter Tree were an ordinary couple with extraordinary ambitions, considering their station in life. Pete was a cook in Her Majesty's Court (Queen Victoria), and his lovely wife Ethyl was one of the scullery maids. In the year 1879, just two short years after their secret marriage, they devised a plan to help better their stations. Ethyl and Pete both had aspirations to become great cooks and open their own business—a combination restaurant and storage rental facility. They began by attempting to "home school" each other in the fine culinary arts as well as the practice of packing and unpacking large quantities of knickknacks into small spaces. While the packing and unpacking was moving along smoothly enough, the cooking lessons were not going quite so well. Pete had all of the access one could ask for with respect to the accouterments necessary for fine cooking, not to mention the queen's food to go along with them.

The one element he lacked was the time—not only to develop his own cooking specialty, but also to school his beloved Ethyl. Ethyl, for her part, was an eager learner, but what with her job dishwashing and the kitchen cleanup, she had precious little time to digest the odd bits that she was learning. It was not uncommon to be interrupted in their learning processes, what with orders to prepare food for the queen's guests or to clean up after some special diplomatic courier who had slipped through the back door right in the midst of a secret cooking lesson. Frequently, when an interruption caught the two budding academicians in the middle of a cooking lesson, they would hurriedly slip the unfinished "practice" dish of partially cooked food into a cabinet or atop a high shelf, with the intention of returning to complete the cooking lesson at a later time. As with all good intentions, none of these went unpunished—evidenced by the plates of growing mold and/or bacteria that would be discovered later that week, or even months later.

The rest of the staff, well aware of the secretive cooking lessons, often came across the "hidden" plates of growing plants or animal life and laughingly referred to the horrid little dishes of slime as "another **Pete Tree dish**."

Suffice it to say that neither Ethyl nor Pete went on to claim any of the culinary fame that they had dreamed of—nor did the business of storing other people's debris come to fruition. However, despite their best efforts at secrecy, word of mouth was never silenced, and the tales of the dishes of living glop took on a life of their own, both literally and figuratively. When the studies of biology and bacteriology found their infancy in Victor Rhein England (Louie Pasteur notwithstanding), it was only natural that the small dishes used to grow scientific cultures would be referred to as **Pete Tree Dishes**, or in non-British English as **PETRIE DISHES.**

POSITION
(FIRST USED: 1879 AD)

Definition: Being recognized as a person duly elected or appointed to provide a specific service or hold an established office

Etymology: This is one of the two terms directly etymologically traced to the bad blood between Will and Shawn Yam as referred to in the etymology of the term **AMBITION**, listed above.

Much like a latter-day story of Cain and Abel (reference: Book of Genesis), Will Yam, in a misguided attempt to usurp the popularity of his fraternal twin brother, posed as his identical twin on the day of the high-school election of student body officers. The attempted ruse fooled only the principal, and the historical outcome was that the phrase **Pose as Shawn** was actually added to the lexicon in 1879, contracted to the spelling **POSITION** and referencing what we now generally define as someone holding a specific private enterprise, social, or civic responsibility.

AVOID
(FIRST USED: 1886 AD)

Definition: To intentionally stay away from, or miss

Etymology: As discovered by Lester Freud in a lab in 1886, the concept of self-preservation is embedded into the fiber of most human beings. The mere thought of balancing on a high wire or stepping off of a precipice will generally make the hairs stand out on the back of your neck or unwind the ones in the neither regions of anyone with a modicum of common sense. It is in our nature to **AVOID** that which we deem dangerous. Some may take guilty pleasure watching others defy sense by leaping canyons on a motorcycle or slipping into a pit of vipers to milk them for antidotes, but those, generally, are the same people who would sooner ride naked on a public conveyance than try any of those stunts at home.

The term **AVOID** actually came about as a result of a common night-mare that typically has the heretofore unsuspecting dreamer falling into a bottomless black pit. He or she awakes startled and in an agitated state, sweating profusely, and gasping for breath. All the person can utter, in the fading panic, is: "**A VOID, A VOID**! I THOUGHT I WAS FALLING INTO **A VOID**!" And that common experience is how the term **AVOID** (as in **AVOID** a void!) came into the language.

ICE CREAM CONE
(FIRST USED 1891 AD)

Definition: An edible container that holds ice cream

Etymology: 1904, in the Coney Island neighborhood of Brooklyn, lived a young lad named Holden Cohen. From the time he turned six years of age, every day during the summer break, his mother, Myrna, would take him to the boardwalk and buy him an ice cream. In those days, ice cream was served on a paper napkin, or if you had an extra two cents, in a paper cup (with a wooden spoon—if you would agree to return the spoon when you were done). Young Holden knew, even at that young age, that there was a better way to serve ice cream.

At the age of twenty-two, after much trial and error, Holden developed a wafer container to replace the napkin and the paper cup. The confection came to be known as the **ICE CREAM COHEN** and for many years it was thought to be so named because it was conceived and developed in **CONEY** Island. Heirs of the patent were loath to concede that origin, and after much legal wrangling, a copy of the original patent application was discovered. It named the invention the **ICE CREAM HOLDEN COHEN**, which was later shortened to the appellation **ICE CREAM CONE** (unless, of course, none of it was true).

BAUBLE
(FIRST USED: 1897 AD)

Definition: An imitation of something precious; an object that sparkles but has no actual value

Etymology: It was in the spring of 1897 when the people of America became officially fed up with the great divide between the "haves" and the "have-nots." It was the Industrial Revolution! It was the birth of the middle class! And, quite frankly, it was simply embarrassing for ladies, who fancied themselves deserving of fine jewelry, to discover that they could not afford the clothes or other sparkly refinements that would present them as ladies of distinction. This was, in fact, the case—especially when they went to browse the shoppes of purveyors of fine jewelry.*

In the cozy shopping district of King of Prussia, Pennsylvania, a little storefront displaying gems and jewelry became very popular with the ladies of the town. Ultimately, a revolution was fomented there, resulting in suffrage—and a precarious footfall was established on the ledge of equality for all shopping women.

The shop in question was run by a Robert Fleecewould and his teenage son Bob. Robert spent the day crafting tiny fake gems out of glass and glue and storing the finished pieces upstairs, where he and Bob slept and ate.

Robert Fleecewould was able to purchase a few "seconds" from the commodities markets that traded in diamonds and gold. Robert designed settings for small pieces of the flawed stones. He crafted them into fairly spectacular rings and necklaces that he displayed in his storefront window. Sadly, the majority of women in town could no more afford these fine pieces of jewelry than they could afford fine furs or a designer shoe—which is where Bob, son of Robert, enters the story.

During the shopping lulls each day, (weekends being the exception) Robert home-schooled his son Bob. So, while Robert fabricated imitation gems and jewelry, his son sat at his side working on his scholastic assignments. When a lady (or gentleman) came into the shop and inquired about this or that piece of jewelry, Robert would show his crafted (real) jewelry. When it was evident that the patron could not afford the "real" stuff, Robert would tell them of his passion for crafting inexpensive "faux" jewelry—and then ask if they might be interested in seeing his collection. Invariably the answer was "Yes!" and invariably Robert would say, "**Bob'll** get them for you." And he would ask Bob to run upstairs and fetch the box of "faux."

Oddly, the expression "**Bob'll** get them" came to be so popular that Robert was able to go national with a chain of faux jewelry stores, which he renamed "**Bob'll**." Eventually the spelling was changed to **BAUBLE**, and to this day, the word has become a reference to "paste and glass" jewelry. But more to the point, it was the beginning of a movement that saw all women (and some men) as equal—in that they could afford sparkly jewelry. Once that glass jewelry ceiling was breached, suffrage was partially transformed and became the first level of equality for all womankind, jewelry-wise.

- *If you really think about it, if there are halves, then everyone left is also a halve. If you halve something, you are left with the other halve. Consequently and logically, therefore, there should be no such thing as a halve not—unless we begin thinking of everything as a hole.*

DEVOTED
(FIRST USED: 1897 AD)

Definition: Dedicated to; to be close too; to be hit in the back of the head; to be committed to something

Etymology: An early golf term (late nineteenth century)—**Divoted**: meaning to be hit in the head, or any other part of the body, with a divot (a piece of earth dislodged—i.e., launched—in the "execution" of a golf stroke) because you are standing too close, or too far; or looked up, down, sideways, etc.

The letter *E* was substituted for fear of being hit in the *I* by the divot. It is interesting to note that the term **DEVOTEE** (meaning a person devoted to…) was first used when the first divot struck the back of the head of a person standing near the tee box. Thus the term **DEVOTED** or **DEVOTEE**. If the player continued with the game after being **DIVOTED** in the back of the head, he could be said to be **DEVOTED**.

CHRONOLOGY: FIFTEEN

(FROM 1900 AD THROUGH 1919)

THE DISINGENUOUS ERA

FLORA SCENTS
AND
FRAY GRANTS

"A TREE WITH A FRAGRANCE SHOULD BE REFERRED TO AS A SCENT-TREE."

CARPET
(FIRST USED: 1900 AD)

Definition: Carpet may be defined as a mat, typically woven. It can be made of any type of fibers that can be adapted to sewing or weaving. Carpet is a floor covering used for insulation and decoration.

Etymology: Well before the first automobile was offered for mass consumption by Henry Ford in 1903, there had been many experimental and one-of-a-kinds. Each was individually built to suit the fancy of the rich and ne'er-do-wells. Some were powered by gunpowder, some by steam, and some even by the wind. But it was not until 1899 that an eccentric and wealthy widow of French extraction named Hedda Bonet commissioned the construction of a steam-powered vehicle that could carry her and her seventeen cats and one Border collie on excursions around the countryside.

Hedda took great comfort in being able to take all of her animals on tours, and she saw to their every need. She had a serious but small sandbox (litter station) with a trap door built into a rear corner of the floor of the vehicle, and she had a suitable feeding station in the other rear corner. The litter station had an ingenious drop-down door that could be opened and managed from the outside of the car when the car was at rest. However, it was not at rest very often, and the excursions were the daily exercise and expectation. The animals became so enamored with the mobile facility that they were sometimes loath to leave it. To this end, Hedda made sure that when the vehicle was at rest, the animal entry door was left ajar so as not to deprive an animal of a single moment of the joy that could be obtained by resting or recreating in their wonderful new quarters. Hedda drove to all of the animal shows, wherever they might be. There were dog shows, cat shows, 4-H events, and of course, all of the nearby fairs featuring the best of the beasts of each county. She and her mobile pet home were the talk of each town that Hedda visited.

In those days of experimental automobile production, the floorboards of a car typically were just that—floor*boards*, and as such they would often be the cause of drafts and just-plain cold air leaking in and making the interior potentially uncomfortable. It is in this respect that Hedda may have been said to be a "Hed-da" her times.

That is because Hedda rarely cleaned the pet areas of her vehicle, and she considered it a contributing factor to why her animals loved the space so much. Simply put: if an animal's scent was present among the growing floor pelt of animal fur, the animal felt safe and comfortable in that space. A by-product of that philosophy was that the car was warmer and quieter because the fur and hair matted on the floor eventually formed a protective "blanket," if you will, of a soft and warming insulated floor covering. Vehicle designers seized upon the concept of a woven blanket for the floors of cars. An additional benefit was that the idea expanded to the floors of homes and offices— and to the dismay of some, even carpeted bathrooms.

It is in this context that Hedda Bonnet quietly became the mother of the modern day **CAR-PET,** which now not only adorns the floors and trunks of our automobiles but also can be found in most every home in America. The development of the term **CARPET** then becomes obvious. It is a direct result of the **CAR PETS** of Hedda Bonnet and the fur that they left behind.

FLUORESCENCE
(FIRST USED: 1901 AD)

Definition: Radiation of visible light through electromagnetism

Etymology: As everyone knows, there are all kinds of sources of light. There is your basic daylight. There is sunlight (akin to daylight). There are spotlights, dim lights, white lights, Camel Lights, iridescent lights, lighten up, light of your eyes, lichen, headlights (not to be confused with head lice), tail lights, by the light of the silvery moon, and so on.

It was not until the invention of light via electromagnetism that the very concept of the ground upon which we walk was shaken for all mankind. As it turns out, this new and special light, which was only recently (in geological terms) identified and "invented," was harnessed into long tubes that burned as light longer (as in length per tube) and brighter than its predecessor—the incandescent light bulb.

These "tubes" of light, when strung end to end in long high school and hospital corridors, focused a new and heretofore unseen light on the condition of the floors of these institutions. It was discovered, much to the chagrin of janitorial services worldwide, that the floors, which were "cleaned" every night of their lives, were still caked with residues from the continuous, relentless, and hapless daily tracking of immense amounts of miniscule molecules of mud and dirt. In a word, they revealed the floor's essence. And it was a troubling day for the cleaning industry—an industry that was, as a result, completely overhauled. It was during the following few weeks that such tools as mops and buckets and hot water and sudsy foamy soaps were invented.

In the process, the new fixtures were named: **Lights of the Floor Essence** (or **FLUORESCENCE**, for short), a name that was to be an eternal reminder to high school and hospital administrators everywhere of what the purpose of hiring a janitorial service was all about, in essence.

DELICATE
(FIRST USED: 1902 AD)

Definition: Frail, easily broken or torn

Etymology: The term **deli-cut** was first used at the beginning of the twentieth century when precision meat slicing machines were introduced to the meat markets and **Deli-Cut**-Tessens proliferating in the streets of New York and Chicago.

The new machines were very precise and could be dialed down to slice salamis to an almost transparent thinness. The one drawback of this thinly sliced meat was that it was easily torn or marred, if not handled **deli-cutly**.

It wasn't much of a jump from frail slices of deli meat to the easily bruised and broken, brittle bones of the aged, the infirm, or anyone who easily injured. The **deli-cut** was expanded to refer to all of the persons or things that needed to be handled as gently as the deli-slicing machines—i.e., **DELI-CUTLY**. The term eventually was spelled differently out of respect for their **DELICATE** natures.

BERRIES
(FIRST USED: 1903 AD)

Definition: any or many of small types and clusters of pulpy fruit usually found growing wild in the forests of the Northern Hemisphere

Etymology: In 1901 Theodore Roosevelt became president after the assassination of President William McKinley. This event, however, did nothing to diminish his love for the great outdoors (Roosevelt, not McKinley) or the impulsive need to spend his rare breaks exploring and hunting. In 1903, prior to serious involvement in turning around the potential disaster that was the digging of the Panama Canal, he was rumored to have been notified of a completely unfounded assertion regarding an allegedly alarming increase of savage bear attacks on the citizens of both of the forested areas of the northern United States and the provinces of Canada.

Despite the fact that none of this story was (or is) true, Teddy headed for the North Country to see if he could help in finding a solution to the huge number of attacks and resulting fatalities. He was able to determine almost immediately that 52 percent of the attacks were taking place forty-five days before the upcoming hibernation periods that bears undergo each winter and that 48 percent of these attacks occurred within the first months after hibernation ended.

The extreme nature of these attacks were of the most serious concern because the majority of the victims were not just mauled and left with memories of an adventure they would not care to repeat. No! The majority of attacks ended in the victims becoming a meal, or series of meals for the bears and for their offspring.

Teddy and his entourage took to the woods of northwestern Wyoming to see if they could determine a way to thwart this new and dangerous evolution within the bear population.

It was on this trip that they discovered that the woods and meadows were a cornucopia of various types of small clusters of pulpy and sweet fruits that grew inside Wyoming's pristine forestlands, glens, dales, riversides, and streams. The men sampled these fruits as they traveled in search of bears and were completely delighted at the delicate and succulent flavors of the varied types of fruits of these vines and shrubs. That was when a brilliant and potentially lifesaving idea came to Teddy.

He had his men collect as many of these fruits as they could store in their rucksacks, and then they continued on their quest. It was only two days later when they spotted several large black bears fishing in a shallow and unrewarding stream. They were upwind of the bears at the time and knew that the wind could shift as the sun began to set, so they immediately began to stage the experiment that Mr. Roosevelt had laid out for them.

First they drew straws to see who would sacrifice his long johns for the experiment. The young man who won the dubious honor stepped behind his steed, stripped down, and then redressed in his hunting gear. The long johns, with his heavy scent, were laid on the ground between Teddy's group and the bears that were still attempting to capture non-existent fish. Alongside the long johns, the men made a pile of all of the succulent fruits that they had carried with them. Now, having staged the experiment, they retired into the tree line to observe the results.

As the sun began to fade and the breeze shifted from the southeast to the northwest, the hungry bears detected a scent that they were familiar with—man steaks! The bears turned as one and began honing in on the scent. When they reached the odoriferous long johns, they attacked as though it contained the savory man that should have been there—but instead, they got a lot of sticky fruit pulp on their paws. And then they licked their four paws clean of the mashed fruit.

It was that moment that changed and perhaps saved the lives of countless people who heretofore, had been destined to swim through the intestine of some hungry bear in some future ghastly mishap.

The bears found the fruit delightful (as we all know, bears are omnivores and quite capable of surviving on fruits, pulps, and other plant life).

For the next few days, President Roosevelt and his team tracked the group of bears, which was headed to their hibernation caves located over the hill and through the dale. Not once did the bears stop to fish; not once did they show signs of aggressive behavior to either of the two lone trappers they came across on their trek. In fact (and this of course is undocumented in the Library of Congress because it is completely untrue), the only thing that they had to eat during the two-day trip was the little clusters of fruits they found growing on the bushes and shrubs along the way.

When the president returned to Washington, he issued a proclamation (PRC 0032526/TR) that allowed the Forest Service to hire four hundred trappers and woodsmen. These fellows were assigned the task of introducing the delights of the herbivore lifestyle to bears across the land. Over the course of the next three years, the mauling and outright killings of humans dropped a full 92 percent. These lives were saved all because of the intrepid determination of one of our great American presidents and heroes.

It was also Teddy Roosevelt who, after some consideration, named the pulpy little fruits **Bear-Ease** (now referred to as **Berries**). To put a fine point on it, **bear-ease** allowed more of the "woodsy-folk," as well as the hunters, to breathe a little easier when in the bear habitat. The **Bear-Ease** also provided essential and quick food for bears and their cubs who came out of a long winter naps into a fruitful spring.

Additionally, it was determined that certain bears preferred certain specific types or varieties of **Bear-Ease**. For instance:

Black Bear-Ease appeared to be a favorite of the black bear.

Blue Bear-Ease perked up a melancholy bear.

Elder Bear-Ease were named for the obvious elder bear.

Boys and Bear-Ease were named for the meal augmented with a human male child.

Cram Bear-Ease (an unfortunate misspelling of "Cran") were for the quick eater.

Goose Bear-Ease were for those bears who preferred to augment a meal with fowl or to sweeten up a foul meal.

Huckle Bear-Ease were for the goofy bears.

Mull Bear-Ease were for the bear that like to take some time to reflect on his life and where it was going

The much beloved Bear-Ease (**Berries**) have become a human staple as well and can be found in produce departments around the world.

(As a tribute to President Roosevelt and his extraordinary work on saving lives and providing the bear population with a new and exciting gourmand world, he was honored with the stuffed animal that we all grew up to know and love as the Teddy Bear [(also a blatant fabrication.)])

SUBMARINE
(FIRST USED: 1906 AD)

Definition: under the water

Etymology: The term **Marine** itself dates back to ancient Greece and was defined as a warring fleet of mariners, or soldiers of the fleet. Most people would suspect that the term **SUBMARINE** found its beginnings with vessels that were used for military purposes and operated covertly. The reality is that the term **SUBMARINE** started out in life as two words that only later were conjoined. There have been misrepresentations of the ships the *Monitor* and the *Merrimack* (circa 1862) as the first **SUB MARINES**, but in fact, it was discovered that the only way to operate completely submerged somehow involved depriving the crew of air—thus potentially creating intolerable stress levels and subjecting the US government to possible lawsuits. The *Monitor* and *Merrimack* were, in fact, not **sub marines** until both vessels were scuttled later in 1862.

The branch of the service referred to as the US **Marine** Corps, did, in fact, engage in the first use of the term **SUB MARINE**. The term **SUB MARINE** did not surface until Commander Alexander Jerry Mander took on the responsibility of reinvigorating the boot camp training of twentieth-century marines. In 1901, the commander initiated a grading scale for the training and disposition of raw recruits. Essentially, if the young recruit could not endure the rigor of the training, he was listed as a **sub-Marine**—that is, not up to the challenge of being a member of the Corps.

By the early 1900s, new technologies were available, and it was not only possible to construct vessels that could operate underwater, but in fact, sailors would not have to supply their own air for these missions. The problem was that these vessels scared the skinny off of most naval personnel—all of whom suspected that the air-pumping devices would fail or that the vessel would slip to the bottom of the ocean, never to see the light of day.

Those young men herein discussed, who had the unfortunate fate of failing to qualify to be **MARINES**, were offered an opportunity to save face by joining the Underwater Vessel Corps. Those young men, the **Sub-Marines**, managed to make the corps work. They were officially referred to as the **SUB-MARINERS**, and ultimately their vessels were called **SUBMARINES**.

GROSS VEHICULAR WEIGHT
(FIRST USED: 1907 AD)

Definition: refers to the total weight of the vehicle and all of its parts

Etymology: This phrase first came into common usage when the modern automobile, with its long, low, and lean design created phenomena held in common by drivers all over the world. As one lowered oneself into the powered and adjustable seats of the automobile, one experienced the sensation that any fat that one had accumulated on one's body tended to stack up in a series of rolls, beginning at the waist and resting, one atop the other in smaller concentric circles. Thus came into modern lexicology one's ***GROSS* VEHICULAR WEIGHT**.

SYMMETRY
(FIRST USED: 1907 AD)

Definition: things in proper proportion, one to another

Etymology: In the very early days of silent film, movie producers frequently operated on a very tight budget. One enterprising prop man determined that when creating a park-like or forest setting in the studio, it was much cheaper to make "half trees" and stand them up next to mirrors—which would then give the impression of a perfectly shaped whole tree due to the reflected image. These "half-trees" were also called **SEMI-TREES** and were all the rage. The term, frequently misspelled as **SYMMETRY**, came to be known as the mirror image of a thing, or a thing in perfect proportion.

ALBATROSS
(FIRST USED: 1908 AD)

Definition: The largest known seabird, commonly referred to as the sea eagle

Etymology: It was a cold morning somewhere between San Diego and Honolulu, and they were arguing about the frigate birds that had been "dogging" the ship for the past two days. Al, as usual, felt he had the moral high ground and was proclaiming that the birds were gooney birds—which, he also claimed, were thought to be extinct. He further argued that if they could catch one of these birds and bring it to the University of Hawaii for confirmation, the discovery would ultimately make them famous. Ross, the calmer of the two, and usually the one with the correct assessment—but rarely the one who would end up claiming victory—insisted that they were frigate birds, and as such were quite common. And besides that, he did not want to be famous! Since neither of them was an ornithologist it was quite surprising that one of them was correct in his assessment. Nonetheless, the argument went on for quite a while, during which Al gathered a net and flung it over a bird as it was making a pass alongside the ship. The net caught the bird and then did a gravity thing that slammed the poor creature into the side of the ship as Al reeled it in.

When they finally succeeded in bringing the capture aboard, the bird lunged at Al (who could blame it?) and grabbed his nose it its beak. Ross grabbed the bird by the neck with one hand, and in an attempt to rescue his friend, grabbed the bird's beak with the other hand, trying to wrestle it loose from Al's nose. Al, of course, was screaming in nasal hysteria, eyes shut, flailing with both hands. When he felt the bird beak begin to loosen from his proboscis, he lunged and bit down as hard as he could. The rest is history. Al bit Ross in the hand, nearly severing two of his fingers. The bird backed out of the fracas in a wily side step that also freed it of the net, and it was off and away. The crewmen who witnessed this tableau looked from one to another in disbelief, repeating over and over: "**Al bit Ross!**" The story became a part of the "legend of the seas," and any big sea bird seen pacing ships during a voyage came to be referred to as an "**Al bit Ross**," which of course was later contracted to **ALBATROSS.**

FROLIC
(FIRST USED: 1910 AD)

Definition: Behavior that is uninhibited and playful

Etymology: It is commonly understood that the **Popsicle** was invented by an eleven-year-old boy. It was in 1905, and his name was Frank Epperson. Years later, his own kids liked it so much that they called it "**Pop's Sicle**" (derived, of course, from the term **Icicle**).

Meanwhile, in Bavaria in 1910, the first **Popsicles** arrived at the ice cream shoppe of the Baron Bjorn Toulouse and Frau Lichtenstein-Toulouse. Because the people of Bavaria were of a cautious nature (some say from the constant threat of avalanche), it was difficult to get anyone to try this new cold treat (which seemed odd for persons with the actual name Lick-en-stein). As a marketing technique, Frau Lichtenstein would wander the streets enjoying the **Popsicle**, for all to see. Oddly, in Bavaria, for a female to suck on, or lick, any food in public meant only one thing. And that thing was that she was having a wonderful time, engaging in merriment and all.

The net result of this obvious enjoyment was that the **Popsicle** also became a hit in Bavaria—with one difference. The **Popsicle**, in Bavaria, was referred to as the "**Frau-Lich**" locally, it lasted only until Frau-Lich's death. Since her death, the treat has been called the **Popsicle** worldwide. The term **Frau-Lich** was morphed into the new term **FROLIC**, which is mindful of the days of Frau Lichtenstein-Toulouse's' playful romps with the **Popsicle** through the streets of Bavaria.

CLASSIC
(FIRST USED: 1912 AD)

Definition: A quality that meets or exceeds established standards

Etymology: As was known and has been experienced by most, if not all, of the children who attended public schools in the United States of America in the twentieth century, one of the most-used and obvious excuses for missing an exam was the claim that the student was sick and would not be in attendance during the announced test. As teachers got wise to the call-in-sick ruse, they began surprising students with what came to be known as the "spot" quiz—which was named after their dogs. The Spot quiz was used primarily to determine what level the students were at with regard to the progression of learning. In the interim, however, entire classes of students would call in sick. The teachers would report the lack of test results to the school administration with the cryptic notation: **CLASS SICK** and a comment about how far students would go to organize the avoidance of a test. And so with the obvious determination of an organized group of students, the phrase **CLASS SICK** came to mean exceeding established norms and standards. It was subsequently truncated to the **CLASSIC** term we now use when shaking our heads in amazement.

MOUNTAINEERING
(FIRST USED: 1913 AD)

Definition: The act of climbing mountains; a person who lives and works in the mountains

Etymology: The term **MOUNTAINEERING** came about as a result of the things that **Mountaineers** do, see, and hear in combination with the term **Mountain**. Several examples are:

a.) **Mountain Earring** refers to any earrings with pointy shapes that are deemed similar to mountains.

b.) **Mountain Ear Ring** is the sound in the inner ear produced by the diminishing air pressure as one climbs higher.

c.) **Mountain Nearing** often refers to the act of a copilot alerting the airline pilot who has dozed off.

d.) **Mountain Hearing** is frequently a diagnoses relating to climbers and the negative effect of prolonged exposure to mountain echoes.

AFFORDABLE
(FIRST USED: 1914 AD)

Definition: A thing that is within financial reach is said to be affordable

Etymology: As everyone is aware, Henry Ford's revolutionary assembly line made the cost of producing cars so economical that the average man was **able**, at last, to purchase a car for just a few hundred dollars. The term **"A FORD ABLE..."** is a product of that phenomenon and became a part of our language meaning "the ability to buy"—i.e., **AFFORDABLE**.

FAUX FINISH
(FIRST USED: 1917 AD)

Definition: A thing that is changed in appearance to emulated something that it is not.

Etymology: A person **pretending** to be a citizen of Finland; someone with a forged or fake **Finish** passport.

FINISHED
(FIRST USED: 1917 AD)

Definition: Done or completed

Etymology: Someone who had recently taken the Pledge of Allegiance to Finland is frequently said to have been **FINISHED**.

POLICE
(FIRST USED: 1918 AD)

Definition: Persons tasked with the enforcement of the law

Etymology: At one point or another we all have the occasional need to be defended from one or another person who infringes on our individual rights. It is hard to believe that most people have, or will, end up as the "subject of interest" by one or more of the law enforcement guardians. For example, consider the speeding ticket, the jaywalking ticket, the parking ticket, the sagging pants ticket, ad nauseum.*

In 1918, when men were first hired to arrest people who went to work even though they had the flu (*the Great Flu Pandemic*), officers were often untrained and a bit overly enamored with their position in the community. That sad sociological fact enhanced their sense of power, and they felt the need to make an example of everyone they came into contact with. The only downside to the job seemed to be their title, which was **Officers on Patrol/Sentry** (commonly shortened to **OOPS.**) As the **OOPS** slowly adjusted to their duties (including a newfound respect for the taxpayers who were paying for the officers protection), they became more of a public servant—which resulted in both taxpayer and public servant being more polite.

It was clear that a name change was in order, and as it happened, the name change came quietly and without any particular planning. Every time there was an interaction with a citizen who was being detained for a minor infraction (and because those were kinder, gentler times), when the scofflaw tried to reason with the officer, typically the word **PLEASE** was spoken with a sense of reverence and respect—as well as a need to get the interaction over with.

Articles were published in the newspapers lauding those officers who managed the public with compassion and respect when working the streets. Not surprisingly, the terms **PLEASE** and **PLEAS** became synonymous with the **Officers On Patrol/SENTRY.** In those days, should one happen to be present on the streets while nefarious activities were afoot, one would hear the call go out: "**HELP, HELP, PLEASE!**" That call morphed into: "**HELP, HELP, PA-LEASE**" and "**HELP, HELP, PLEAS.**" Those calls drove the change from **PLEAS** to the current appellation **POLICE (Po-Lease).**

*Caution: *Speaking in foreign tongues may actually get you some jail time if Homeland Security Officers are involved or if the language is French.*

CASTING ASPERSIONS
(FIRST USED:1919 AD)

Definition: Making nasty or derogatory comments about a person, directly or through inference.

Etymology: In April of 1919 a movie producer who liked to be referred to as DW, or just The W, hired an up-and-coming director to shoot a movie about the biblical story of the Tower of Babel and the great King Nebuchadnezzar. The W's vision was of a glorious time, a glorious land, and a story of the enchanting and industrious people of the Tigris and Euphrates valley (it was not discovered until much later—i.e., 2006—that Babylon was actually located in today's Iran). His new director, a man known to the history books as Curmudgeon Caruthers (also known as Cee-Cee) was a disingenuous, sullen, and mean-spirited fellow whose gestalt embraced the "kill or be killed" edict. He was raised by a step uncle, who, in fact, was a native of Persia—modern day Iran—and who was the fertilizer that fed the morose personality disorder of a younger Curmudgeon.

So it came to pass that as Curmudgeon interviewed and hired or rejected applicants who wished to act in the soon-to-be-produced movie, a trend was becoming quite noticeable to The W. Each person Curmudgeon hired seemed to be as sullen and morose as he, and each applicant Curmudgeon dismissed tended to be bright, alert, talented, and alive with just the kind of spirit that The W was expecting Cee Cee to be casting for in his film. The W questioned Cee Cee about his selections. Caruthers explained to him that he had personal experience with the people from that region of the world (specifically his step uncle) and was casting people who were like his step uncle (a cantankerous Persian coot) in an attempt to add realism to the film. After explaining the sour, nasty personality of his stepuncle to The W, Caruthers was told in no uncertain terms to **STOP CASTING AS PERSIANS**! Caruthers lost his job and ultimately was blackballed from the casting and directing business. From that point forward, the phrase **CASTING AS PERISANS** came to mean something negative— i.e., **CASTING ASPERSIONS**.

CHRONOLOGY: SIXTEEN

(FROM 1920 AD THROUGH 1936 AD)

THE FALLACIOUS ERA

< REVEL ANTS
SHOULD NOT
PEST DECIDE...>

"A MAN SUING FOR DIVORCE MAY HAVE SOME QUALITY OF WIFE ISSUES..."

CARNAGE
(FIRST USED: 1922 AD)

Definition: The aftermath of violence, the wreckage of life and, or property. Slaw-tar.

Etymology: We see it every day. The slaughter on our highways—the images on our TV screens of smashed and scattered remains of cars and trucks that have crashed, debris spread across the roads and into the fields. It is a documented fact that prior to the 1900s, not one death was caused by, or happened as a result of, the automobile. Shortly thereafter, as the death, damage, and injury count took an astronomical leap—all a by-product of the of the **Age of the Car**—the term **CAR-N-AGE** came into the lexicon as a dependable way to describe the newest way for members of civilized society to accidentally kill themselves.

CARCASS
(FIRST USED: 1923 AD)

Definition: a term referring to the unsightly physical remains, or decaying corpse-like globs, of biological materials

Etymology: This term came into common usage after the single-family automobile was a common sight in every driveway in America.*

It might be easier to understand the etymology of this word if we break it down into its component parts.

> Component 1.) The first three letters of this word are identical to the term we commonly use to refer to the automobile—i.e., **CAR**.

> Component 2.) The last four letters of this word are **nearly** identical to the term we commonly use to refer to verbally venting frustration—i.e., **CUSS**.

As indicated in the etymology of the phrase **Gross Vehicular Weight**, when any driver of a vehicle who is not within specific fitness guidelines lowers himself into the **CAR** and feels the sensation of the rolls of fat stacking up as he positions himself in the seat, it is not uncommon to hear variable-pitch swearing emanating from the driver—or, as common usage would have it—the clearly audible **CAR-CUSS**.

The combination of the two components—the **CAR CUSS** (as properly pronounced; and **CARCASS** as properly smelled)—came to refer to the unsightly globs of biological materials stacked up under a shirt or blouse. The term was later co-opted by the medical and forensic communities to refer to anything corpse-like.

sometime in mid-1937

RECTIFIED
(FIRST USED: 1923 AD)

Definition: To have adjusted or fixed

Etymology: The first thing most people do, when involved in a car crash, is bleed. Not that there is anything wrong with bleeding, per se. No. Wait! Bleeding is one of the most popular forms of pre-death. If you think about it, the statistics for people in car accidents would be severely reduced if they made cars today as they did in the old days. In the old days, cars were made of heavy steel, and they crumpled on impact only if the other crash vehicle(s) were made of heavier steel. In the 1920s, the first person to decide that she could make a living out of fixing crashed cars was a woman named Lynda La Rue. Lynda was a welder by choice, but she saw what she considered to be easy money after being in a crash herself. She was not injured, primarily because she was driving on the wrong side of the road and clipped a bakery delivery truck, which flipped before it could cause any serious damage, although the pies and cakes were a total loss.

The baker was slightly injured and furious at Lynda for damaging his only vehicle. Lynda promised to fix it—and found the process fairly easy. She returned the truck in pristine condition the following week, and the baker was so happy that he promised to be the food host for her next two birthdays.

Lynda, for her part, went home and immediately drew up plans for her new business. She put up posters and notices all over town advertising her company, which she called **WRECK DEFIED**. She even rented two billboards (one at each end of town) that announced that **WRECK DEFIED** could rebuild crashed cars for less than a quarter of the price of replacing them. She **defied** anyone to present her with a vehicle that she could not fix.

Her business became the household phrase **Wreck Defied**, which has come to mean something that can be, or is, fixed. After consultations with the Word Police, it was determined that **RECTIFIED** would be the best compromise on an addition to the WPD (Word Police Dictionary).

RELIABLE
(FIRST USED: 1925 AD)

Definition: Trustworthy, dependable, able to leap tall buildings, etc.

Etymology: People are said to be **RE-LIE-ABLE** when they have the capacity to keep each lie they have told compartmentalized in their brain, so that at any given moment in any given year, they can bear witness to a previous lie… remember and repeat it perfectly. They are persons you can rely upon. In a word, they have **RE-LIE-ABILITY**. They have proven to be **RELIABLE**.

RELUCTANT
(FIRST USED: 1926 AD)

Definition: Not wanting to do something, being unwilling.

Etymology: For many years circuses and circus performers spent the off seasons (winter) in camps in the state of Florida. It was during the winter hiatus that performers would polish and practice their acts. Most camps had a **special** tent to reinvigorate the spirit and motivation of performers who had experienced a "negative" season. Examples would be those entertainers, for instance, who may have fallen off of the high wire; or perhaps the lion tamer who had taken a right paw to the jaw. Those types of experiences tended to sour performers, and they were reticent to give 100 percent in the face of a potentially life-ending experience. The special tents were referred to as **Re-Luck Tents**, and they served to provide the added **"motivation"** (sometimes Mafia style) required to reinvigorate the acts that had gone bad.

Being sent to the **Re-Luck Tent** meant that you needed to renew your **luck**. This decision was based on the indications that you were emotionally unwilling to give your best for upcoming performances. The reputation of the **Re-Luck Tent** was such that most performers were reticent to go into the tent. They were disciplined until they agreed to undergo the **Re-Luck-Tent** "re-education." Even though they were sometimes disinclined to participate in the "training," upon release from the **Re-Luck-Tent** experience, they were ready to give their all again. Their **Luck** was renewed. As a result of the overall success of the program, the **Re-Luck-Tent** became a popular reference in business seminars. Ultimately it became another entry into the Lexicon as **RELUCTANT**.

(Another term that got its start in the Florida circus winter circuit was **INTENSE,** meaning driven as a result of being under pressure; pursuit of a goal to the extreme.

One can derive the interrelationship of the terms **RELUCTANT** and **INTENSE** oneself if one adequately understands the methodology of the **"re-education,"** or **"re-lucking"** (if you will), of the **RE-LUCK TENT** circus performers. Their re-education not only took place **IN TENTS**, it was also high-pressure, sometimes excessive, and as such gave birth to the term **In-tents, which was reissued as INTENSE.)**

And finally, the term **INTENT,** meaning more focused.

(The **"re-education"** programs for the unlucky circus performers were persistently recommended even if they seemed disinclined. However, the term **Intent** comes from the understanding of all of the other circus employees—the ones who had, as yet, no reason to participate in the **RE-LUCK TENT**. If you went **In Tent**, you were going to come out more focused and single minded in your performances—if for no other reason than to avoid having to go **In Tent** again – thus the term **Intent**.)

PARENTHESES
(FIRST USED: 1926 AD)

Definition: Curved marks, left and right, enclosing a group of words, or an idea separate from the main body of text

Etymology: **"Don't-ah you just-ah love-ah the Italian-ah accent-tah. It's ah got-ah ah-ah sort-tah cadences-ah to it-tah—No-ah?"**

If you carefully translate the term **PARENTHESES** from the Latin directly into the Italian, you have ***PARENTAH-THESEAH***—or in English, **PARENT OF THESE**. While there may be some skepticism regarding the research that produced these results, please remember the dedicated and painstaking research that I vaguely alluded to in the forward of this work. And if you are still a doubter, consider that even visually, on the page, the term describes the image of two adults—the sloped lines on each side of the group of words represemble the parents surrounding their KIDS just as real parents would enclose and protect their kids.

We can therefore assume that the Italian (***PARENTAH-THESEAH***) has morphed into an oft-ignored sign that represemble "parents embracing kids"—and is the very foundation of our struggle to generate and keep our civilization alive. Could you get any more profound!

NUPTIALS
(FIRST USED: 1929 AD)

Definition: a term referencing the uniting of two in marriage

Etymology: Prior to the ravages of the Dust Bowl, which created a great migration to the west, the small city of **Where** came into flower in the northwest portion of the Oklahoma Panhandle. The city was limited in growth potential because of the landlock created by of the state borders of Colorado to the north, New Mexico to the west, and the Punchasocket River to the south and east. As more people moved into the region, it was inevitable that they would have to settle the lesser lands south of **Where**. A new township was incorporated south of **Where** and named **Under Where**.

In the mid-1920s a man named Curtis Sea opened **Under Where's** first candy store, which he named **N**ummies **U**nder **P**roduction, also known as **NUP**. Curtis was somewhat of a candy genius and invented a hard-candy wrapped gum. The cleverness of this new candy was that it could be easily shaped and colored to resemble jewels. For instance, one of the most popular items available from **NUP** was a necklace that appeared to be a string of pearls. The wearer could, over the course of the day, remove one of the "pearls," quietly suck on the outer shell until the candy was gone, and then chew the underlying gum. One necklace would last the wearer for a full day. Curtis made six different types of necklaces as well as a number of edible bracelets and rings. The line of candy was named **NUP Chew-Alls.** He eventually opened a Shoppe in **Where** after the city elders came down to **Under Where** to encourage him to grow his business.

When the banks began collapsing in 1928 and people were losing their livelihood both on the farms and in the cities, it became quite common for young men to visit his stores to shop for engagement and wedding rings. There was no money for real gems, so **NUP Chew-Alls** became all the rage for a few short years. Sadly, Curtis died in 1937, and his business died with him—but his legacy lives on to this day. **NUP** and **Chew-Alls** were united to form the term **NUPTIALS**—a word rich in the history of our country and in the wedding plans of our young citizens.

ARTISAN
(FIRST USED: 1930 AD)

Definition: Someone who is skilled at a handicraft

Etymology: This term is another that has morphed into a much broader, more all-encompassing concept than originally defined. The term originated on the beaches of Brazil in the 1930s, where the Rio de Janeiro city fathers sponsored sand-sculpture contests each September. The local newspaper (The *Rio Day Lee*) featured a full-color photo section on the last Sunday of each September, with a broad header reading **ARTY SAND CONTEST**. The entrants had the entire month of August to build sand sculptures, and barring any meteorological interference, the judges judged on the last Saturday of September.

The contest was world famous, and entrants came from every nation on the globe. If you won the **ARTY SAND**, you were considered as talented as the "best sand artist ever." Over time, the arty sands of Rio washed away as the tides ebbed and flowed, but the term **ARTISAN** will forever remind us of the nostalgic magical transformations that took place on the beaches of Rio in the thirties.

FUTILE
(FIRST USED: 1930 AD)

Definition: Something that has no point or is not worth doing

Etymology: This term has its roots in the construction of the Empire State Building in 1930, the year before the building was scheduled for completion.

Unlike today, in those days, jobs that middle-class Americans did not want to do were relegated to the rank-and-file immigrant laborers.

In this particular situation, the job was laying the floors of all 102 stories of office space in the building. Tile were delivered to Grand Central Station by rail and then transferred by truck to the site.

The winter lingered late in 1930, and the second train of the fifty train-loads of marble tiles derailed in an ice storm near Albany, New York, holding up the forty-eight trainloads behind it. At the Empire State Building, Miguel, the crew manager of the immigrant floor layers, was running out of tiles and did not know what to do. Miguel was not entirely conversant with the English language, but he got by. When his boss asked him what the holdup was, all Miguel could say was: "**FEW TILE…!**"

And the rest, as they say, is history. "**FEW TILE…**" became the catch-phrase for the next couple of years whenever there was a job to be done but nothing to work with, or a job with no useful purpose. In the mid-1950s, the term was contracted to a single word: **FUTILE.**

CARRY-ON *(LUGGAGE)*
(FIRST USED: 1932 AD)

Definition: Typically refers to luggage not checked, but rather carried aboard an airline flight

Etymology: Commercial flying did not really "take off" until the 1930s, when airline companies had the foresight to hire young gentlemen (referred to as stewards) to help passengers on and off of the aircraft (when it was at rest). They also assisted with stowing handheld luggage and serving beverages at appropriate times. Up until then all carry-aboard luggage was referred to as **Handheld**. Not infrequently, one would find that passengers would surreptitiously smuggle aboard wrapped meat or some other form of spoilable food that they planned to consume during the long flights.

Typically, 50 percent of those packages never saw the inside of a stomach and were forgotten about. It was not uncommon for the stewards to find foul-smelling packages of unconsumed meat or fruit (much of which was days, and sometimes weeks old) rotting under a passenger seat—or tucked deep into a crevice in an over-head compartment.

Along with the spoiled foods came the problems of the foul smell and potential infestation. On September 7, 1932, at the urging of the developing airline industry, as well as concerned flyers, Congress enacted the **Carrion** Bill, which required the airline to inspect the handheld luggage of passengers boarding any domestic flight. They were charged with the responsibility of immediately removing any packages suspected of containing any consumables. Bringing your own food onboard was specifically banned and is, in fact, the reason that the industry-of-old ultimately took on the responsibility of pro-viding food to in-flight passengers.

Political cartoonists took advantage of the situation, and many dis-tasteful images of enormous vultures hovering over in-flight passen-ger planes, searching for rotting food, were spread across the Opinion pages of the nation's newspapers. As a result, the food in the hand-held luggage became the **Carrion** of vulture fame, and the term, to this day, still brings to mind the wrapped meats that innocent travel-ers carried with them before airline food service became an expecta-tion. To further separate the passenger from the thought of uncon-sumable food reeking beneath their seats or within their handheld luggage, the term morphed from **CARRION** to the term **CARRY-ON.** (Author's note: This was a hard lesson learned, though airlines have apparently forgotten it and have again abandoned the responsibility to feed passengers. It is not, therefore, foolish to expect the eventual return of CARRION **in the Carry-On.**)

ALONE
(FIRST USED: 1934 AD)

Definition: State of being unencumbered by others; doing something without the assistance or interference of others

Etymology: Prior to the Great Depression of the thirties, no one was ever in a situation where they did not have someone else's attention, someone's hand to grab, or someone's opinion with which to disagree. As the Great Depression rolled over the landscape, crushing people's hopes of maintaining their jobs or keeping their homes, it became more and more difficult to pay for the basics: food, shelter, and asphalt. The less they had, the more they needed. It was fairly common to see long lines extending outside of financial institutions and extending down the sidewalks and gutters of every major city in the country. They had long since given up the struggle to withdraw money from their accounts because it had been long since there was any money left in their accounts.

The problem was that people needed loans, and few had collateral with which to barter. Banks are composed of people too, and one might have thought that applying for a loan from people with whom you had entrusted all of your money would be a fairly easy transaction (if not somewhat embarrassing). However, "No Collateral, No Loan!" was the battle cry of the bankers. People began asking one another—sons asking fathers, nieces asking aunts and neighbor asking neighbor—for the loan of money that did not exist.

People became weary of anyone who seemed to be approaching them—for fear that they would again be asked for money. The constant pleading, even from total strangers became a depressing nuisance, and people began avoiding one another to prevent embarrassing moments. The cry "**A LOAN? A LOAN?** My Kingdom for **A LOAN!**" became commonplace, and most people sought out areas where they would not be accosted by others seeking help. Once in a while you might hear voices near the barn. A single soul would be found sitting alone on some fresh straw, saying "**I got your loan right here! Now go away and leave me alone!**"

Thus did the cry for "**A LOAN?**," with a minor spelling adjustment, become a term that meant you had found peace: **ALONE**—that you were one, **ALONE** unto yourself.

FORBIDDEN
(FIRST USED: 1935 AD)

Definition: An action or thing that is not allowed

Etymology: Government contracts are put out to bid. Bids are accessed based on how close or far they are from the actual cost of manpower and equipment. A contract is underbid if the competing bidder places or puts a bid in that is less than the CM&E (Cost of Manpower and Equipment). This is called putting a **One-Bid** in. A **One-Bid** classified as the best of all bids. If the company puts in a bid that is relatively equal to the projected costs of the project, it is called putting a **Two-Bid** in. A **Two-Bid** represents a bid that is relatively even with the projected cost of the project. Putting a **Three-Bid** in suggests to the analysis that you are less likely to be awarded the contract because your bid is high and not in line with the existing financial goals of the contract.

Corruption sometimes walks hand in hand with government. Regrettably, it is not uncommon to receive contract bids from campaign donors who agree to slip some financial incentive to the contracting agent as a quid pro quo for granting the contract. These types of bids are those that far exceed the actual costs of those projects that are already underbid. They are strictly illegal and can end up in jail time. Analysts can identify these bids because they are so out of place from normal expectations. Consequently they are classified as putting a **FOUR-BID IN**. A **FOUR-BID** is always placed under scrutiny and is how the term **FORBIDDEN** is derived.

PECAN
(FIRST USED: 1935 AD)

Definition: Another nut, most profitable of the "P"-Nuts

Etymology: Not infrequently we hear (while begging not to hear) conversations that are sometimes referred to as Toilet Humor. Although typically tasteless, some (particularly boys in their teens) get good belly laughs - while the rest wonder where the humor is and why it is so appealing to others. It is therefore a difficult task with which I am burdened regarding the term **PECAN**.

It may be blatantly obvious to some readers that the term **PECAN** is just the sort of word that would invite giggles from the high schoolers among us. However, my task is to accurately speculate on the origins of words, and the term **PECAN** requires us to put aside bathroom humor and understand how it is possible that this nut can "crack someone up." There are seeds of truth in some of the "humor" connected with the history of the term. For example, if you are a teenage boy, you know that the **PEE CAN** is a place to empty your bladder.

However, if you are a moderately serious adult, you are also aware that the toilet is an important part of your life, and if you are a male who has ever had urinatus-interruptus—and consequently consulted a physician—you are aware that eating certain snack foods while on the **Can** will distract your clenching muscles enough to allow you to (as we say) release.*

It is commonly understood that men prefer to stand rather than sit while releasing because of the "relax" vs. "contract" muscle potential to "hold you up." This explains the common recommendation from doctors worldwide to keep cans of nuts available while you are actively engaged in "relaxing." The **PEA CAN** is the perfect fruit (if you will) of the nut tree because it is a bit larger than the **PEA-NUT** and as such fills a can with a lower count of nuts. That makes the **PECAN**** a more profitable nut for bathrooms than the aforementioned **PEANUT**. **PISS TACHIOS** are also some of the nuts you see hanging around the bathroom and serve the same function even though **PECANS** tends to get more juvenile chuckles and are more cost efficient.

Cashews are not in the mix or commonly found in the bathroom. Their primary medical use seems to be involved with people who need encouragement to sneeze (and people who generally like the physical experience of sneezing). It is not recommended that you share anyone else's cashews. ***

* Generally speaking, physicians' tend to discourage eating in the bathroom

*** The **PECAN**, the **PEANUT**, and the **PISTACHIO** were all named with the target **PEE** as a prefix in an effort to be the most widely sought-after OTC PEE inducer.*

*** We will take a pass on the complicated debate current underway in urological circles regarding the Peedy-Attrition sometimes associated with an enlarged prostate.

CHRONOLOGY SEVENTEEN

(FROM 1937 AD THROUGH 1937 AD)

THE APPALOSSOCENTRIC ERA

< *1937* >

"OBSTETRICS IS THE ONLY WING IN THE HOSPITAL THAT PROVIDES WOMB SERVICE."

MELANCHOLY
(2ND ETYMOLOGY 1937 AD)

(This term was first used in 9,372 BC).

The second etymological school of thought on the term MELANCHOLY is as follows:

Definition: a state of mind resulting in a mild to severe depression; a sad, sometimes empty feeling

Etymology: The collapse of the stock market in 1929 was followed by the Great Depression of the early 1930s. Along with all of the problems those events generated, we weren't much further along toward recovery when the drought in the Midwest led to the dustbowl of 1934. With all of the bad news engendered by these events, one would think that the etymology of the term **MELANCHOLY** could be traced directly to this time in our history. And, in fact, that is the case, but not for the reason one might assume.

Along with the Dustbowl came the abandonment of family farms, resulting in mass foreclosures. One of the few staple crops of the states of Kansas, Oklahoma, and northern Texas was the melon. This crop was not only devastated during the Dustbowl era—it was very nearly annihilated! The only threats to a good melon harvest prior to the drought and Dustbowl were the melon predators. From badgers and raccoons to rogue chickens, it was not uncommon to see substantial predator-generated losses to the seasonal melon crops.

One way the farmers dealt with the threat was to utilize trained dogs (almost always **Collies**) to ward off would-be melon raiders on any given night. The Collie Protection System (CPS) worked well and helped keep profits up and losses down.

With the devastation caused by the dustbowl/drought and the resulting mass migrations of farmers to California and points farther west, the **Melon Collies** were left without crops to guard. For the **Collie**, the sense of a loss of purpose had a devastating emotional impact and, in fact, is how the term **Melon Collie** (or **Melancholy**) came to be synonymous with a depressed state.

*(It is interesting here to note that with the abandonment and loss of the melon industry in the Midwest, there was no further reason to label these depressed and out-of-a-job dogs with the moniker of **Melon Collie**. In fact, in 1935 a survey was taken of all working and nonworking collies across America, and it was determined that no dog was more bored than the displaced and unemployed **Melon Collie**—and it was at that time that they were renamed the **Bored'er Collie** to reflect their state of mind. As these dogs went through rehab and were retrained to herd other animals, the Bored'er Collie became known as the Border Collie.)*

AFTERMATH
(FIRST USED: 1937 AD)

Definition: The remnants following an event that may be defined as destructive; what is left over

Etymology: The origin of this word is so obvious, especially to persons not inclined to mathematics, that it is almost embarrassing. The word came into being as a result of eons of children and adults who were not mathematically disposed and who flunked, or just barely passed, proficiencies in mathematics. Those of us with no apparent gift for numbers know only too well the anguish and angst-ridden pain of Post-Traumatic Arithmetic Syndrome, or PTAS (later revised to Parent Teachers Association Sessions). Each drill and test was a cataclysmic cacophony of cerebral calamity (CCCC) in each and every one of our lives. The night terrors, the fear, the anxiety, the horrific heart tremors, and cold sweats—yes, even the dyspepsia—were all a result of the emotional crisis that we all endured after math. Accordingly, the destructive term **AFTERMATH** shall forever haunt us and shall live in infamy until such time as it just doesn't add up.

ANOREXIA
(FIRST USED: 1937 AD)

Definition: A condition typified by a profound lack of, or loss of, appetite

Etymology: In the early days of competitive body building, two adoring parents were at the top of their game, having won the 1937 World Championship trophies for male and female bodybuilders. They were Bunny "Flex" Rex and Buster "Pecs" Rex. Their daughter, Anna, who was seven years old at the time, wished with every fiber of her being that she could build muscle like her mommy and daddy, and, in fact had taken the crown for Miss Fit that same year.

But Anna had a problem.

The pediatrician called it "a problem with a simple solution" because there was no specific medical term for it. Anna had no appetite. Her doctor told her to "just go out there and eat something," but Anna had no interest in food. Without the proper nutrition, she could not exert the energy she needed to build muscle like her mommy and daddy.

It is alleged that her pediatrician wrote about her lack of appetite in *JAMA (**Journal of the American Medical Association**)* and referred to her case as **ANNA REX**, adding the letters *EAH* to her medical chart to signify *Early Appetite Hiatus*. So it is from the doctor's notes that the disorder **ANNA REX EAH** was first diagnosed. As in all evolutions, some doctors considered themselves rebels and branched out by documenting Anna's problem as: Insufficient **A**ppetite—or **ANNA REX-IA** The term had a certain ring to it and became the designation adopted by the AMA—but with the alpha code **ANOREXIA.***

> *** Author's note**: *The pediatrician, in conjunction with the AMA, made the changes in spelling from **Anna Rex IA** to **Anorexia** to protect the child's identity; therefore, so should you. The author urges you not to speak of this to anyone.*

ASTEROIDS
(FIRST USED: 1937 AD)

Definition: a heavenly body

Etymology: As with any heavenly body, **ASTEROIDS** (**ass steroids**) are something many people aspire to. **Ass steroids** are commonly known and discussed in the circles that aspire to well-toned bodies—but with little or none of the work required to produce results manually. Typically these steroids are injected into the buttocks twice weekly to, in common parlance, "plump it up"—that is, to round and firm the posterior.

The upside of **ASTEROID** injections is that it solicits admiring glances from members of the opposite sex. The most common downside of **ASTEROIDS** is an increased chance of hemorrhoids. Please consult with a physician before ASSuming the process will work for you.

AVOCADOS
(FIRST USED: 1937 AD)

Definition: The fruit of a West Indian tree; the alligator pear

Etymology: The **AVOCADO**, remarkably, got its name from a game a two-year-old West Indian child played back in early 1937. Apparently the child, after wandering around in the orchard one afternoon, discovered the overripe fruit on the ground. He came back to his momma with a soft avocado (In those days the fruit was referred to as **Snack Dip**) stuck onto each foot in such a way that his toes were buried in the soft, ripe fruit. When his momma asked him what he was doing wearing snack dip on his feet, he gleefully asked in his baby talk: "Have I got toes, Momma? Have I got toes?" And then he would giggle and ask the same silly question of anyone who would listen. This, folks, was as cute as it gets. Henceforth the fruit was named **Have-I-Got-Toes**. For simplicity's sake, and for obvious marketing concerns, **Have-I-Got-Toes** was contracted to the term we now use: **Av-I-got-toes**, or as we here in the colonies pronounce it, **AVOCADOS**.

BAHRAIN
(FIRST USED: 1937 AD)

Definition: The name of an island country in the gulf of Bahrain, off of the coast of Saudi Arabia.

Etymology: Most Middle Eastologists agree that the independent kingdom of Bahrain, which has been heavily courting tourism over the last two decades, was named Bahrain in a misguided attempt to suggest that rain is not welcome. Obviously, the desert climate supports less than three inches of rain per year; however, the Madison Avenue marketing company that invented the name

"**Bah! Rain!**" really missed the mark—and was ridiculed by the mon-eyed tourists who frequented the baccarat tables and high-end spas that attracted them to this storied kingdom of old. The marketing company, prior to being fired by the ruling monarch (Bahrain is a constitutional monarchy), also tried to stimulate the tourist trade by claiming that "**Bah! Rain!**" was ruled by a Grand Pooh-Bah who, according to the Gilbert and Sullivan operetta *The Mikado*, was "The-Lord-High-Everything-Else."

The fear was that "**Poo-Bah!**" suggested an avoidance of the distaste-ful but necessary use of toilets. Concern grew that this may be a nation that either disavowed and/or was void of toilets and toilet facilities. The results were a "Dis-Ass-Tour" (pun not intended...*well, maybe*) for the marketing company as well as the Bahrain gaming industry. Over time, the situation has improved, and the now-named **BAHRAIN** is an epicenter of Mideast tourism.

CRUSTACEAN
(FIRST USED: 1937 AD)

Definition: Sea creatures with an exterior shell

Etymology: It was not so long ago that people, in general, expressed some sympathy for the creatures they harvested for food. To the extent that it was possible, some went so far as to adopt one or the other of those creatures and kept them at home as pets.

Most people agreed that they enjoyed the taste of the meats of some of these creatures—lobster, crab, and shrimp—but were repulsed by the need to remove them from their shells. The sickening sucking sound as these innocents were literally ripped from their shells made even the most macho of men sick to their stomachs. It became clear that those who were trying to make an industry out of the capture and sale of these creatures had to do something to buoy up sales.

In 1937, a man named Henry Smelt came up with the idea of affixing tables to the decks of the fishing vessels and removing the "**crusts**" of these animals during the return trip. When the boats docked, they could then sell the meat of these creatures without the odious proposition that the consumer would then have to hear that sickening sucking sound. The idea was an overnight hit. Henry named the de-shelling tables the **Crust Station**, and over time, all of the shell "fish" were referred to as the **Crust Station Fish**. Later, these animals were all grouped together for the purposes of scientific study and named **CRUSTACEAN** in honor of old Hank Smelt's **CRUST STATION**.

GLOBAL WARMING
(FIRST USED: 1937 AD)

Definition: A potentially disastrous increase in worldwide temperature

Etymology: In the beginning of winter in 1937, Thomas Edi "sun's" son, Eddy, invented a child's toy that he introduced to the children of our northern neighbor, Canada. Eddy wanted to unite form and function. His toy, which he named the **Glow Ball**, was a ball the size of a modern day soccer ball, and it contained an ingenious series of smaller balls inside. The interior of this **Glow Ball** was, in fact, crowded with sixteen smaller balls, and the interior of the **Glow Ball** as well as the exterior of each of the smaller balls was plated with a deli-thin slice of steel sheeting. The thin steel sheeting was altered with magnet sheeting (harvested from the Magnut trees in Central California). Eddy's thought was that if a child of the northern country was unable to go outside to play during the winter months, he would have enormous amounts of excess energy to expend. The **Glow Ball** would provide a release for that energy. The toy was intended to be rolled rapidly, frequently changing directions. The internal friction would cause the ball to warm rapidly, and given enough rapid movement, would begin to glow as the steel and magnet-plated internal balls made contact with one another and the inside of the outer ball. An expensive marketing campaign was undertaken to take advantage of the Christmas season during the remaining three months of the year. The problem was that neither a child nor an adult could typically sustain the energy required to keep the **Glow Ball** moving enough to get it to warm. Secondarily, the noise created by the crashing balls was almost unbearable. What usually happened was that the over exercised user ended up exhausted, complaining of a headache due to all the noise, and was left profusely sweating,—thus the **Glow Ball** *Warming*. The phrase ***Glow Ball Warming*** came into common use as of 1938—a mocking term for a failed invention. In the latter half of the twentieth century, the scientific community co-opted the term to describe the causes of climatic change. They, of course, changed the spelling to **GLOBAL WARMING** to avoid any patent infringement claims.

LONELY
(FIRST USED: 1937 AD)

Definition: Deserted, solitary.

Etymology: In the tradition of Robin Hood and the Lone Ranger, **Lone Lee** wanted to be a do-gooder. Because he was unclear on the concept regarding where and when to do actual "good," he was forever butting into the affairs of his neighbors and acquaintances (he had no actual friends). Nonetheless, he continually tried to find opportunities to single-handedly "save-the-day." And no surprise, the more he tried, the more people shunned him. So instead of becoming a legend like his heroes Robin Hood and the Lone Ranger, **Lone Lee's** legacy was reduced to a misspelling of his name. The name **LONE-LEE** was changed to the term **LONELY** and came to mean someone yearning for human contact.

MUSICAL (BROADWAY)
(FIRST USED: 1937 AD)

Definition: A play using music and lyrics as a unifying theme

Etymology: As we all know, **Music** was invented in early 1937 in response to the first major outbreak of Mad Cow Disease (MCD)—the term **Music** being a contraction of the two words **Moo** and **Sick**. As you are also aware, the last ice age ended in the spring of that year with the glaciers receding up the Hudson River and restaging in northern New England. In those days, as verbal history explains it, cows were driven in large herds from the colder northern New England states into New York, and then onto Manhattan. The trail for these cattle drives became very wide as more New Yorkers required post-Ice Age beef. The trail was referred to as Broadway, which simply described how wide it had become.

It should here be noted that during the ice age, our pre-ancestors in New York would have to make do with frozen cattle, which they pulled along the Broadway on primitive sleds. The cows would be hit with a sled* hammer several times, and the hundreds of frozen pieces that resulted would be tied to sticks. These frozen treats were referred to as Cow, or Moo Sickles.

During the first outbreak of Mad Cow Disease in early '37, the farmers and the drovers would tend to the sick cattle by humming soft melodies in the fire lit evenings. Eventually, people would put words to the tunes to reflect events in their lives—thus the invention of not only **Music** (**Moo Sick**), but also of Lyrics **(Leer Ricks)**. It was shortly thereafter that they began weaving a story line around a group of "tunes" and acting out the story while the cows moaned in the background. On any given summer evening as you traveled down the Broadway, you would come upon as many as a dozen groups acting out these plays with music.

It was late in August of that year. Mad Cow Disease had ended, but people continued to invent new "stories in moosick" and enact them for gathering crowds along the Broadway. It was also then, to honor the memory of the Ice Age treat the **Moo Sickle**, that people co-opted the term to describe what they were doing—and thus was invented the Broadway **Moosickle** (**MUSICAL**). Since then, many popular **MUSICALS** still recall the spring and summer of '37, such as: *The Sound of Moo Sick, The Moo Sick Man, Oaklahomoo, Meat Me In St Louie, A Cow Rush Line, The Cow and I, Les Miserable (Bovine Edition), Cow Melot,* and *Man of La MunchYa,* just to mention a few.

*A Sled Hammer was a hammer that was carried in a sled. It had a heavy iron peen, which was originally used to break up frozen cattle and was eventually called a Sledge Hammer when it became an effective tool for people making glue (see etymology of **Moocilage***).*

PERSPIRE
(FIRST USED: 1937 AD)

Definition: To excrete fluid through the pores of the skin; to sweat

Etymology: There is evidence that the Eskimo culture dates back to somewhere between 5000 and 3500 BC. But it was not until early into the twentieth century that female Eskimos discovered what ladies from the Middle Ages forward had known for centuries—and that was that a bag (then known as a handbag) was an indispensable accouterment to a lady's wardrobe. It wasn't until mid-1937 that Eskimo females began to experiment with the handbag. The practice was touted as a marvelous way to carry items from igloo to igloo, and when lined properly, it could be a wonderful way to carry fish from ice hole to igloo to bonfire and back.

The handbag (or purse) became the proud possession of every female Eskimo until problems began to arise. Because of the extreme cold, every Eskimo hand was covered with a mitten. It was very difficult to open, reach in, find, and hold onto any item that might be stored in a purse without taking off your mittens. The few unfortunates who did just that suffered from extreme frostbite! Typically, everything in the purse would freeze once you stepped outside of the igloo, so the purse items became unusable until thawed. Sensibly, Eskimo kept their hands shielded in mittens, and in their pockets, while they were outside. Consequently, purses became virtual millstones around the necks of their owners. In effect, the purse had no value when used outside. It took only one winter season for the Eskimo ladies to realize that there was a reason that no one before them had adopted the purse "habit" in the frozen north.

As a result, a special day (the first day of spring) was selected to formally discard the "purses of the north." On that day, Eskimo ladies from Canada, Alaska, Greenland, and Russia came together for an official burning of the purses. A huge pyre was built. Everyone formed in a circle around the pyre and watched the conflagration of purses transformed into ash.

The pyre was so great and the heat so intense that every single Eskimo watching began to sweat—which is something you ordinarily do not see happening that far north. The event became known as the great **Purse Pyre**. And it was then that the physical act of sweating was given a name—i.e., you were said to **Purse Pyre**, or as we now spell it, **PERSPIRE**.

SEA LION
(FIRST USED: 1937 AD)

Definition: a creature belonging to the family of Otariidae; typically of the seal family Zalophus (sounds like *Zalo-phus*) Californiacus.

Etymology: The scientists who were given the responsibility for the naming of this particular sea mammal had to endure great confusion, bitter feelings, and petulant grandstanding before finally settling on the name **SEA LION**. Even after the then-universally respected and multi-faceted **Scientific Institute of Nature, Ulcers, and Sobriety** (**SINUS**) ratified the decision in 1937, they spent many years arguing about the misguided and misdirected spelling of the creature's new name.

The only rationale, at the time, for the name **SEA LION** had been the inclination for this seal to find a comfortable (of sorts) place to get out of the sea and then promptly lie down (based on the empirical body of evidence, it was determined that this trait may have been due to an lack of legs). Sightings of this slippery slug were commonplace. On the coast of California (over six hundred plus miles of sand, rocky outcroppings, marinas, and gift shops), it was considered uncommon not to see these creatures lying somewhere within one's field of vision. Often, the local police would receive phone calls wherein the caller would say, "I **see** huge slug-like creatures **lying** on the wharf, and I am afraid for my wife!" However, the only harm ever recorded from **sea-lying** behaviors were the boats that sank due to the weight of these creatures sun bathing on the decks of anchored or moored vessels.

In any event, the hullabaloo surrounding the naming of these creatures was created because it didn't seem appropriate to call them: **SEA LYINGS**. And so, the struggling scientists of **SINUS** took liberties with the English language and officially named the creatures **SEA LIONS**.

STABLE
(FIRST USED: 1937 AD)

Definition: a building used to keep domesticated animals out of the weather

Etymology: The term was derived in mid-1937 by the actions of Jonathan Wise the Lesser, who owned and operated a cow farm (as he called it) on the rocky slopes of the Scottish north shore. John was not particularly successful in his endeavors and would probably have been much better suited to watching farming than to pursuing it. In any event, Jonathan had about twenty head of dairy cattle and one newly acquired bull. He kept the animals on a windswept pasture of about thirty acres and was having a terrible time managing the bull. He had hoped that he could teach the animal certain basic commands, starting with heel, sit, and stay. But as you may have guessed, the bull was having none of it and wandered at will over the entire thirty acres.

John decided that trying to teach a bull three commands at once was perhaps too ambitious, so he settled on one command with which to begin the training. He bought a stout rope, which he managed to tie around the perplexed animal's neck. He firmly tied the loose end around the nearest fencepost. He then grabbed the rope and with a firm jerk, shouted **"STAY, BULL!"** As you can imagine, it took only one jerk of the rope to alarm the already confused animal, which simply turned and walked away, dragging a ten-foot stretch of fence with it. After repairing the fence, Jonathan tried the same tactic using several alternatives to the fence post. Two sapling trees were uprooted immediately after the shouted command to "**STAY, BULL!**" along with an auger buried several feet into the soil. Jonathan's final attempt to train the bull was when he decided to tie one of his cows to the bull. As it happened, the cow and the bull just walked off together when they heard the command. John, not being as dumb as a casual observer might assume, went radical on the concept of training the bull to stay!

He began construction of an enclosed building with a fenced pen to keep the bull in when he didn't want it to roam at will. Obviously, and with some glee, he pronounced the enclosure a **STAY BULL** and was elated when the bull had no choice but to remain caged. Oddly, the concept caught on, and people far and wide began constructing their own **STAY BULLS**—and used them to keep other kinds of animals (such as horses and pigs) penned.

Ultimately the term **STAY BULL** was contracted into the current spelling **STABLE**. To this day, the **STABLE** still serves the purpose of keeping an animal in one place, as originally intended by that misguided farmer, a.k.a., animal trainer Jonathan Wise the Lesser.

STAKEOUT
(FIRST USED: 1937 AD)

Definition: A phrase commonly used to refer to the law enforcement practice of waiting for or luring UNSUBS* into the open, in an effort to capture and hold them until such time as they can be proven guilty, or alternately, released, based on insufficient evidence.

Etymology: It was not until the very middle of the beginning of the twentieth century (1937, to be more specific) that the phrase **STAKEOUT** came into common usage. However, the concept goes back many millennia and was, in effect, a very successful creation of men of the Stone Age. In fact, the "two steps" of the **STAKEOUT** (which we will review forthwith) are visually represented in the pictographs found on the now-famous cave walls of **Pictograph Cave State Park** in the Great State of Montana. The park, not far from Billings, has several caves, the most prominent of which is the so-called **Pictograph Cave**. The site became prominent in 1901 after Teddy Roosevelt was alleged to have found prehistoric artifacts, not the least of which was a series of wall-chalked stick figures apparently showing how they lured a saber-tooth tiger into a pit—a pit which we can only assume was used to "store" (if you will) live food for later consumption.

As was omitted in his personal journal, Theodore Roosevelt made no mention of discovering the pictographs while seeking shelter in the cave during a nasty thunderstorm on one of his exploring and hunting forays along some of the lesser-known trails in the Montana wilderness.

The speculation was further embellished with the fabrication that the pictographs gave Theodore an idea for trapping grizzly bears[**]— which were the only North American bears that he had not yet captured—and consequently that he did not have mounted on the wall of his rather sizeable den. In any event, unfounded gossip has it that based on his interpretation of the pictographs, and with the help of his hiking staff (which was the precursor to the much smaller Swiss Army Knife which had a shovel "blade" as well as a pistol "blade" and a swing-out peg that could be used as a toilet paper holder or a coat hook, depending on the situation). Theo dug a pit measuring 12' x 12' x 12'. The pit was covered with branches and leaves. Theodore used additional branches and leaves to cover the entrance of the cave (which he then dubbed a hunting "blind"). As mathematics would have it, the blind was exactly 12' from the hidden pit. Theodore then pulled an enormous, 6 lb. slab of rib eye out of his food bag and secured it in the air, 12" above the pit, via a rope slung over a high tree branch. That evening, Teddy's cook and all-around handyman-slash-companion, Hu, who was sitting with him in the "cave blind," asked Teddy how long he thought it would take to lure a grizzly into the camp.

Teddy turned his head to answer, and no sooner than you could say "a can of beans," there was a loud thump, and Teddy turned to see the tail-end of a 400 lb mountain cat disappear into the forest. While it doesn't need to be said, the sad fact was that the steak, formerly known as "dinner," had departed between the teeth of the big cat.

Teddy muttered an expletive! Hu said: "What?" Teddy said in exasperation, "Oh, I don't know, Hu! I don't know!" Then Hu, whose command of the language, though laudable, was also sometimes laughable, and who had missed witnessing the event but now saw an empty space where the slab of meat once rested, asked, **"STEAK OUT?"** Teddy responded by affirming that **steak** was now **out** of the question for dinner, and in turn asked Hu: "What have we got to eat?" The aforementioned "can of beans" was heated up for dinner that evening.

This event—i.e., using a ruse as a lure to wait for, snare, and then slay an animal—had been in use, but had been unnamed as a technique since the Stone Age. However, because of the fame of Mr. Theodore Roosevelt and his sidekick Hu, the term **STEAK-OUT** became a commonly used hunting term to define, in a slightly less depressing way, the loss of dinner in a failed attempt to entrap an animal. It wasn't until the 1930s, with the onset of the days of bootlegging, the Great Dustbowl, Great Depression, and the ubiquitous soup lines—along with the concomitant rise in criminality via the gangster era, that law enforcement stopped using actual steaks and began applying the principles of *psychology and deception* to the **STEAK-OUT**. It should be noted that with that evolution of policy, the **STEAK-OUT** became a much more effective tool in capturing and prosecuting criminals.

It was also in 1937 that the Beef Council aired its own "beef" to security organizations worldwide, complaining that the subtle suggestion of a relationship-linkage between **crime** and **steaks** was materially harming **steak** sales. Congress acted immediately with the historic HR Bill 90120, which passed both parties unanimously and was signed into law in 1937 by the other Roosevelt. The law required that all **STEAK-OUTS** relating specifically to criminal justice issues be heretofore referred to and spelled as **STAKE OUT**.

It should be noted that there was an immediate hue and cry from the lumber industry. They issued a proclamation that such a change in spelling would be disastrous—and in a not too subtle play on words predicted that huge financial losses were at **stake!**

There was no sympathy from Congress.

And yet, as predicted, the sale of wooden **stakes** saw a drop of 15 percent to 45 percent in the three years following the enactment of the new law. That decline in sales drove the tent industry to convert from a lumber-based **tent stake** to a metal **tent stake**. However, what was lost in sales of lumber has been clearly made up in new dollar sales of coffee and donuts for the hundreds of thousands of dedicated police persons on **STAKEOUT** duty throughout the land***.

Police-speak: Unsub = Unidentified subject

*** It is important to note that no grizzly bears were harmed during the development of Theo's "Bear Snare."*

**** There is no actual evidence that anything stated above is true, although it did not feel like fiction when I was composing it!*

CAPABLE
(FIRST USED: 1937 AD)

Definition: having the potential to do a thing or perform an act.

Etymology: Superman, Batman, Robin, Spiderman, Captain Marvel, Captain America, and many other superheroes conceived of first as comic book characters, then as TV heroes, and then refined as movie stars, all had several things in common: One—they looked good in tights, and two—they went from mild-mannered citizens to Doers-of-Good and Defeaters-of Evil by changing from their ordinary clothes to their Super Hero Suits, and finally by donning their **Capes**. The wardrobe change made them able to fly, lift heavy objects, see through walls, and in general put a rude but heartwarming end to the doers of evil.

Thus we have the etymology of the word **CAPABLE**, which was a combining of the Super Hero **Cape**, and how it powered and enabled the Super Hero's to do the good deeds that we all admire. They became **CAPE ABLE**, as we used to say. Now, anyone who can perform a given act is determined to be **CAPABLE** specific to that act.

PACEMAKER
(FIRST USED: 1937 AD)

Definition: to set a pace; an implant to keep the heart stimulated

Etymology: frequently confused with **pedometer** (SEE: etymology for **Pedometer**)

PEDOMETER
(FIRST USED: 1937 AD)

Definition: to measure steps; a device to count and measure steps

Etymology: frequently confused with **pacemaker** (SEE: etymology for **Pacemaker**).

CHRONOLOGY: EIGHTEEN

(FROM 1938 AD THROUGH 1949 AD)

THE SULFURIOUS ERA

‹THE WAGES OF

THIN

IS

METH›

ABDUCT
(FIRST USED: 1938 AD)

Definition: To take away forcefully, to kidnap

Etymology: The place was Delaware, the crime was culinary, and the victims were simple farmers. In 1938, Delaware was the duck capitol of the Delaware region. These rather innocuous quackers were used for cooking in most of the best restaurants in America.

A farmer named Reynaldo Singletine raised ducks, and though many people raised ducks, Reynaldo's claim to fame was the quality of the duck meat that he sold. Reynaldo worked his ducks—groomed them, if you will—as he prepared them for market. Reynaldo wanted his duck meat to be firm and delicious. To that end he spent hours each day "stirring the ducks," as he liked to say. He would walk them around the duck pens during his every spare moment. He allowed the ducks brief food and water breaks and a two-hour rest period. Aside from a healthy eight hours set aside for sleep, he "walked" them daily. The ducks were wracked with chest heaves for fourteen hours of every day that they lived in Reynaldo's "workout" yards. The result was **ripped duck abdominals**. Because of this, it was said that Reynaldo's ducks were exquisitely meaty. They were the only "brand" of duck abs that the gourmands of New York, Chicago, and Newark would eat. They delighted the palette as "Duck à L'Orange," "Duck de la Renta," and "Duck des Crete's."

Of all the duck trucks used for shipping in all of the land, Reynaldo's duck trucks were the only trucks that were hijacked with regularity when the monthly shipments were fork lifted aboard and dispatched to the restaurants in New York, Chicago, and Newark. It was a well-known fact that crime bosses sent their goons to steal those duck loads of prime fowl. If the crime bosses discovered that one of their associates had hijacked a truck that did not have the proper **ab-duck** pedigree, the associate would find himself swimming with the fishies (out of duck and out of luck)! He was then said to be the victim of an **AB DUCK SHUN**, which referred to stealing duck breasts that did not "meat" the rigid quality expectation of the gourmand standards of the mob hijack teams. Thus those duck abs were, in effect, shunned.

As is patently obvious by now, the term **ABDUCT** was coined, if a bit translationally knurled, from its forerunner, the **Ab Duck.** They were **one** of the tastiest treats that The Post-Prohibition Era produced—and for two decades the meat of the AB DUCK was worth the risk of ABDUCTION.

SELFISH
(FIRST USED: 1942 AD)

Definition: Total immersion in the "self"; concerned with self without regard to others

Etymology: The Theory of Relativity states that the Neanderthal and his buddies were our relatives. Some people insist that just because the idea is dressed in the skirt of a theory, that does not make it so. They therefore conclude that it is just idle conjecture (and we don't have to believe it). Some insist that the theory is true and that if records had been kept - we would have direct proof that we are related to the Neanderthal.

Therein lies the solution. If there are two opposing sides to a theory (especially when the disagreement is within the same family), then it can be said to be "relative"—thus proving that a theory is relatively correct.

There is, however, another way to approach this thorny issue. It involves going back to the days of early man, or the late ape, or the day the thing that slithered out of the sea to breathe heretofore un-inhaled air did just that. The sea was teaming with life when man first stepped in it. It was cold and foreboding—but it was full of edible creatures that were easy to cook and chock full of other, smaller fishes who managed to lose their way. (Bones were an issue, as were scales, but the first people to begin consumption of seafood didn't yet know that bones and scales did not have to be chewed, gnashed, and swal-lowed—although the lesson on scaling and deboning didn't take long to learn.

The other good thing about fish was that they were free, like air and water. All you had to do was wade in and wait until you felt them nib-bling at your leg hairs (razors for the shaving of leg hair - disposable or otherwise, didn't come along until years later). You then grabbed them, smack them upside a rock, and voila! Fresh Fish! Catch of the day.

As we got more organized (somewhere in the late 1930s–early 1940s), some thoughtless entrepreneur who had missed out on the Invention of Fruit Stands decided that he could catch fish, clean 'em up a bit, and open a Fish Stand. In fact, it was a great idea. It was an idea that has stayed with us into the twenty-first century. However, it had one major drawback. The big negative was that it drew the ire of fisher-persons around the world because up until then, fish were free for the taking. People were vehemently opposed to the selling of fish for personal gain. Riots, arrests, and alas, some deaths were the rule rather than the exception while governments tried to sort out this new phenomena.

The Divided Nations (founded in 1942 as a pre-cursor of the United Nations), in one of its most controversial judgments, ruled that while it smacked of capitalism with a capitol "ISM," it was nonetheless legal for any person to harvest and sell the fruit of the ocean. They did, however, note for the entire world to see, that the collection of the fruit of the oceans is for all men of every nation. "It is not without reservations that we have approved that any person can at any time sell fish for their own personal gain."

Over next few months, the rioting diminished. However, normalcy was not restored until a still-angry populace was able to "recoin" the phrase SELL FISH into the single word **SELFISH**, which would be forever described as the act of plundering and selling fish for personal gain—without concern for others.

CONSUMMATE
(FIRST USED: 1945 AD)

Definition: The completion of an act in the best, most positive way

Etymology: The words we use to express ourselves come from a never-ending supply of sources, not the least of which is insects. For instance, we get the term fly, or to fly, from none other than the pesky little bugger referred to as (yes, you've guessed it) the fly. Another would be the worm, which worms its way into a few of our conversations. Then there is the bee—"to bee or not to bee"—and the mosquito, whose sting we have named after a barbed bush known as the familiar (and semi-same named) mesquite.

All of this leads us to the term **CONSUMMATE** and from whence it came. Anyone who has spent time studying the science of entomology (and who hasn't?) understands the complex interactions of the lives of bugs and how they, in turn, have helped new word-buds blossom on the tree of language.

The term **CONSUMMATE** is the ultimate in a descriptor when applied to the romantic actions and aspirations of the praying mantis. Everyone is awed because the little critters appear to be praying. But despite the piety, these insects consummate their little praying mantis relationships only after the female (who has worked up an appetite) chows down of her recent paramour. She finalizes a pregnancy by giving in to one of the more bizarre cravings in the insect world: she eats her recent ex. She eats him from antler to wing tip, nose to hoof, chewing carefully as she goes. She is the ultimate example of the descriptor **Consume Mate**, or as we now refer to it, **CONSUMMATE.**

MARVELOUS
(FIRST USED: 1946 AD)

Definition: Something that is first rate, top of the line, best of the bunch

Etymology: At the founding convention of the **MUTUAL ADMIRATION SOCIETY** in Pittsburg during the summer of 1946, a conversation between two members was recorded. It went as follows: "You're a Marvel!" To which the other replied, "No! You're a Marvel!" Upon which they agreed, with a group hug. They then declared that everyone should "**MARVEL-US**"!

A motion was made to the rules committee to adopt **MARVEL-US** as the motto of the society. It was unanimously adopted. The rest is history—except the spelling, which was adapted to the more elegant (non-phonics appropriate) spelling of **MARVELOUS.**

ATTENTION
(FIRST USED: 1947 AD)

Definition: Stiffening of the body in an upright and rigid manner to indicate full compliance to military command.

Etymology: It is wholly unclear which one of two early historical references accurately depicts the underpinnings of the term **ATTENTION**, though both clearly have military roots.

The first, like the second, seems to be a contraction of the term we use in today's language. It is simple and pure in its military form. When soldiers were compelled to dutiful diligence and prepared for being ordered into combat, they were expected to **shun** their tents and grab their weapons and form into orderly lines. Thus **A TENT SHUN** was an early military order to prepare for battle.

The second interpretation goes to the need to be alert and vigilant. The call to **A T**ENSION required the soldiers to stand in rigid and **tense** formation to receive orders. It is equally possible that **A TENSION** was, therefore, the root and etymology of the term **ATTENTION**.

MYSTERY
(FIRST USED: 1948 AD)

Definition: Something that is not fully understood; baffling

Etymology: The first tree farm in recorded history was established over a burned-out forest in the somewhat barren hills of eastern Oregon in 1922. According to recently disclosed records, the land was deeded to a Miss Ann Thrope, twenty-seven, who tended to shy away from both neighbors (one on each side of her property) and family. She had no one who would be verified as a friend.

Because Miss Ann did not interact well with others, she was determined to return her father's patch of one hundred acres to the forest that it once was. Her first step was to have a fence constructed around the entire property. She hired an industrial auger company to dig each hole, which were laid out clearly in a plan that included post holes for each of the trees she was planting, as well as the ten-foot-high fence with which she intended to close off her forest. She had exactly 9,855 fledgling spruce trees delivered (the number of trees was based on the number of days she had been alive). Her house was in the middle of the property, and her intent was to live amid the fenced forest. Therein, any requirement to interface with other humans was entirely under her control.

As a token to the outside world, Miss Ann Thrope had two trees planted astride the entrance gate to her property. She felt a sense of exoneration to the world at large with these trees greeting those who passed by the portal to her realm.

The trouble began in her fifty-third year. Miss Ann was strolling through her kingdom when an unauthorized burst of sunlight by the entrance gate caught her attention. Upon examination, she discovered that someone had physically removed one of the trees at her portal!

She had no interest in getting the sheriff involved in this misappropriation of her property. She climbed into her Ford Roadster and drove over every roadway in Eastern Oregon. Her search for the missing tree (possibly one of the two most important trees in her life) lasted seventeen exhausting days. Her anger turned to tears. She went from determination to helplessness. Finally she returned home, drove through her half-portal, and locked herself back into her private space.

In her diary, Miss Ann wrote of the horrid people who had ruined her life by taking her tree. She referred to the lost plant as "my lovely missed tree." Though Miss Ann is no longer with us, her tree farm and her entrance gate, with the one missing tree, stand in tribute to her oddness of character. Her **MISSED TREE** was transformed into the term **MYSTERY** and is in use even today. Her apparent fear or hatred of social interaction has become known as **Miss Ann Thrope**, or **MISANTHROPE**.

PERCHERON
(FIRST USED: 1948 AD)

Definition: A large draft animal

Etymology: It was thought for many years that the draft horse was so named because of the fact that if one ran by you, you could feel the draft that it caused. That draft theory was debunked by scientists when they discovered that pretty much anything that passed you rapidly also created a draft, and no one had named them draft iron horses, draft cheetahs, or, for that matter, draft dodgers.

It wasn't until the "taming" of the American West from the mid-1830s through the 1890s that we really discovered why these large animals were referred to as draft horses. In those days large animals were highly prized and typically raised in groups of four or more. While they were expensive to maintain during the spring and summer, their true value was captured during the blustery and wintery months, and are credited with preventing many an early settler from freezing to death during inclement weather.

The early settlers would construct their wilderness homes of whatever available woods were handy. As those were the days prior to the invention of caulking and other sealant substances, during cold and windy days, the farmers would line the large horses up against the ranch house along walls where the worst drafts came through.

The huge and warm bodies of the horses would block the winds from seeping through the walls and as a result, would keep the rooms from being drafty all of the time. Thus the appellation **the Draft Horse**.

However, this is not the complete story. One of the breeds of these huge draft horse is the **PERCHERON**. The **PERCHERON** is a glorious animal often reaching seventeen-plus hands high (depending on the size of the hand being used for measuring). **PERCHERONS** are classified into three groups depending on the height of the horse's back. They are, in order of height, the **Basic PERCHERON**, the **Tall PERCHERON,** and the **Quite A PERCHERON.** These classifications were, again, strictly based on how tall these splendid beasts were. The actual name **PERCHERON** came from the interaction between a child and her dad.

For her twelfth birthday, little Charlene, who loved horses (the more the better, and the bigger the better) got a very special present. Charlene's dad took her to visit a rancher friend of his. Of course this man had four draft horses and as a favor allowed Charlene to be hoisted up onto one his biggest animals. As she sat atop her dream animal, her dad said: "Charlene, that's a very **high PERCH YOU'RE ON**!" The name stuck, and to this day those marvels of horsedom are referred to as **PERCHERON**. That **High PERCHERON** became that standard by which all of the other groups (Basic, Tall, and Quite A,) were measured.

RESEARCH TEAM
(FIRST USED: 1948 AD)

Definition: A group of people looking for anything from answers to artifacts, evidence to etymologies

Etymology: Originally the concept of a research team was a narrowly focused one. Typically when someone lost an item or became lost, a team of individuals was sent out to search for and find what was lost. They were referred to as a **SEARCH TEAM**. On those rare occasions when they did not succeed in their mission and returned empty handed, a crack team of highly trained persons would be directed to go out and **RE-SEARCH** for whatever, or whomever, was missing. They became known as the **RE-SEARCH TEAM**. That name was morphed in to the term **RESEARCH TEAM,** which was broadened to include any kind of search.

TERRA COTTA PIECES
(FIRST USED: 1948 AD)

Definition: Glazed or unglazed fired clay used especially for statuettes, vases, and architectural purposes (as roofing, facing, and relief ornamentation)

Etymology: You might be surprised to learn that the term **TERRA COTTA** came into being because of a very dangerous road in southern Peru that "treks" over the Andes Mountains and ends at La Paz, Bolivia. As you know from the above definition, **TERRA COTTA** is fired clay. It wasn't always thus.

In the early days of its history, the **Death Highway** was given its name because of the heavy loss of life that resulted in many severe accidents. Most deaths were the result of drivers becoming impatient with the long, hot, dusty pass and consequently trying to pass each other on blind turns—along the ten-foot wide dirt and gravel road (which was etched out of the sides of the Andes Mountains). All too frequently they would crash and burn as they tumbled hundreds to thousands of feet into the valleys below.

Local villagers, upon hearing the crashes, would scramble down the mountainsides in futile attempts to rescue the living. Typically, the vehicles would careen down and their fuel would ignite, exploding into fireballs and subsonic booms. Everything that came in contact with the burning vehicles was also torched.

Because everyone was poor in the isolated villages along the Death Highway, the brave men who attempted to rescue the ill-fated crash victims would bring as many charred pieces of the wrecked vehicles and explosively fired clay as they could carry and drag back up the mountainside. They would then use these pieces of blackened metal, melted plastic to add to and reinforce their adobe dwellings. Some would exercise their creative sides and incorporate the pieces into their garden fountains or walled courtyards. Eventually, it was discovered that even the scorched and burned clay found at the sites of the vehicle fires seemed to be harder and more durable than even the clays used to construct their adobes. As a consequence, experimentation with clay, molds, and fire resulted in a product that was perfect for creating ornamental decorations for the adobes and gardens.

Because this whole process came into being as a result of the savage destruction evidenced by the rubble remains of broken vehicles, and because the common warning for people who planned to travel the Death Highway was "**Don't do it! That road will tear a car to pieces,**" this wonderfully decorative by-product was named **Tear a Car to Pieces,**" or in Spanish: "**TERRA COTTA PIECES.**"

CHRONOLOGY: NINETEEN:

(FROM 1950 AD THROUGH 1960 AD)

THE SPORIFIC PERIOD

< YOUR DOG NEEDS TO BE

RE-FIR BRUSHED >

THE TERM "YOUTH" IS A CONTRACTION OF THE WORDS: "YOU" AND "THUG."

TESTOSTERONE
(FIRST USED: 1950 AD)

Definition: The male sex hormone

Etymology: The first "men's game" was throwing stones at one another to see how many of the competitors' team could be sidelined and sent to the Emergency Cave. This was a direct offshoot of the stone-age carnage, where perfectly reasonable cavemen would attack the neighboring tribe with a big pile of rocks to steal their furniture.

Looking forward to the Middle Ages, the main improvement in the game was that it was played by tribal warriors who practiced how far they could throw a lethal stone. By the seventeenth and eighteenth centuries, soldiers would, both in training exercises and battle, attempt to toss cannonballs directly into the cannon from varying distances. Successful timing on the part of the cannon-fuse guy would result in a barrage of cannon balls in the direction of the opposition. If the cannon toss was not up to par, the opposition would usually overrun the defenders and win the day. Consequently, it was very important that the soldiers be instructed to accurately put (toss) the ball (or shot) into the hole at the front of the cannon. But the mastery of the cannon toss, as such, was a short-lived skill that went into hibernation with the abandonment of the cannon fuse, which was replaced with triggers and pre-loaded gun powder.

Thereafter, the military abandoned the cannonball toss as a training exercise. In the meantime, the newly formed Olympics Committee declared that the cannon toss would be made into a track-and-field Olympic sport. They decided to call it the shot put. The cannon balls (or shots) were made a uniform size, and the game consisted of "putting" (or tossing) the shot (cannonball) as far away as possible.

In the thirties and forties of the twentieth century, and primarily because most of the men were off fighting a war, ladies got into Olympic sports. Typically, they had to train under the tutelage of older male coaches and track-and-field assistants. The rules for ladies were somewhat different than for the men, insofar as they were allowed to have one of the assistants help them lift the shots and to help keep them in balance as they wound up to "put" (or toss) the lead balls.

An amazing breakthrough came in the 1947 practice tryouts when a young lady declined the assistance of the assistants. Theresa (Tess) Throckmorton of Great Britain was somewhat, shall we say, stout and brash—and without apology. She stepped into the ring, hefted her balls with no sign of strain, and "put" them. Tess brought home three gold medals from the London Olympics in 1948, although critics claimed that she was "already at home," considering that she lived in London at the time.

Most people were astounded at this historic development, and Tess became a household word. The usual context was when the guy of the household tried to get out of a chore such as taking out the garbage in a rainstorm. He would be told in no uncertain terms (usually by his wife or his mom) to **"TESS UP!"** Ultimately, though, the greatest honor came to Tess from the scientific and medical communities. In 1950 they named a newly discovered male hormone after her. They, of course, called it: **Tess Tossed Her Own**. The spelling was simplified in 1951 to **TESTOSTERONE**.

(Authors' note: All of these activities were a precursor to the school-yard game of dodge ball, beginning with the caveman's inclination to throw stones at his neighbor's barking dog, through the nobles of the Middle Ages having "Throne" Room furniture, and into the twentieth century, whose politicians would throw insults as if they were cannonballs.)

CATALINA (ISLAND)
(FIRST USED: 1951 AD)

Definition: One of the Channel Islands off of the coast of Southern California. It is sometimes referred to as Santa Catalina Island.

Etymology: A little-known type of cattle was bred specifically to graze across the hillsides of much of Northern California and some of the Channel Islands. The actual breeding of these "hillside" cows was done on a small island off of the coast of Southern California. In order to create an animal efficient enough to feed off of the steep hillsides common to the island and other California environs, exhaustive steps were taken to breed an animal that had shorter legs on one side. Today as one travels the back roads of California's Sonoma, Napa, and Mendocino counties it is common to see these animals grazing calmly on steep hillsides. They appear to be perfectly upright and apparently level. They were nicknamed **Side-Hill-Gougers** and have become so commonplace as to no longer elicit wonder or curiosity from the passing traveler. Their legs on one side generally are six to twelve inches shorter than the two normal legs. This efficient animal originated from breeding farms on the scenic island we now call **CATALINA ISLAND**, which is a contraction of the term **Cattle-Leaner,*** the name of the company that bred them. (Note: Santa Cattle Leaner was a Christmas marketing gimmick that never caught on.)

* *It should be herein noted that the pastime of cattle tipping got its start with the occasional side-hill-gouger that wandered onto the flatlands. The comical appearance of these leaning cows inspired unsympathetic youth to give them that last little shove. The malicious bump would knock them off of their delicate center of gravity and onto the ground.*

TRAILER
(FIRST USED: 1952 AD)

Definition: an unpowered wheeled conveyance towed by powered vehicle

Etymology: Man has taken advantage of the invention of the wheel in many ways since the caveman harnessed a wooly mammoth to a covered oxcart and called it his home away from home. Trailers became popular and increasingly stylish with the release of the movie *The Long, Long Trailer* in 1952. Travel trailers are considered the "road" housing used to travel to wilderness campgrounds and have some of the same benefits as one-star hotels. They were and still are a way to "hit the dusty trail." They are reminiscent of the pioneer days, of the Calistoga wagons and of the great western migration of the 1800s. In fact, the term **TRAILER** was derived from the two words that describe the memories of those great treks—that is, **Trail Lore**.

DUDE
(FIRST USED: 1953 AD)

Definition: a term specifically referencing a "city slicker" who vacationed on a farm or ranch to get the ultimate western outdoor living experience; a colloquialism used to greet a person of either sex, as in a "buddy" or "pal"

Etymology: The first "ranch vacation packages" were similar in many ways to the current military "boot camp" experience. They were specifically marketed to men who wanted to emulate the activities of early ranch hands and cattlemen. These men could then claim to be as fit and hardworking as their ancestors. The ranch vacations required that the men sleep in bunkhouses and arise at 4:00 a.m. to milk the cows and feed the horses and sheep. At 7:00 a.m. breakfast was typically served off of a chuck wagon in one of the pastures. The men would arrive at the designated spot to eat and to drink strong coffee (it was not uncommon to find that the brewed coffee was strong enough to eat). Frequently, because of the early hours outdoors, their clothes and hair would be damp from the early-morning dew. It was said at the time that they were **dewed**, which went a long way to prove their manhood. The term morphed into the current spelling **DUDE**, and the ranches became known as **DUDE** Ranches. The current colloquialism uses the term **DUDE** as a casual address or greeting to any other person.

PILFERAGE
(FIRST USED: 1953 AD)

Definition: To filch. To steal from somebody.

Etymology: There are many kinds of **rage**. There's your ***out***-rage, your ***en***-rage, your ***cou***-rage, or your ***ga***-rage…ad nauseam. But the **rage** with the longest history, is, of course, your **PILFER-RAGE**. Ever since the first man to steal from his neighbor was discovered and confronted, the rage from the theft immediately awakened what would always be an assault on the trust of the entire community.

Put another way, when all that you own is a club, a cave, and a piece of cloth to cover up your hoo-ha, nothing short of murder is more of an assault on your dignity then the theft of your hard-earned possessions. So the early term "pilfer" was always followed by the term rage. When language was streamlined in early 1953, the two words were joined to form what we now know as **PILFERAGE.**

SOUTH POLE
(FIRST USED: 1953 AD)

Definition: A frozen, barren place beyond the southern edges of civilization

Etymology: Krakow is located just north of the fiftieth parallel. It is this parallel that separates Northern Germany from Southern Germany, North Czechoslovakia from South Czechoslovakia, and more importantly, North Poland from South Poland. While it gets quite cold during the winter in South Poland, it does not get nearly as cold as it does at the "bottom of the world," which may be correctly referred to as Antarctica. However, in Poland, everyone who lives south of the fiftieth parallel is referred to as a **SOUTH POLE** or as **SOUTH POLISH**.

UNDER ARREST
(FIRST USED: 1954 AD)

Definition: A phrase used by law enforcement officials to indicate that you are being detained in their custody.

Etymology: In the days of Sheriff Andy Taylor of Mayberry, if you disobeyed a law, you might be told that you were going to "cool your heels" in the "hoosegow," or spend the night in jail, or that you were going to be locked-up—or any number of other colloquial phrases to advise you that you were no longer a free citizen. The whole point of being imprisoned is to give law enforcement a chance to get you in front of a judge to establish guilt and punishment.

The phrase **give it a rest** applied to all who were remanded into custody, in that, until such time as the system determined your fate, you had no other option but to sit and stew in a jail cell—or **REST.** When the Miranda Law was enacted, the phrase "give it a rest" was changed to the legal speak: "being held **under a mandatory rest period.**" In common parlance the phrase **under a mandatory rest** was shortened to **UNDER A REST**, or **UNDER ARREST.**

CARDBOARD
(FIRST USED: 1956 AD)

Definition: Thick paper that is used to produce boxes and other "hard paper" packaging; frequently created from recycled paper products

Etymology: The term CARDBOARD originally referred to people who received so many greeting cards that they tired of them. They were said to be **card-bored.** Most of the cards were ultimately dis-carded into recycling centers that produced "paper" or card "bored" boxes from the dis-cards. The very term **discard** was a direct result of getting rid of both "dis" card and "dat" card. Over time **CARD BORED** has morphed into **CARDBOARD.**

PLAY DOH
(FIRST USED: 1956 AD)

Definition: A substance invented for when you are of a mind to mold

Etymology: For people who don't have, but would like to have, money to burn, or (**Play "Dough"**) fun money. It is rarely confused with **Plato**.

APPARENTLY
(FIRST USED: 1957 AD)

Definition: An idea or fact that appears to be true but is unverified

Etymology: Many things that we take for granted are a result of hearsay. One might wonder why the majority of the population trusts undocumented sources enough not to question the authenticity of the newfound information.

Genealogy has been discovered as the root of this data malaise. It has been determined that every human who occupies or has occupied space on this planet has, at his or her root, a genealogical tie to the commonality of accepting and expecting that what one is told to be true, is in fact true. As every child knows from the earliest cognitive awareness, his or her parents impart not only physical and emotional security, but also the sense that they are in command of the ability to understand the rational as it pertains to the minds and hearts of others. This is in addition to the actual operations of physical reality.

Consequently, when a parent tells a child that such a thing as turning on the gas stove without igniting the burner can cause death and mayhem, the child believes it to be true because it came from an unimpeachable source: **A Parent**.

However when that parent fabricates an answer or explanation, he or she can create an aura of childlike distrust and misunderstanding. So the oft-used term **A PARENT-LEE*** refers to something that has yet to be physically verified by that child (until then it is considered a parent lie..).

> ** It should here be noted that the one exception to the etymology provided above is when the said parent is actually named **LEE**, in which case the reference is then to **a Parent Lee**.*

CHILDHOOD
(FIRST USED: 1957 AD)

Definition: The period of human growth when the human is considered to be young and deviant

Etymology: It goes without saying that the time we spend growing from infant to teenager is possibly the most formative of all epochs in our individual histories. Most of our parents might request that some of the words and phrases be expunged, had they kept a diary of "terms of endearment" that they uttered as they were fully engaged in raising us. It is, in fact, more and more common to see youngsters in serious trouble during significant periods of their growth as children. It is not uncommon to find parents turning over their responsibilities as directors of our psychological growth to teachers, therapists, managers of juvenile detention facilities, and perhaps worst of all, to Facebook.

So it is within this context that the term **CHILDHOOD** came into being. In days of yore, children were raised with a work ethic; raised to respect and obey their elders; to maintain the expectations of decorum and to grow up to be models of civility. It has come to pass, with the sociology of permissiveness and entitlement that many of our young people no longer aspire to be models of virtue and cordiality. Instead, many (beginning at age four and running right up to, through, and well beyond the proverbial age of reason) rebel, act out, strike out, break glass, carry the cat around by the tail, stay up late watching the likes of Fallon and Letterman, throw food at one another, scream, stamp their feet, and in effect emulate the vile and prurient traits of hoodlums. It is from this unsocial behavior that the terms **CHILD** and **HOOD** (a truncated version of **Hoodlum**) have become inextricably interwoven. Thus, sadly, **CHILDHOOD** is now an accepted term in our modern-day lexicon.

FOREWORD
(FIRST USED: 1957 AD)

Definition: A guide for what is to come; frequently used as an introduction for a book or play; the opposite of backward; to make progress.

Etymology: As everyone knows, the hit TV series **_LEAVE IT TO BEAVER,_** which ran between 1957 and 1963, was a weekly, half-hour peek into the life of an "average" family as seen through the eyes of a pre-teen by the name of Beaver Cleaver. His dad, **Ward Cleaver**, was played by the actor Hugh Beaumont. It was said that Hugh insisted that the producers provide him with not only the expected script prior to each preshow walkthrough, but also a series of specific directions from the writers.

These directions were to indicate any expectations that they might have of a sense of the state of mind and predispositions that the character, Ward, was expected to emulate. He needed to know, in detail, all of his interactions with all of the other characters in the show. These specific directives were placed in a binder each week. The binder was clearly and permanently titled **For Ward** (*Cleaver*). It was the writer's weekly instructions of the direction each show was to take, specifically for Ward Cleaver. Since then, of course, **For Ward** has been adjusted to the term **FOREWORD**, and has come to mean the pre-amble or explanation of what is to come in most books of nonfiction.

SATELLITE
(FIRST USED: 1957 AD)

Definition: In modern terminology, **SATELLITE** refers to man-made electronic devices that orbit the earth while bouncing data, transferring information, or spying at will

Etymology: In the second half of the twentieth century, as technology advanced and man was able to propel vehicles from the earth to the moon and/or in an orbit around earth, it became common to launch devices into orbit that would circle the earth and bounce communication signals from one station to the next all around the world. This allowed increases in signals for (*listed in order of importance*) TV, telecommunications, and defense.

On dark nights, it was said, one could sit outside and scan the black void in search of these seemingly tiny devices. Sometimes one would be lucky enough to see them moving across the sky. More often than not, the sky observer would sit for hours, if not until daylight, attempting to spot one of these space vehicles.

Because of the fact that the ardent observer might go all night and through dawn of the next day in search of a sighting, these space communication devices were named **SAT TILL LIGHT** or in common parlance, **SATELLITE**.

CRACKDOWN
(FIRST USED: 1959 AD)

Definition: Colloquial terminology, usually specific to law enforcement; focus of specific criminology

Etymology: Urban mayhem stemming from opium dens common to the turn-of-the-century opium-oriented communities through Prohibition in the early 1920s, followed by every form of illegal behavior and substance abuse known to man (and some plants) engendered the need for substantial, and precisely schooled, law enforcement. As men and women were trained to specific types of crime intervention and sent out into the streets, they were often distracted by other types of emergencies, be it the taxicab fetal delivery or the snatch-and-grab opportunist. All of these distractions made it difficult for these brave men and women to impact in a significant way the obsessive behaviors of the druggies, not to mention their penchant for stealing to support their expensive habits. It was not until the age of crack cocaine that the system turned really ugly and in a way provided the breakthrough needed to focus teams of police on these troublesome but determinate problems.

One police officer in Scranton found a way to focus on crack dealers. With each encounter, Chester "the Taser" Tester, as he was called, would draw and steady his Taser and call out: **"Step Away From The Crack. This Is Your Last Warning: Put The Crack Down!"** Very, very effective! So much so that, as a matter of fact, the Scranton police officer was awarded the National Medal of Menace, and Chester's phrase **"Put the Crack Down"** actually morphed into the term **CRACKDOWN**, which was used through all law enforcement branches to describe all manner of organized police crime focus.

DECADENT
(FIRST USED: 1959 AD)

Definition: A state of moral decline; moral turpitude

Etymology: As is well known in the cruise industry, cabins on the eighth, or "Emerald" deck, are usually called Obstructed Ocean View cabins, meaning that they are a bit larger than inside cabins and that they have a window—but as noted, the view is obstructed by lifeboats. Usually the deck above (called Deck Nine) has a fairly good accounting of suites, where it is not uncommon to find shipboard guests holding gracious parties in the evenings. The net effect of all of this is that passengers on the Emerald Deck typically want to emulate, if not surpass, their "bigger brothers" in the suites above. This would be OK except that their attempts usually end up taking partying to the extreme.

As a result, "Emeralders," as they have come to be known, throw quite rowdy all-night bashes that spill out into the passageways of deck eight—where the bacchanal might carry on until sunrise. Because of these morally bankrupt festivities, drink glasses are broken, food and wine are spilled on the carpets, dings and dents are accidently (and purposely) bashed into the narrow corridor walls and doors on the deck as the partygoers and the party throwers thrash, trash, and act out their ideas of what it's like to have larger cabins.

The cabin stewards and deck hands referred to the nightly damage as **Deck Eight Dents**"—and as a result, the new term **DECADENT** was added to our language.

CHRONOLOGY: TWENTY

(FROM 1960 AD THROUGH 1999 AD)

THE EON THAT BECAME AN EPOCH ERA—PERIOD!

< NOTHING COULD BE FARTHER FROM THE TRUTH... >

"THE ATTEMPT TO INCORPORATE WATCHES INTO BELTS FAILED BECAUSE IT WAS CONSIDERED A WAIST OF TIME."

KARAOKE
(FIRST USED: 1963 AD)

Definition: an electronic device that provides music to popular songs as an accompaniment for fledgling singers

Etymology: It is a widely held belief that **KARAOKE** is a Japanese word and a Japanese invention as defined above. It is said that the etymology of this word comes from the Japanese **KARA**—meaning empty—and **OKE**—which is short for okesutora (or orchestra). This is silly on the face of it. In the first place, everyone knows that kara comes from Karo Syrup, and oke is short for the people who live in the state of Oklahoma. It is sometimes used as a pejorative reference similar to what was once known as a **Yahoo**. Furthermore, the Irish would take serious umbrage at any suggestion that **KARAOKE** was anything more than the invention of one of their own who spent a lonely life in the fogbound highlands, who loved to sing, and who, one boring afternoon, developed a recording device that played her favorite music so that she could sing along. It is, furthermore, an insult to every Irish man, woman, and child that the lass's name was co-opted by heretofore unknown parties and changed to the absurd spelling of **KARAOKE** when it should have been spelled **CARRIE O'KEE**.

OBFUSCATION
(FIRST USED: 1963 AD)

Definition: The act of confusing or bewildering another

Etymology: Given the definition, it is somewhat amusing that this particular word began life (if you will) as a secret office memo aimed at confusing a woman who spent most of her career spying on her fellow office workers or gaining their confidence only to report negative incidents to the managers—all in a misguided attempt to promote her own career. Once it was discovered that Cate M. (full name withheld to protect her identity) was relaying comments and grumblings to management, one of her co-workers sent a memo to the rest of the team using a shorthand code that translated literally as: **Office! Cate—Shun**. Her peers would always clam up when they saw her coming toward the water cooler. When it was impossible to avoid Cate, the conversation would become so nonsensical or intentionally convoluted that she would walk away in a state of bewilderment. Thus was the evolution of what was a secret office memo. It was transmorgafied from **Office! Cate—Shun!** to the term **OBFUSCATION**, which was rightfully intended to confuse and bewilder office snoops everywhere.

PACIFIST
(FIRST USED: 1964 AD)

Definition: opposition to war or violence as a means of settling disputes

Etymology: The term **PACIFIST** came into the lexicon as a description of what a nonviolent person is—that is, someone who can get **past a fist**, where the fist is a symbol of violence.

DEMEANOR
(FIRST USED: 1970 AD)

Definition: The physical manifestation of one's state of mind; behavior; comportment

Etymology: This word was born into the lexicon in the 1970s during a TV interview on the iconic program ***The Walton's***, after John Boy asked his TV dad (coincidentally also named John) why the family dog was always trying to bite him (John Boy). His dad asked John Boy what he was doing when the dog got nasty, and John Boy responded that the dog growled and snapped when he was poking it with a sharp stick (apparently the stick was sharper than John Boy).

John Walton put a hand around the boy's shoulder and said to him, in an ad lib that still holds true today, "Son, the more you gonna poke that poor dog with a stick, the meaner he is gonna git." John Boy, just barely eighteen, wrote down a one-word reminder to himself to stop poking the dog. The word was **DEMEANOR** because John Boy couldn't spell all that good and needed to "git" himself some "edjamakasion." Nonetheless, children of the seventies began referring to behavior, in whatever form, as **DEMEANOR**. And the rest, as they say, is verbal history.

DISDAIN
(FIRST USED: 1971 AD)

Definition: To look down upon; to consider something "less than" with respect to others.

Etymology: when you are **dissed** (**dis-respected**) you are said to have a **dissed-stain** until you even the score.

ADMONITIONS
(FIRST USED: 1982 AD)

Definition: warnings, whether written or verbal

Etymology: It is not without cause that mothers advise their children not to play outside at night in a war zone. But giving such advise was not always obvious to some mothers.* On the eve of the outbreak of the **CRISIS** (nobody actually declared a war) between Argentina and Britain over the territory called the Falkland Islands, most mothers called their children in at sunset.

The first use of a new word, **ADMONITIONS**, came about as a direct result of this military conflict. A secret British group known only to a few as the Falkland Elder Council of Espionage and Secrets, or FECES, met in chambers to discuss the impending invasion of the islands from the Argentinean forces (not to mention a potential subsequent outbreak of mayhem). It was decided that while the best defense was a good offense, until the British got their Command-Royal Army-Protocols (CRAP) in defensive positions along the coast of the two hundred islands that made up the Falklands, the immediate solution was to increase the amount of munitions wherever possible. That meant mines, mines, and more mines – even if you do mind. While the request for a shipload of mines was being processed at Her Majesty's Royal Naval Academy, FECES was advised that there could be harmful and unintended consequences to planting all of the mine fields that were being planned.

In the long run, the crisis never flowered into a full-fledged war. Nonetheless, between the two adversaries, some twenty-five thousand land mines were deployed, and most of the ordinance has yet to be unearthed or destroyed. Consequently, Falklinians keep their children inside at night and are forced to tiptoe around the island in constant fear that an errant sheep will blow them all to kingdom come.**

The most enduring lesson of the crisis was that against good advice, both sides decided to add munitions. The word **ADMONITIONS** was coined directly as a result of the warning not to **ADD MUNITIONS**.

*Under the heading of **LITTLE-KNOWN ETYMOLOGICAL FACTS**, we might stop here to comment that the phrase "some others" was a direct offshoot of the phrase "some mothers," when the fact is that those others were not actual mothers.*

***None of the underpinnings of the above etymology can be documented as fact, or even as fiction. So either enjoy it or move on.*

GENE POOL
(FIRST USED: 1983 AD)

Definition: Hereditary soup referencing the combined genetic strengths and weaknesses of a given group of people

Etymology: At the inception of the study we now refer to as **genetics**, a very bright couple determined that some commonly shared human characteristics were inherited. Wade N. Poole and his wife, Lividea Poole, were the first geneticists to trace absolute links between the genetic characteristics of generations of both humans and simians. They worked with ten other scientists on these heretofore unestablished theories. They were specifically working on the blue-eyed trait in the family history of Wade and Lividea.

It was only by a stroke of luck that at the same time, all of the group were leaning toward absolute discovery links—Wade and Lividea dotted the last "eye" with the birth of their daughter, Jean—and the subsequent confirmation, through their own family tree, that the little blue-eyed Miss proved their theories. And while at first, it seemed a bit "Poole-ish," little **Jeannie Poole** not only proved the hypothesis, but by sheer happenstance of birth also became the model, with a few minor changes, for the subsequence intermediate naming of the term **JEAN POOL**. However, her new little brother was the icing on the cake, genetically speaking, and his name, **Gene Pool**, was the actual progenitor of the phrase that we know today as the **GENE POOL**.

VANISH
(FIRST USED: 1985 AD)

Definition: Something or someone that becomes invisible; to disappear

Etymology: It was inevitable. Beginning in the mid-1980s, kids growing up in the United States of America became truly advantaged. Not only did they have the benefits of a by-and-large free education, they were also the first generation that didn't have to figure out how to get themselves (walking uphill both ways) to their schools, sports programs, and home again, like all of their predecessors. The age of the soccer mom was upon us. While some called it "false entitlement" and others referred to it as "parental protectionism," it was the beginning of a movement that may yet end up "bringing the school to the student" as opposed to bringing the student to the school.

The real impact on twenty-first century sociology has yet to be determined; however, it clearly had an impact on the automotive industry. It seems that every family now requires two vehicles. One is used primarily to get Dad back and forth to work and the other to ferry kids to school and to after-school activities such as soccer practice followed by Band-Aid practice, if not band practice itself. Indeed, if you examine the purchase invoices for vehicles (SUVs, vans, and minivans that are designed to carry large groups of kids) during the period from 1985 to the present, you will find a spike in sales that has not been seen in the automotive industry since the end of the Second World War. It included the development of such vehicles as the Hummer (at the high end, and the Bummer on the other end), the Jeep, and other SUVs (such as the Dodge Caravan and even the PT [Personal Transport] Cruiser). It became the age of transformational transportation, and it was gearing for the new millennium crush of the babies of the baby boomers.

If you have ever had the misfortune to get caught driving through an area that has a grammar school—before the first bell or after the last –you will completely understand the impact of the soccer mom phenomena. Gridlock is a word commonly used to refer to the conundrum of hundreds of moms in their vans, picking up or dropping off their charges. It is awesome to behold.

Sadly these activities have spawned a new word in our vocabulary. It is a word that aptly describes the frightening horror of hundreds of youngsters trying, all at the same moment, to identify at the end of the school day which of those waiting vehicles is piloted by their mom. The fact is that from the vantage point of a seven-year-old, all of the vehicles look alike. Panic, like a mild acid, begins roiling in their bellies as they scan a sea of vans awaiting their passengers. When asked by school staff to describe the vehicle their mom drives, it is not uncommon to hear a tearful response of "It's sort of …van-ish." And thus is our language burdened with a new term, **VANISH**, which refers to the blending in and disappearance of a child's ride home (or anything else that appears to disappear).

INDEPENDENCE
(FIRST USED: 1990 AD)

Definition: The ability not to have to depend on another; to be self-governing

Etymology: Most people believe that the term **INDEPENDENCE** came into common usage with the American Revolution and the subsequent establishment of the American Constitution. Sadly, they could not be farther from the truth. The real genesis of the term **INDEPENDENCE** lies in the mid-twentieth century and can be directly associated with the development of the adult diaper.

As everyone who has suffered from it knows, incontinence is belittling and embarrassing and can frequently leave one in a "sticky" situation. As a result, before the invention of the adult diaper, most folks who were burdened with the problems of incontinence needed to either be constantly be near a water closet, or they needed to stick (if you will excuse the expression) close to home. Many incontinent people required caregivers to help them with the cleanup, both at home and when out and about.

When adult diapers were introduced and Depends became all the rage, it was not uncommon to see senior citizens who had heretofore kept to themselves and hidden away in locked bathrooms, dancing for joy at the prospect of being able to "shop" now, "mop" later. The joy was seen from the coast of Maine to the shores of San Diego, and the dance was given the name **IN DEPENDs DANCE**. Of course, when the dust settled and people became comfortable with each and every Depend they tried on, its use became a matter of course, and the phrase **IN DEPENDs DANCE** was modified to **INDEPENDENCE** (It is important to note that it was at this time (early 1990) that Congress agreed to quietly rename the cherished **Declaration of Freedom from the English Monarchy** to the **Declaration of Independence**).

DECORATION
(FIRST USED: 1992 AD)

Definition: Something colorful and out of the ordinary that is added to create a festive mood

Etymology: The nation of Croatia has, as its western border, the Adriatic Sea. Croatia created a "precedential" form of government in 1991 after separating from Yugoslavia. When the "precedent" is seated every four years (mostly during meals and at conferences), he is said to be the "setting Precedent."

One of the more precedent-setting moves came in 1992 when the parliament, in an effort to stimulate a sagging economy and create jobs, initiated a government-sponsored cruise ship industry. The government purchased mothballed cruise ships at scrap value, sailed them to Sibenik, and then thoroughly rejuvenated them. In order to maximize employment opportunities for their own people, they staffed the cruise ships exclusively with Croatian citizens. In an overzealous attempt at job creation, the Bureau of Cruises hired 120 cruise deck staff positions over and above the actual needs onboard each ship.

Each of the three ships had six passenger decks. The extra crew were split into groups of twenty and assigned to specific decks. They were required to dress in the brightly colored medieval costumes of their ancestors and simply stand in appointed positions, smile, answer questions, and when needed, direct passengers, upon request, to various locations about the ship.

Sadly, in the long term the project failed, due partially to a misunderstood declaration from the Croatian precedent—in which he stated that "Cruising is, at best, a sea-zonal issue." However, the biggest failure happened when the tide ebbed in Sibernik's newly dedicated harbor and two of the cruise ships tipped over onto the mud flats. While it appears that managing a cruise industry in Croatia was not meant to be, the colorfully costumed **Deck Croatians** appear to have been the inspiration for our present-day term **DECORATION**

BERING STRAIT
(FIRST USED: 1994 AD)

Definition: A fifty-eight-mile-wide narrowing of the waters between the Arctic and Pacific Oceans that separates Russia and the USA.

Etymology: In 1993 President W. Clinton declared that "Don't ask, don't tell" was the new policy of the United States military. He invited commanders of each service to find a way to keep the message of "Don't ask, don't tell" in the forefront of their mission—without compromising the need to focus on the tasks at hand. Each commander was to develop a "Don't ask, don't tell" awareness program*

The navy took this policy change seriously and after several months decided that posting subtle hints on the ship bulletin boards would be of most help in reminding the young sailors to "**mind their mannerisms.**"

The first signs posted read simply: **"The Gulf of Hunu"** and they (the signs) were everywhere on every vessel afloat. The fleet admiral selected **"The Gulf of Hunu"** as a reminder because he hoped that seeing the phrase posted everywhere on the ship would remind the sailors that some of their brothers-in-arms were "torqued" a bit differently. **Like—Who Knew!** After getting more questions than answers, the brass decided to switch it up and post the **"Bay of Wassup"** as a more direct reminder. Everyone was well aware that liberty in **Wassup** could find the lone sailor in a bar with as many guys with "twinkling" eyes as there were gals ready to help relieve the stress of sleeping shipboard.

Nonetheless, there was no discernible change of awareness for the naval "Don't ask, don't tell" program. The final attempt to influence the sailors was a new sign reading **"BERING STRAIT,"** again to subliminally hint at the hidden message to **"Keep your BEARING Straight!"** With this sign, the message finally worked. From the lowly sailor on the deck where you shovel poop, to the marines wading ashore at Unalakleet, every naval man felt a sort of inspiration to uphold the dignity of their service by keeping their chins up, doing their assigned jobs with grit and determination, and keeping their "**Be(a)ring Straight**."**

* I am making most of this up.

** No sailors were outed in the fabrication of this etymology. In deference to Vitus Bering, after whom the actual strait was named, and because of sound decision-making regarding subliminal advertising, the spelling of "Bering" was not changed. If you are confused about the meaning of any of the above statements, just move along; there is nothing to see here....

RELENTLESS
(FIRST USED: 1995 AD)

Definition*: proceeding without remorse; unyielding, hardened and persistent*

Etymology: This term came into the lexicon in the mid-1990s and was reinforced in 2008 in the wake of the crash of the housing market. Banks and other lending institutions revised their manifestos to include dealing with those folks who found it necessary to walk away from their houses and mortgage loans.

Lending institutions did not wish to summarily refuse to reinstate customers who defaulted on predatory loans, so they adopted a policy they referred to as **Re-Lent Less**, wherein they would reissue loans to past customers with the caveat that those customers would be lent less than other customers. These banks and mortgage companies were said to have a **RELENTLESS** policy.

CHRONOLOGY TWENTY-ONE

(FROM 2000 AD THROUGH .... ?)

A NEW MILLENIUM

< *THERE IS NO XCUSE...* >

"IF YOU HAVE A FRIEND NAMED JACK, AND YOU GREET HIM IN AN AIRPORT ('HI, JACK!'), YOU COULD GET JAIL TIME."

ALGORITHM
(FIRST USED: 2000 AD)

Definition: a technique established to solve specific mathematical problems

Etymology: In the run-up to the 2000 presidential elections, and through some clever, albeit marginally ethical press releases, candidate Albert Gore was mocked as the self-described "inventor" of the Internet. While the publicity regarding the alleged "inventing" helped in undermining Mr. Gore's credibility as a contender to the presidency, additional "pseudo-information," which thankfully was not released, would have been the time bomb that would have ended the candidacy midstride. Specifically, it was never actually alleged that Al Gore invented the already well-established relationship between mathematics and music. It was left unsaid as to the specific steps to which such a relationship should and could be applied, but through significant unspoken innuendo it was clear that the process was secretly called **Al Gore Rhythm**—and it is certain that the post-2000 AD term **ALGORITHM** came into being as a result of the aforementioned nondisclosure.

COMPLEMENT
(FIRST USED: 2003 AD)

Definition: Something or someone that completes the whole; some-thing that combines with another to complete

Etymology: To a certain extent we are all competing for financial secu-rity. It is difficult, at best, to manage the process in good economic times. When there is financial insecurity, it seems that the unpleas-antness flows like a rushing torrent down to our feet, ruining our only pair of good shoes.

When your boss calls you into his office for coffee to discuss how good you look today and how your smile means the world to him, warning bells should be going off in your head. If he then transitions into a discussion of possible "downsizing" and the "cutting of corners," it frequently is an opening for him to lighten his burden by negatively impacting your compensation. He may ask you to take a cut in pay or to pay more out of pocket for health care—or he may even, dare I say it, eliminate your job. Frequently it is all done with a brace of smiles and "friendly" pats on the back.

If this happens, it is common to engage in a healthy debate with the man before stomping off in a fiery rage. Nine out of ten employees spend the remainder of the day in what is referred to as the "deep-seethe." When you arrive at home, the slamming of doors is expected, as is, in some cases, the weeping and gnashing of teeth. Having been swallowed up in a sea of emotions, one can only wait until one's loved one(s) arrive home so that one can have a shoulder to cry on. One also tends to vent during this process, usually in some form of rage that includes characterizing one's (ex) boss as an evil, sinister, psychopath who has always had it out for one.

This whole process is documented in psychological studies as the **Lament for lost Compensation**, or the **Comp Lament**. Because it all

started out with that invitation to have a cup of coffee and trade pleas-
antries, people are well warned to look out for the **COMPLEMENT.**

ECONOMIST
(FIRST USED: 2003 AD)

Definition: a person claiming expertise on the subject of the economy

Etymology: This term has truly had an etymological evolution since its
inception during the post-Depression era, when it began as a concept
about the financial well-being of the individual. The term **ECONOMY**
(from which **ECONOMIST** derived) was originally spelled **ECONO-ME**
to denote the ultimate subject of economic growth—i.e., financial
transactions that would benefit the individual—ME. (It is true that a per-
centage of the populace could not grasp financial underpinnings and
growth, and as a result feared anything to do with managing money.
From that fear comes the next stage in the evolution of this concept,
namely the emergence of a new word/phrase: **ECONOM-ICK**!)

Nonetheless, the managers of material wealth were, for years, granted
the approbation of the elite. With the notion of elitism came the general understanding that the market was above the common man.
Beginning with the birth of the twenty-first century and the expensive boondoggle in Iraq and Afghanistan and the crash of the dollar, the rising prices of all commodities were tied directly to the cost
of oil. Economic disasters lurked behind every door! It was not until
the middle of the Bush administration that the term **ECONO-MISSED**
was used to describe treasury secretaries and their ilk, and thus the
term became a part of the lexicon.

But that was not to last long. As a result of the spiraling cost of printer
ink, the term **ECONO-MISSED** was truncated even further to the

cheaper spelling: **ECONO-MIST** (which gives a "misty-eyed" and tearful memory to the days of pre-recession), and then, in another cost cutting measure, the dash was completely removed to simply read **ECONOMIST**. It is woefully rumored that should another cutback occur, the term shall simply read **ECON-NO.**

MILEAGE
(FIRST USED: 2006 AD)

Definition: One of the forms of measurement of distance in the United States of America. Example: inches—feet—yard—mile

Etymology: *(This etymology is a correction to this frequently miss-defined term.)* Mileage is the age of a car based on the miles driven (therefore, seventy thousand miles is the mile-age of the car)—not, as some would have you think, the amount of miles you get to a gallon of gas. That's why the term is spelled with **age** at the end. We should be referring to the amount of fuel consumed as **GAS-AGE**. However, we do not—to the delight of the auto dealers and the oil industry, who would rather the consumer not focus on the **GAS-AGE** or the **MILE-AGE** of a vehicle but rather on its "coolness" factor.

AWFUL
(FIRST USED: 2007 AD)

Definition: Atrocious, dreadful

Etymology: (See **Offal**)

OFFAL
(FIRST USED: 2007 AD)

Definition: Odoriferous waste meat (rotting, etc.)

Etymology: *(*See **Awful**)

❖   ❖   ❖

CURSIVE
(FIRST USED: 2008 AD)

Definition: The style of handwriting in which the letters are joined in the fashion of script

Etymology: The art of writing in script is rapidly fading from our culture. The insurrection of the block-printed words of the twentieth and twenty-first century are changing how we communicate. The transition has taken us from quill and ink to household typewriters and from typewriters to keyboards. Keyboards have been truncated by PDIMs (Personal Device Interface Module) and texting—and all have progressed to the point that script has become just a fancy advertising gimmick.

While we ponder the vicissitudes of this unplanned replacement of scripting, it might be a good time to note that pharmacists are still required to learn the art of script writing merely to be able read the doctor's "handwriting" on prescriptions. Nonetheless, script writing has always been the softer of the two writing options. If you "bold" your **printed diatribes**, the starkness holds a certain "**shouting**" quality. If you issue your *diatribe in plain script*, the words seem to absorb and filter out (like a sieve) any intended harshness.

It was for that reason that the art of writing in script was understood as being something of a **"curse"** *sieve*—because the power of the curse dissipated as "handwriting" softened any intended vitriol. It is, indeed, also the reason that the act of script writing itself came to be referred to as the **CURSE** *SIEVE* form of communication. The term is still in use by the more refined readers as **CURSIVE.**

PARENT
(FIRST USED: 2009 AD)

Definition: The biological progenitor

Etymology: The term **PARENT** is a prime example of a word that sprang (*springed?*) from a practical need (*kneed?*). When the Medieval Times kind of fell apart due to the **MARCH** of the ages (*which actually occurred all eleven months of that year*), regular people (i.e., not the people of the upper crust of the earth, but rather those of the streets, muddy drainage ditches, and hovels, yearning to be free) moved away from the city centers in attempts to eke their living in the fallow fields of the suburban outskirts. With this migratory abandonment of rental agreements and leases, stunned landlords and property owners were at a loss as to how to replace their needed property incomes before going "belly-up" themselves.

Providentially, it was during this same time period that an entrepreneur stepped up and advertised an introductory offer (including two free sets of steak knives, as well as a Hog Wash Cleaning Kit—for a limited time only!) that he called **the Kin-Sue Rental Manual.** This one-of-kind, never-before-offered, **Manual** was dedicated to various suggestions on how to market abandoned rental properties. It advocated a number of solutions, not the least was the use of deadly force. Other inquisitional types of behavior were detailed—many of which included the loss of hair (via fire) and the removal of fingernails—which were then converted into tiny spoons to delicately spread miniscule amounts of seasoning on your steaks and chops.

Notwithstanding the less "gracious" options for keeping renters renting (not the "renting" as in the renting and tearing of garments, although there was a fair amount of that going on during this period), **The Manual** also offered an opportunity to advertise vacant properties in some creative ways. Specific to our journey of discovery, word wise, and the most popular and useful technique was to post signs on doors, on windows, and in the public square advertising that "this" or "that" property was available to couples expecting a child. One of the main advantages of renting to a "pregnant" couple was that they could place like-minded renters in proximity to one another and eliminate the noise complaints from couples without children.

The advertisements usually began with the big, bold words **PAIR RENTAL: With Room to Expand and Grow Your Family.** That was usually all it took to find renters. Of course, the term became very familiar and morphed from **PAIR-RENT to** the now popular **PARENT** and **PARENTAL**. And the rest is, as they say, history

SUCCULENTS
(FIRST USED: 2012 AD)

Definition: Plants that have fleshy leaves that preserve moisture; juicy

Etymology: Plants that we now refer to as **SUCCULENTS** are plants that have been on the earth since before the beginning of time (time, for our purposes, is defined as anything happening in recorded history since the invention of the clock). **SUCCULENTS** have also been considered by scientists to be the smartest of the plant species. There are two primary reasons for that assumption. The first primary reason is that they store liquid, which allows them to survive through periods of drought. The second primary reason is because they have names such as Cochlospermaceae, Xanthrorrhoeaceae, and Phyloccaceae. These names are hard for humans to pronounce, even in the ancient Latin. So while **SUCCULENTS** stretched their syrup-laden leaves on balmy afternoons along the shores of Amalfy, the learned senators of ancient Rome were trying to understand how to pronounce their tongue-twisting names.

Yet even before leather was invented (which would later be used as watchbands which would revolutionize the concept of time as we know it), these plants were engaging in cross-species symbiotic inter-actions that would shock even the most liberal of plant lovers.

In the warm Mediterranean climate lives a fairly rare species of ant called the Lasius Carniolicus (again with the Latin). The English equivalent of Lasius Carniolicus is "luscious meat," although the so-called "luscious" meat tastes more like a lemon drop. The ant reverse hibernates from June through October to escape the hot, muggy Mediterranean climate. But just two months before the rainy season unleashes, the "lemon drop" ant awakens and seeks the stored mois-ture of the **SUCCULENT'S** leaves to quench his thirst and to see him to the rainy season. Large caravans of red ants seek out the moisture-laden plants and, when they find them, suck out rejuvenating liquid via a stiletto proboscis. The ants literally triple their size with the sweet juice of the plants.

The ants like to spend their days lying in the sun on the beaches of San Tropez and Cannes, though any beach will do. The beaches pro-vide the ant with easy access to food because the beaches are never far from one or more varieties of **SUCCULENTS**. However, the con-stant exposure to the warm sun has a chemical effect on the now big-bellied ant, and the biologically altered liquid that the ant so unapologetically sucked out of the plants begins to harden inside the ant. Too much sun, sand, and plant juice make a lot of very dead ants littering the beautiful sands of the Cote d'Azur. Nonetheless, the natives of those beach towns spend hours collecting the dead ants in late November to mid-December. The ants are de-armed and de-legged and popped into the freezer. Once frozen, they are removed from cold storage, and the juices of the plants are mixed with the enzymes of the ants. This combination makes a delicious lemon-drop-flavored Christmas treat for both children and adults alike. The actual term **SUCCULENTS** springs from this Mediterranean Christmas treat, which is called **SUCK YULE ANTS**.

ZEBRA
(FIRST USED: 2012 AD)

Definition: Heretofore, the **ZEBRA** has been an African animal similar to the horse but covered in black-and-white stripes

Etymology: **Zee Bra** is a stylish, black-and-white-striped intimate apparel item from *"Zee Boudoirs"* of Paris.

AFTER WORD(S)

XCUSE

Xenophobe* sounds like a word describing people who are afraid of all things Zee (example: Little Johnny and his dog Spot were both afraid of ZEE TOILET TISSUE). I, on the other hand, distrust the word XENOPHOBE itself because it begins with the letter *X*, though, in fact, it is pronounced with the ZEE sound. To my mind, a word beginning with the ZEE sound should be a word beginning with the letter ZEE. There is no excuse for any word that begins with the ZEE sound but is spelled with the letter *X*.

This also suggests to me that the people responsible for translating our words from the Phoenician to the Greek, to the Latin, to the English, were either lazy or overworked. Perhaps they were suckered into phonics as a way of speeding up the process of inventing words. If that is indeed the case, we can easily make a connection between the ancient Phoenicians and the process we call phonics (note the spelling similarities: **Pho**enicians/**pho**nics. Note also that the proper phonic pronunciation of the *Pho* in Phoenicians and the *Pho* in phonics should be: *Foenicians* and *Foenics*. That is because words can also be our *frien*imies.

So the very best example of how phonics works (or doesn't) would be the actual word **Phonics**. Note that the proper phonic pronunciation of the *Pho* in **Phoenicians** and the *Pho* in **phonic**s should be: Foenicians and Foenics. That is because words can also be our frienimies. But apparently the proper spelling and pronouncement would be too much work for the Phoenician, Greek, Latin, or the English. We are then left with the Primary Directive of Spelling 1.0, which is: never spell it the way it sounds—or you are going down.

In a 1,568-page dictionary, there are fewer than two pages dedicated to all words starting with the letter *X*. Out of a total of eighty "**X**" words (including the word "**X**," which is one of the few letters of the alphabet that is its own word), forty-two words—which is more than half—begin with the **ZEE** sound. Compounding the *X's* problem, many words that sound like "X" words begin with the letter *E*. Nonetheless, they actually, I should think, belong in the province of the letter *Z*. Some examples are: Example, Exceptional, Exert, Exhaust, Exfoliate, Exercise, Exonerate, Exempt, Exist, Execute, Exit. And so again, I ask, in reference to the Phoenician, Greek, Latin, and English: What is their **XCUSE**?

*   * Xenophobe actually refers to people who fear other people when those other people are perceived as different. Wouldn't it be great if xenophobes could, with an equal amount of gusto, fear words that sound different than they are spelled? Maybe then we could all just get along.*

PUNISH

Punish is one of those words that has no historical date that I can find to actuate its leap into metaphysical existence. Nonetheless it is one of those words that, by their mere utterance, become what they mean.

As an example: if you say that something is "punny," you are saying that it is both like a pun and/or that it is humorous (sounds like funny). If, therefore, you decide to capitalize on the similar sounds and meanings of words such as CLASSIC and CLASS SICK, you might get groans from your target audience because that was "sort of" pun-like, or as we have said, **PUN-ISH**.

Those groans are a human's most effective way to discourage, and in fact, legally **PUN-ISH** you. Concomitantly, the use of words that are similar in sound but not in meaning is what we refer to when we say that your comparison was, or wasn't **PUN-ISH**—a.k.a., like a **PUN**.

Therefore, and in conclusion: if you want to **PUNISH**, say something **PUN-ISH**.

I urge you all to carry on bravely while I continue to X-pose more etymological root derivations and deviations. In the meantime, I leave you with this thought:

TIME!

Oh fleeting spectered joke on me!

Yes—Time!

A lie…a lost reality!

You're neither here nor there,

not soon nor past…

But always out of reach.

No grasp on you can I achieve;

But ponder at the sudden loss,

And lose right there

so suddenly,

The matter of my pondering!

The End (of TIME)

TABLE OF ETYMOLOGICAL CONTENTS

Made in the USA
Charleston, SC
12 October 2013